Highest Praise for M. William Phelps

"M. William Phelps dares to tread where few others will: into the mind of a killer."
—*TV Rage*

"Phelps is the king of true crime."
—**Lynda Hirsch, Creators Syndicate**

"Phelps treads dangerous ground like an Amazon jungle guide—fearless, compassionate, insightful."
—**Geoff Fitzpatrick, Executive Producer of *Dark Minds***

WHERE MONSTERS HIDE

"A chilling real-life tale of murder and madness that reminded me of *Fatal Vision*. This is narrative nonfiction of the highest order, a sumptuously scintillating tale that greets us in *fact* with the character types we're used to seeing in the fiction of Lisa Gardner, Harlan Coben, or Lisa Scottoline. Superb in all respects."
—**Jon Land** in *The Providence Journal*

"Riveting, emotional, a mystery from cover to cover . . . A nonfiction thriller of the highest literary caliber."
—**Gregg Olsen,** #1 *New York Times* bestselling author

"Phelps solidifies his mark as the Eminem of true crime: in-your-face truth, spoken from a journalist who holds nothing back."
—**Steve Jackson,** *New York Times* bestselling author of *No Stone Unturned*

I'LL BE WATCHING YOU

"Phelps has an unrelenting sense for detail that affirms his place, book by book, as one of our most engaging crime journalists."
—**Katherine Ramsland**

IF LOOKS COULD KILL

"M. William Phelps, one of America's finest true-crime writers, has written a compelling and gripping book about an intriguing murder mystery."
—**Vincent Bugliosi**

"Phelps consistently ratchets up the dramatic tension, hooking readers. His thorough research and interviews give the book complexity, richness of character, and urgency."
—**Stephen Singular**

MURDER IN THE HEARTLAND

"Drawing on interviews with law officers and relatives, the author has done significant research. His facile writing pulls the reader along."
—*St. Louis Post-Dispatch*

"Phelps expertly reminds us that when the darkest form of evil invades the quiet and safe outposts of rural America, the tragedy is greatly magnified. Get ready for some sleepless nights."
—**Carlton Stowers**

Also by M. WILLIAM PHELPS

WHERE MONSTERS
HIDE

M. WILLIAM PHELPS

PINNACLE BOOKS
Kensington Publishing Corp.
www.kensingtonbooks.com

PINNACLE BOOKS are published by

Kensington Publishing Corp.
119 West 40th Street
New York, NY 10018

All Kensington titles, imprints, and distributed lines are available at special quantity discounts for bulk purchases for sales promotions, premiums, fund-raising, educational, or institutional use. Special book excerpts or customized printings can also be created to fit specific needs. For details, write or phone the office of the Kensington sales manager: Kensington Publishing Corp., 119 West 40th Street, New York, NY 10018, attn: Sales Department; phone 1-800-221-2647.

PINNACLE BOOKS and the P logo are Reg. U.S. Pat. & TM Off.

ISBN-13: 978-0-7860-4473-3
ISBN-10: 0-7860-4473-X

First Kensington trade paperback printing: April 2019
First Pinnacle mass market printing: March 2020

10   9   8   7   6   5   4   3   2   1

Printed in the United States of America

Electronic edition:

ISBN-13: 978-0-7860-4474-0 (e-book)
ISBN-10: 0-7860-4474-8 (e-book)

This book is dedicated to . . .

Matthew Valentinas:
friend, manager, agent, lawyer, "therapist"

&

Sonya Cosumano, LMFT:
for helping me work through the most difficult time of
my life

Three may keep a secret, if two of them are dead.

—Benjamin Franklin

PROLOGUE

Every year, between the third week of June and the third week of July, the Mitchell's satyr butterfly emerges from hiding, exposing her fragile, coffee-colored wingspan, in only two states: Michigan and Indiana. An endangered species, the satyr is an elusive, unique, devious creature, using yellow- and orange-ringed eyespots located near the tips of her wings as camouflage to hide in plain sight. Catching a glimpse of this unusual, uncommon caterpillar-mutated-into-flying-insect is more rare than a Sasquatch sighting. The primary threat to the satyr's survival is habitat loss and modification. As an adult, she does not eat or drink—and there is very little known about how she reproduces. Only during her flight period, after breaking free from the chrysalis entombing her, will the satyr mate, lay eggs, and, with her life's purpose now complete, die—a process that takes no more than two weeks. It is one reason why those looking to catch even the slightest glimpse of her have such an incredibly frustrating, difficult time.

PART 1

THE MISSING MAN

1
MOVING ON

CHRIS REGAN JR.'S CAR WAS loaded with nearly everything he owned. For the past several weeks, Chris had slept on the floor of his Traverse City, Michigan, apartment, nothing left inside but life's core essentials: iPhone and laptop, coffeepot, pillow, a few blankets for keeping warm. At twenty-six years old, Chris Jr. was ready for a change. He and his father, Chris Regan Sr., had discussed moving in together for the past year. They'd decided to leave Michigan, where both had lived for most of Chris Jr.'s life.

"Fresh start," Chris Jr. said. "Something different."

"Yeah," Senior responded. "Sounds good to me."

The previous winter, 2013, Chris Jr. had taken a trip to Florida. He'd gotten his hands on an ice-cream truck from a friend and drove it fifteen hundred miles south. He wanted a change of scene, if only for a few months, but also to see what opportunities were available outside Michigan. An avid photographer, along the way, Chris took scores of photographs. He'd passed through towns and cities he would have never known existed—or had a chance to ever see—had he not driven. When he returned to Michigan four months later, just as the spring of 2014 broke, Chris had nowhere to live. He'd given up his place in Traverse City. So his father allowed him to sleep in the basement of a house Senior was renting. On some nights they'd get together, sit and talk. Chris Jr. would pull out photos he'd taken during his trip.

"Let's just do it, son," Chris Sr. said one night. "The two us. Get the heck out of Michigan and live somewhere else."

Chris Sr. did not have to twist his son's arm. Chris Jr. loved the idea. The cold, dark, gloomy winters up north were something both could easily leave behind. Chris Jr.'s brother, the father's only other child, lived far enough away in Rochester, Michigan, outside Detroit, anyway. Senior had been divorced from his sons' mother for just a few years. The four of them hardly ever saw one another. They had no family up north. Why *not* move? What was holding them back?

"Where, though?" Senior asked.

"Texas?" Chris Jr. suggested.

"No. Not a chance."

"South Carolina?"

"Maybe, Chris," the father said.

"Asheville, North Carolina, has always been on my radar as a place I kind of want to live, Dad."

They both looked at each other. Rolling off the tongue, Asheville sounded delightful, as if it were meant to be. They'd visited before. Camping. Cycling. Hiking trails. So much to love about a town that seemed to celebrate the eccentricities of life! Where art trumped the fast-paced style of modern living,

Junior soon moved out on his own, downstate from Upper Michigan, where Senior now lived. He rented his own apartment. And they continued discussing a move to Asheville. It almost seemed like a plan now.

"What about Colorado?" Senior suggested over the phone one day, still tossing out locales.

"No."

"Yeah, too cold and snowy still."

"Asheville, Dad. I'm telling you," Junior reiterated. "Remember, we camped there. Rode our bikes on the trails."

"Right. It's gorgeous, Chris." The father paused. "Okay, it's decided. Asheville it is, then."

"Yes."

Asheville offered the most opportunity for both. Especially where it pertained to hobbies and life outside work. Both were avid cyclists, mountain biking, mostly downhill. Chris Jr. had dedicated most of his life to cycling, having started riding at the age of three with the help of his dad. Senior was an expert cyclist and had won trophies while racing in the air force. He'd actually traveled and lived all over the world, where he enjoyed a second passion, scuba diving. The son had worked in cycle shops all his adult life. So finding a job for Chris Jr. in North Carolina was not going to be a problem once they got settled.

AS THE MIDDLE OF October 2014 settled in, Senior had a job lined up in Asheville. He'd signed a contract with a company he was excited to get started with. In fact, he had a scheduled October 15, 2014, drug-screening test for the new job. Still packing, with boxes everywhere, Senior was working toward being ready to leave on schedule. His apartment in Iron River, Michigan, where he'd relocated, was in a bit of disarray.

"Exciting," Senior told his son one night on the phone during that second week of October. "Look, first one there wins, okay?"

"What?" Junior said.

"Whoever arrives last buys the other a steak dinner."

The son laughed. He lived a few hundred miles closer and was planning on leaving a day earlier than his father.

"You're on, Dad."

Just west of the Blue Ridge Mountains, known for its art scene and historic architecture, the picturesque, mountainous terrain of Asheville offered nothing but gorgeous Americana scenery, as well as endless photography subjects.

"It's going to be great, Dad."

"It is. I cannot wait. So excited."

As much as he was looking forward to moving and starting a new job, Senior was ecstatic to be reconnecting with his oldest boy. Living together. Getting to know each other as adults. Even though both his boys were older, Senior's divorce, like any, had been difficult. Since the split in 2010, Junior and Senior had bonded, but Senior was looking forward to forging that into a close friendship, while watching his son grow.

Chris and his father spoke or texted every day during this time. Junior later recalled, during the fall of 2014, as they discussed the move, they never failed to communicate at least several times daily. They spoke constantly over a twenty-four-hour period.

"I'm at work, can't talk right now," Senior would say if he was busy. "I'll text you later."

And he always would.

* * *

AS CHRIS JR. STOOD and stared out the window of his apartment, looking at his car fully loaded with his possessions, a trickle of excitement stirred. He was eager to get on the road. He looked at his watch. It was late in the day, October 15, 2014. The sun was just dropping below the horizon. The only bit of awkwardness Chris Jr. felt on that day—and it was minor at the time—was that he'd not heard from his father all day long. He'd texted and called. But had not gotten a response.

The next morning, October 16, Junior opened his eyes, grabbed his iPhone, and rubbed the sleep from his eyes. After acclimating himself to getting up, Junior stared at the iPhone screen.

Not one text or call from his father throughout the night or that morning.

Standing, walking to the bathroom, Junior stopped in the hallway. He felt a pinch in his gut.

Something's wrong. I just know it.

2

NIGHT SHIFT

ENOUGH, CHIEF LAURA FRIZZO decided. *That is enough for today.* It was twenty minutes to five o'clock. Frizzo's sergeant, Cindy Barrette, would be in soon to begin her shift: five p.m. to three a.m. Frizzo should have been out the door two hours ago, on her way home. Except, well, when it came to work, Frizzo had "a problem leaving," she said.

The job.

Always pulling her away from life—something one signs up for as the chief of police in a small town.

October 27, 2014, was a brisk autumn evening in Michigan's Upper Peninsula. As Iron River Police Department (IRPD) chief Laura Frizzo walked out of the station house's front doors and began locking up, out of the corner of her eye she saw a car pull up. She put the key into the lock, turned it to the right, latching the glass doors with a metallic snap. Standing there, Frizzo made a point *not* to look at the vehicle or make eye contact with its driver. Her workday was supposed to be over.

Get in your car. Go home.

As Frizzo walked, she could hear the car engine shut down, the driver's door creak open.

Don't turn around, the chief told herself. *Don't look up. Don't make eye contact. Walk to your car.*

As Frizzo reached down to open her car door, unable to help herself, she glanced up. The woman who had parked in front of the building now stood at the locked precinct doors, pulling on the handle, cupping her hands around her eyes, peering inside, frustrated nobody was around.

Frizzo could see the woman was anxious.

Then the woman turned. Stared directly at the chief.

Laura Frizzo saw "help me" written all over her face.

"Yes, ma'am, of course—what is it?" Frizzo said, rushing toward the woman.

The blond, middle-aged woman seemed more upset and worried than frazzled. "Yes, I . . . I . . . ," she tried to say.

Something's not right here, Frizzo knew.

"Why don't we go inside and talk," Frizzo suggested.

And there it was: the rub of being a cop—it's not what you do; it's who you are.

Thirty-four-year law enforcement veteran, IRPD sergeant Cindy Barrette was due in at any minute for her ten-hour shift, Frizzo knew. As she and the woman walked in, *What was another couple of minutes waiting with some-one in need?* the chief considered. Soon as Cindy arrived, Frizzo could hand her whatever problem the woman had and continue on her way home.

"My friend," the woman explained to Frizzo, "it's my friend Chris. I think . . . well, he's missing. I've made several attempts to contact him . . . and . . . well, um, I found his car . . ."

At the time fifty-three-year-old Chris Regan Sr.'s disappearance was reported, Laura Frizzo, with eighteen years behind an IRPD badge, was the first woman in Upper Michigan to be named police chief. She had held the highest job in the IRPD since January 1, 2014. Ten months. A single mother, the forty-five-year-old self-proclaimed "gym rat," lifting weights five days a week if she had her way, was in better physical shape than most twenty-year-old females. During working hours, Frizzo wore her brown hair tied back in a ponytail, curly ribbons dangled over to one side, naturally flowing down her shoulders. Frizzo carried a wholesome look about her, with the chiseled facial features of a model. Still, she was street-tough and strong-willed. Make no mistake, Laura Frizzo could handle any situation she might find herself in as a cop in a small town replete with the same problems plaguing the rest of the country.

Frizzo's career in law enforcement began with the Grand Rapids Police Department (GRPD) after she was graduated from the Kalamazoo Police Academy. Although her reign as IRPD chief would end in controversy—Frizzo having no idea in this moment the impetus for that personal and politically driven public shitstorm had just begun—most of the town's three thousand residents respected the chief and believed Frizzo was the most qualified person for the job. She was liked by many and praised for her tenacity, integrity, and overall experience as a peace officer.

"Take a seat," Frizzo said as she and the woman walked into the precinct. "Let's talk about this."

Iron River, Michigan, sits about 140 miles north of Green Bay, just over the Wisconsin state line. The town butts up against the edge of the Ottawa National Forest, far west of the most northern tip of Lake Michigan, due south of the middle point of Lake Superior. This is

Fargo-like country, complete with a touch of the "you-betcha" accent. The snow in winter can accumulate hip-high without warning, the air cold and dry as a freezer burn. There are over three thousand miles of snowmobile track throughout the state. Several Native American reservations are scattered about the immediate area around Iron River. It's quiet. Secluded. Wide open. Generally flat. Friendly. Homey. And totally Midwestern. Yet, despite Iron River being such a small town, the heroin (opioid) epidemic, like mostly everywhere else, has sucked up any serenity the landscape and law-abiding citizens might offer. Meth has become a problem for the IRPD, too. With this, of course, come the burglaries, larcenies, B&Es, home invasions, and associated violence.

"All sorts of problems, not enough police officers," Frizzo said.

Still, all that police business being part of a normal IRPD day, people up here don't go missing without reason, and even the most unassuming local cops can become the biggest pains in your ass if you're trying to deceive, take advantage of, or break the law. Though they might don wool caps with Elmer Fudd earflaps during the coldest months, ten pounds' worth of winter boots, and heavy, parka-type down coats with furry collars, these cops are quiet and resolute. When someone walks into a PD talking about a missing friend or family member, cops don't roll their eyes and shoo them away, thinking the person is overreacting. They listen. Respond. Make a promise to find out what happened.

"Please explain what is going on," Frizzo prompted the woman.

Just then, Cindy Barrette walked in. "Evening. What's going on?"

Good, Frizzo thought. She could turn the case over

and get home at a decent hour for a change. If it turned into something bigger than a worried-over-nothing friend, Cindy would call, and Frizzo could jump back in.

The chief explained to her sergeant the facts she gathered, telling Barrette if she was needed in any capacity, Barrette should just call, adding, "I'm heading home." Then, to the woman, "My sergeant here will take a statement from you, ma'am. We're going to do whatever we can to help."

Frizzo took a breath, grabbed her things for a second time, and headed out the door.

As she explained the events that led her to the IRPD, fifty-three-year-old schoolteacher Terri O'Donnell said she had known Chris Regan, the so-called "missing man," since the early '80s, when they met in a bar while Chris was in the service. They lost touch, but reconnected through Facebook and started dating after Chris's divorce. By April 2014, Terri and Chris had decided to stop seeing each other romantically, but remained close friends. So much so, they still saw, or at least spoke to, each other two to three times per week.

"I am very family-oriented, he was not. He also had a few problems I couldn't get around. The relationship didn't work out. But we would still text, talk on the phone. Sometimes I would see him at the store," Terri told Barrette.

That store was Jubilee Foods in downtown Iron River. Terri O'Donnell's parents owned the store and Chris rented a small one-bedroom apartment nearby. They'd often run into each other in the store or parking lot. Say hello. Catch up.

As Terri spoke to Barrette, she was certain of the last time she saw Chris Regan. Almost two weeks before, on

October 14, 2014. Since that day, Terri said, she'd texted Chris, driven by his apartment, banged on his door. She'd called and called and called. But came up short every time. This was so unlike Chris. Terri could think of no reason for him to avoid her.

"He was very good at returning calls and texts," Terri said.

Barrette encouraged Terri to take a breath. Slow down. The sergeant took her coat off, hung it on the back of her chair, sat down, and took out a standard UD-3E form.

"We're going to file a missing person's report."

"Okay," Terri agreed, nodding her head.

"What makes you think he's not answering his phone?"

"It goes directly to voice mail."

Terri was firm on the date: October 14.

"How so?" Barrette asked.

"Well, on that morning, I spoke to a friend of mine who works with Chris . . . and he had said that was about the last time Chris had shown up at work."

Chris *never* missed work. He went in at five a.m. on most days and stayed until three, four, or five p.m. Nearly two weeks now and no one at the job had seen or heard from him.

"Also," Terri mentioned, "his storage unit in Caspian is still full of his belongings."

Something was off. The entire situation had a bad feeling about it, Barrette felt, without sharing her feelings with Terri.

"When was that—the day you spoke to your friend?"

"October twenty-third."

"Parents? Kids?"

"His folks are deceased. He has two sons."

Chris worked at Lake Shore, also known as Oldenburg

Group Incorporated, a large employer in town. Oldenburg, a private company, manufactured defense and mining equipment.

As Terri explained Chris's situation, she told Barrette he was planning a move to Asheville, North Carolina, but wasn't scheduled to leave, as far as she knew, until November 1. Terri believed Chris was going to pick up one of his two sons along the way (having no idea they were going separately). Still, Chris had his dream job lined up. He was looking forward to the change. Starting a new life away from Iron River.

"He was excited to begin a new chapter and move to North Carolina," someone close to the case later commented. Chris Regan was an air force veteran. North Carolina was a state he had been stationed in previously. "He loved the outdoors, wine, particularly biking, and his kayak. He took his camera with him wherever he went to record his adventures."

Most unsettling, Terri explained, was that Chris's car was not parked where he usually left it in the apartment complex lot. "I just found out Chris had a drug test scheduled on October fifteenth in relation to his job, which he did not show up for," she added.

Barrette's concern grew.

"When I spoke to Chris's coworker, my friend, he told me he thought he'd seen Chris's car at the park-and-ride in Bates," Terri said.

Part of Iron County, Bates Township is directly east of Iron River, about a ten-minute, five-mile drive. Odd that Chris would park his vehicle there. He loved that car, a Genesis Sport. Why would he leave it in Bates for this long? Terri O'Donnell wondered.

Terri said: "So I went up there to see for myself if it was actually Chris's car."

"What did you find out?"

"It was late last Thursday night. I saw it. Definitely his vehicle. I looked inside and saw some of his personal belongings. So that next day, Friday, I tried again to contact him—because I actually wanted to get into his apartment to see what was going on."

Terri thought maybe Chris was home, had somehow gotten hurt, and could not get hold of anyone. Or he'd taken terribly ill and was unable to communicate. On top of that, two items in particular inside Chris's car struck Terri as belongings Chris would never go without—his water bottle and a second bottle he used as a "spittoon" to regurgitate spittle from chewing tobacco. Both were on the front seat. A knee brace Chris had been wearing was also on the passenger seat. Seeing all of this alarmed Terri. She never saw Chris without them. Seeing it made her nervous. Why would he leave his car parked there and all those personal items behind?

"What did you do next?"

"I went after work on Friday to Jubilee Foods to see if I could get a spare set of keys to Chris's apartment. I wanted to go in and see if he was okay."

"Did you get in?"

"I also texted him to tell him I was going in—I was going to do this. I was concerned maybe he was injured or hurt inside the apartment."

"What did you find out?"

"I wasn't able to get inside the apartment on Friday."

"Why not?"

"Well, the extra set of keys to his apartment was not in the, um, lockbox, where they keep them. That set is missing."

Cindy Barrette sat in front of Terri O'Donnell, took notes, building on that UD-3E. It all had an air of suspicion. Terri was obviously distraught over her friend having not been heard from in so long. This did not feel like an adult disappearing on his own, getting away from family and friends for a few days to cool off or be alone.

It had a far different pulse.

Chris Regan had left his life in the middle of it—without telling anyone.

He had vanished.

3
DAD

CHRIS REGAN JR. WAS beyond concerned. Days, then a week, had gone by since that morning he opened his iPhone and did not see a call or text from his father.

Then two weeks.

Not a word.

They'd been talking about moving. Junior had his car loaded. They had a place to live set up in Asheville. Now Junior was pacing in his empty apartment, wondering what to do. Who should he call? His brother and mother, only because they lived so far away, rarely spoke to Senior. Would Senior, an adult, even be considered a missing person if Junior called someone? He was conflicted and confused.

Still: *Something is wrong.*

Chris Regan Sr. grew up in Northville, Michigan, which is divided by Oakland and Wayne Counties, an area suburb of the Detroit metropolitan region of the state. Chris met his wife, who lived in Rochester, while they were in high school. They were married not long after graduation: a quintessential American, Midwestern family.

"I remember camping a lot," Junior recalled. "My dad showed us lots of love. Took us places. He introduced us to the outdoors. He put me on my first bicycle. I've always had cycling in my life."

In the air force, Senior was a CAT 2 racer, mountain bikes. CAT 2 is a classification for serious cyclists that has to be maintained by entering races and scoring enough points.

"It's like a step below pro," Junior said. "He was very successful while being on the Air Force Road Racing Team."

Sailing was another outdoors passion senior adored, whether on a Sunfish, small lake craft, or a big boat on the ocean.

"He loved being on the water."

That love for the water led Chris into scuba diving, which he took as seriously as he did most anything else.

"While he was in the air force, he spent, like, eight months on the island of Micronesia, where he did lots of scuba diving in what he told me was one of the best locales in the world to dive."

The Federated States of Micronesia is a country actually spread out like blots of ink across the western Pacific Ocean, comprising more than six hundred islands in total. It is often described as "diver's heaven."

When Junior and his dad trained on mountain bikes together, it was a time that later brought about the best memories from the son. Senior was a motivator. He pushed his boy to the max—but in a healthy, positive way.

"Come on, Chris!" the son could hear his father screaming from behind while heading up a trail. Junior had hit a wall of fatigue, his legs burning with pain, throbbing with discomfort. "Don't think about your legs, son. Just keep

pushing. Don't give up! Don't give up! Think about win-
ning."

Junior pulled out that last-ditch effort.

"Pedal! Pedal! Pedal!"

Sometimes Dad would even catch up to his boy on the
trail and literally push him up a steep hill with one hand
on his back, the other on the handle bars of his bike.

"You got this. Come on, son. You can do this!"

MEMORIES CAME FLOODING BACK to Junior as he thought
about what to do. His father had completely fallen off the
radar. They were talking four or five times a day about
moving and the life ahead of them in Asheville. Then,
overnight, nothing.

Not a word.

Chris Jr. hadn't re-signed his lease. He was working
his final few days at a cycle shop in Upper Michigan.

"Everything was in my car. I'm ready to go."

Senior was going to beat him down there and win the
bet, Junior knew, because Junior, it turned out, could not
leave until November 2. He knew his father was starting
work in Asheville on November 1.

"So excited," Senior had said that last time they chat-
ted. It was getting cold in the Upper Peninsula, so it was
really slow at the bike shop. Bored, Junior would often
call his father to just shoot the breeze and wax about
Asheville.

"Yeah, Dad. So many trails. Lakes. Camping. The
mountain biking we will do."

But all he heard now was silence—and it became deaf-
ening as each moment passed. Louder, in fact, than anything Junior had ever heard in his life.

4
PARK-AND-RIDE

LAURA FRIZZO WAS ON her way home. She had not thought too much about the fact that Chris Regan had been missing now for two weeks—and how significant that time span alone could be. Frizzo was focused on getting home to her son. Putting dinner on the table. Unwinding.

It had been a long, exhausting Monday.

"It just didn't register with me at the time," Frizzo recalled. "I just turned it over to Cindy, thinking Chris Regan probably told someone where he was going—and that he would eventually turn up. That would be the end of it."

Still, as part of her daily routine, Frizzo reviewed each of her officers' daily logs from the previous night/afternoon, read through all of the reports generated during the day, and followed up with whatever needed to be done. She communicated with her officers mostly through e-mail, mandating a face-to-face interaction with the staff at least twice a month. Another task Frizzo put on herself as chief was writing police policies and procedures. "Because," she said, "there were absolutely none put in place by prior chiefs. . . ."

Doing all of that allowed Frizzo to keep a fairly accurate pulse on the happenings within the department—and crime in general—at all times. And as she considered the name Chris Regan, and thought more about it that night on her way home, hearing from Terri O'Donnell where Chris had worked, an internal bell went off.

Frizzo lit a Marlboro Light. Took a drag.

I know that name . . .

In fact, before arriving home, after turning the case over to Cindy Barrette, Frizzo had heard from her sergeant about the car. "Listen, I'm going to take a ride over to Bates Township on my way home to check it out. I'll also call Lake Shore," Frizzo said. "I know the director there very well. I'll make a couple of other calls, too. If I have anything, I'll get hold of you when I get home."

"Okay," Barrette said. "I will follow through here and we'll talk later."

As Frizzo drove toward Bates, she kept going back in her mind to Lake Shore, where Chris Regan worked. Frizzo had taken a call from the director of Lake Shore the previous month. Something about an employee who was scared of her husband and had not shown up for work. Lake Shore asked if the IRPD could take a drive by the woman's house and conduct a wellness check.

Something told Frizzo the two were connected: Chris Regan and this call the previous month.

Pulling into the park-and-ride, Frizzo spotted Chris Regan's two-door gray Hyundai Genesis.

The chief drove up. Parked. Got out. Took a quick walk around the vehicle, shining her flashlight, peering inside.

"Right away," Frizzo said, "I knew something was off. I felt Chris Regan had not parked this car himself."

She also had the feeling that the car had been there for a while.

5

MESSING AROUND

THROUGHOUT THE PREVIOUS WEEKEND, October 25 and 26, leading up to that Monday evening, October 27, when Terri O'Donnell drove to the IRPD, Chris Regan's former girlfriend worked her contacts at Jubilee Foods to see if she could get into Chris's apartment to have a look around. Terri spoke to the manager of the store, Zach, and her father, who managed the apartments. Zach told Terri he would get hold of the local locksmith, Willard, who promised to make a spare key so they could get into Chris's apartment. Meanwhile, Terri called and texted Chris several times; she received no response again.

Going back a few days before that, on Thursday, October 23, Terri spoke to one of Chris's coworkers.

"Have you heard from Chris at all?" Terri had asked.

"I have not. But I did see his car parked in Bates at the park-and-ride."

"I'm worried about him."

Chris's coworker snapped his fingers, "Hey, you know what? Now that I think of it . . . he's been romantically involved with someone at work. Her name is . . . um . . . Kelly. I believe Chris said she's estranged from her husband."

Earlier on that Monday, October 27, Terri heard from Willard in the form of a text: **Key is ready.**

"So after work," Terri explained to Sergeant Cindy Barrette as they continued filing the missing person's report, "I got hold of my mother and we went over to Chris's apartment."

Terri tensed up. Just the thought of what they had seen inside the apartment upset her.

"It's okay, ma'am," Barrette consoled. "We'll get this figured out. Please continue."

Terri explained how she had driven directly from Chris's apartment to the IRPD on that Monday night, October 27, now convinced more than ever something was wrong.

"When we first entered, I saw a folder on the floor. The apartment is very disheveled. Cabinet doors open. Dirty dishes. Things lying around. It all alarmed me."

"Why?"

"Chris never kept his apartment like that. He kept things *very* neat. His dishes were always done. Things were always put away. He is very organized."

Sergeant Barrette studied Terri for tells—any type of involuntary body movements indicating how she was feeling.

Mystified was about all Barrette came up with: "She was concerned and upset."

"You indicated he was leaving soon for a new job in North Carolina," Barrette asked Terri. She also wanted to know if the boxes and messy apartment were perhaps an indication of Chris packing for that trip.

"There were suitcases on his bed and boxes in the front room," Terri explained. "So he had started to pack. But things were very, *very* messy."

Her sense was the mess had nothing to do with Chris packing.

"What makes you suspicious something's off here, Miss O'Donnell?"

"The car. Chris would never leave that car of his in that lot for days at a time. He loves that vehicle."

Terri O'Donnell believed the inside of Chris's apartment spoke of something having happened to him. It felt as if he had been plucked from this environment in the middle of going about his life. Terri was certain this was *not* the way Chris would have left it. She had, in fact, helped Chris pack once when he moved from his house in Suttons Bay not long before. He'd packed one room at a time and had kept everything "very organized," she told Barrette.

Barrette asked about the folder on the floor. What did it contain, and where was it in relation to Terri walking into the apartment? She had actually pushed the folder out of the way with the door when she first walked in. The folder contained medical documents. She took a look inside. She found information about Chris taking Percocet—he'd suffered a knee injury that past August and his doctor had put him on the drug—and the drug screening he had to undergo for his new job.

Walking in, looking around, seeing dirty dishes "crusted over," as Terri put it, cabinets opened, various personal items everywhere—it was out of character for Chris.

"I knew something happened to him."

The gut speaks—and rarely lies—of what *is* and what is to come. Terri O'Donnell, who knew Chris Regan better than most of the people in his life then, stood inside Chris's apartment on October 27, 2014, and had a sinking feeling she was never going to see Chris Regan again.

Terri told Sergeant Barrette one more thing.

"What's that?"

"I've heard rumors Chris is messing around with a married woman from his work."

Barrette asked Terri to sign the UD-3E. Then requested if she would mind taking a ride over to Chris's apartment.

6
WHISPERS

CHIEF LAURA FRIZZO WAS one of those cops who could not let things go. She'd heard a few new details from her sergeant, Cindy Barrette, about Chris Regan's sudden disappearance. She'd stopped at the park-and-ride to check out his vehicle. Call it a cop's intuition, but Frizzo had a bad feeling about the way in which Chris's car was positioned.

Heading home, Frizzo thought again of that incident she had gotten involved in the month before, late September. It involved another employee at Lake Shore, thirty-two-year-old Kelly Cochran, the same married woman Chris Regan was allegedly seeing. Kelly Cochran was an electrical assembler working on the manufacturing line. A rough-around-the-edges type, Kelly had a series of butterfly tattoos (various sizes and shapes) along both arms, up onto her shoulders. She had black hair cut just below the neckline, with a rugged, beefy, power lifter's frame, broad, thick shoulders, and pronounced trap muscles. Kelly and Chris had met at work and started secretly hooking up not long after Kelly was hired in May 2014. For Chris, seeing Kelly was a "step down," someone close to both of them later observed: "Chris was a bit more of an upstanding guy in the community. He did not want anyone knowing he was dating Kelly Cochran. They were from two different worlds. She was married."

Kelly and her husband, Jason Cochran, a very overweight, bald-as-a-knee thirty-six-year-old, had moved to Iron River earlier that year from Hobart, Indiana. Jason was the tough-looking, outdoorsy type. Hunter. Fisherman. He had a reserved gait about him. A lot more seemed to be going on behind the large-framed glasses he wore than he would ever let out.

After walking in the door of her home, tossing the keys on the counter, Chief Frizzo recalled the name Kelly Cochran. Then a second name: Laura Sartori, who, with twelve years on the job, was Lake Shore's human resources generalist. Frizzo remembered how, back in late September, the IRPD had been called to do a "wellness" check on Kelly Cochran at her home after Kelly had called work to say she feared for her life. Kelly and Jason Cochran lived in Caspian. Five minutes south of Iron River, past the Iron River Country Club, Caspian was just out of Frizzo's jurisdiction, so the chief turned the wellness check call over to the local sheriff. Sartori had phoned Frizzo and explained that on September 27, 2014, Kelly called work and explained her "husband threatened to kill [her] and then kill himself." That next day, September 28, Kelly failed to show up for work. A report was generated on September 29.

"I cannot reach her by telephone," Laura Sartori had explained during her initial call into the IRPD about Kelly. "I'm worried about domestic violence inside the home."

"Why is that?" the responding officer asked.

"Because Kelly has come to work in the past with

marks consistent with a domestic assault. I've also heard of her husband making comments about harming her if she ever left him."

An officer took a ride over to the Cochran house that afternoon, September 29. Knocked on the door.

A dog barked from inside, but no one responded.

The officer took a walk around the property and noticed a light on, no vehicles in the driveway. Bending down on one knee for a closer look, he could tell "there were fresh tracks leaving the driveway."

He then went in search of a few neighbors to talk to.

"I saw Jason leaving earlier this morning," said the guy next door. "Probably going fishing. I have not seen Kelly."

LAURA FRIZZO GOT SETTLED inside her home on the evening of October 27. Thinking more about that September 29 incident report, she called Laura Sartori.

Sartori knew Chris Regan well, she said. He'd worked at Lake Shore/Oldenburg since December 13, 2013. As an air force veteran, Chris had a job that was high pressure, with major responsibilities. He was team leader for military assembly, overseeing all aspects of the company's larger military projects.

"He's very dependable," Sartori said. "He dots his *i*'s and crosses his *t*'s. . . ."

A guy like that, Frizzo thought, *would not just disappear on his own without letting someone know.*

The fact that on October 16 Chris did not show up for work confused her, Sartori explained to Frizzo. Chris had put in for October 15 off. Yet, when he failed to show on October 16, didn't call or tell anyone he was taking the day off, Sartori developed a whisper of concern.

No one had seen or heard from him since—and that whisper turned into a mild scream.

"It didn't make sense to me," Sartori said.

As Frizzo thought about it, she wondered: *Have Chris and Kelly run off together?*

Sartori explained how she got hold of the sheriff who had done the wellness check on Kelly Cochran back in September and he reported back to her that no one had been found at the Caspian address where Kelly Cochran lived. The house was empty.

"Allegedly," Sartori told Frizzo, "Chris Regan and Kelly Cochran were having an affair." Still, that information, Sartori warned, was from the rumor mill of a large workplace environment.

Since a few different sources reported Chris and Kelly were an item, Frizzo now felt it was likely true.

But what did it mean, actually, in the scope of a missing person's investigation? Affairs happen. Especially in the workplace.

Frizzo called the deputy who had conducted the wellness check and asked him for Kelly Cochran's address. Maybe Chris was living with her? Perhaps Kelly had tossed her husband out and Chris had moved in? Maybe they *had* taken off together? Was Kelly Cochran planning to move to North Carolina with Chris? Affairs brought out the worst in people. Lives were turned upside down. People did things they wouldn't normally do. How one reacted to his or her life imploding underneath the weight of an extramarital affair was not predictable. Add a jealous husband into the mix and, well, motive for violence rises to the surface.

"I don't have the address on me," the deputy said. "But I can explain how to get there."

7

ABSENCE OF MALICE

CINDY BARRETTE AND Terri O'Donnell drove to Chris Regan's apartment at 514 North Fourth Avenue in Iron River on the night of October 27, 2014. It was five forty-five p.m. when Terri let the sergeant in with the keys she'd gotten from the locksmith.

After having trouble finding a light switch, Terri walked the sergeant into the kitchen, found a light over the sink. Turning it on, looking around, Chris Regan's ex-girlfriend said, "This doesn't look like Chris's apartment at all—you know, it's all . . . it's all disheveled."[1]

"When I first entered," Barrette explained later, "it appeared that there may have been some packing going on. There were boxes in the living room area and in the kitchen and in the dining room. There were notes pertaining to, like, a to-do list for moving."

The apartment was disorganized. Personal belongings

---

1. Most of the real-time dialogue in this book is verbatim, taken directly from a host of Axon body-cam videos the Iron River Police Department recorded during the course of this investigation.

everywhere. Chris had left himself reminder notes all over the place. Most referenced the move to Asheville and what he needed to bring with him.

A detail-oriented guy.

Terri pointed to a bottle of medication sitting on the stove. "This is just one," she explained. "I'll show you his meds for his heart and stuff."

They walked toward the bathroom, stopping in the dining room.

Barrette took out her digital camera and snapped photos of anything she felt might be significant. As she did that and Terri explained items they were looking at, Barrette noticed Chris's laptop was still powered up and sitting open on the table. A coffee cup and several other items one might use during the course of daily life—calculator, stapler, highlighter markers, clipboard, magazines, hand creams, a candle—were next to it. The chair was pushed out from in front of the laptop, as if the person sitting had stood up and left.

The sergeant found an e-mail Chris had recently received from his future employer about a drug-screening appointment. He'd printed it out. Didn't say much, other than when and where. It seemed, from the available information, that maybe Chris Regan decided to leave for North Carolina early without telling anyone. In truth, Chris did not owe anyone an explanation regarding how he conducted his life, when he was taking off, or where he was going.

"He did plan on one of his sons moving down to North Carolina with him," Terri said as they walked through the apartment.

Terri found a cell phone on the table. Plugged it in. Barrette looked through it. Got the numbers for both of Chris's kids, along with additional contact info.

Making it into the bathroom, after Terri opened the medicine cabinet, she noticed at least eight prescription medications inside, sitting on the shelves.

Barrette photographed each one. Staring at it all, she became even more concerned.

Why would a man leave without taking his medications?

Seeing this quashed the early-move theory. Chris Regan's meds—some of them necessary for keeping his blood pressure in check, which he needed to take every day—were still in the cabinet.

Barrette slid the shower curtain to the side, looked down. In the bathtub was a scrub brush and what appeared to be a dried, crusty brownish-red covering of scum near the drain.

Something is off here.

In the bedroom, on the bed, two suitcases sat with the lids opened, nothing packed inside. Tucked on the side of Chris Regan's bed, in between the box spring and bed frame, easily accessible to the person sleeping on that side of the bed, was an aluminum baseball bat.

In the living room, Barrette found several phone chargers plugged into wall sockets.

A large box was in the kitchen, positioned in front of the stove. She noticed one cabinet drawer full of miscellaneous household items; it was pulled all the way open and appeared to have been rummaged through. On the counter above the drawer were a few small notebooks, one opened. A pen. A pair of prescription eyeglasses.

A handwritten calendar Barrette located had a few interesting notes, which Terri O'Donnell confirmed were written by Chris: *resign* sketched into the date of October 14; *last day of work* penciled in on October 23.

Barrette stopped and stared at the kitchen counter a moment.

"Toothbrush and toothpaste are in here?" she said aloud. Then turned toward the door into the apartment.

He walks out the door, no doubt planning to return . . . but never comes back.

A ceiling fan was still on in the living room. Barrette walked over to a window. Pulled the blinds to one side.

"Was this window left open?" she asked Terri.

"Window *was* open . . ."

They wandered around the apartment. Terri worked her iPhone to search for Chris's kids on Facebook. Couldn't come up with anything right away.

"It's just creepy," Terri said at one point.

"Yeah," the sergeant agreed. Then: "Let's go down and look at the truck."

"Yes. Let me show you the truck. . . ."

They worked their way out of the apartment.

As they walked, Terri said, "It's amazing what you know about somebody when you really start thinking, eh?"

"Oh, sure, honey, sure," Barrette said as they shared a brief moment of laughter in an increasingly tense situation.

The small white Mazda pickup Chris owned was parked on the north side of the apartment building lot, a kayak strapped to the top of the vehicle. It appeared to have been sitting in the same spot for a long time.

"So he hasn't drove this for a while?"

"No . . . ," Terri said.

"So what was he going to do with it if he took the insurance off?" Barrette wondered.

Terri said the truck was for winter use only. Chris was

likely going to sell it anyway, seeing that he had the other vehicle he was driving to North Carolina.

"Oh, yeah. Okay."

Barrette found nothing within the truck.

From Chris's apartment, Barrette said she was heading out to the park-and-ride to have a look at Chris's car. Terri said she'd meet her out there.

Terri arrived first. As Barrette pulled in, Terri was talking to a guy whose car was parked near Chris's Genesis.

"Been here for a long time," the man said to Terri.

"Have you seen anyone around the car or anything like that?" Terri asked.

"No."

Barrette stepped out of her cruiser, flashlight in hand. She noticed Chris's Hyundai parked on the north side of the lot, its front end facing north. It wasn't as though whoever was driving the car had been in a hurry to park it. Quite to the contrary, actually.

Shining her flashlight inside the vehicle, Barrette walked around, looking for anything out of place.

"There were a couple of water bottles in the console," Barrette said. "A hat and pair of gloves kind of wedged into the seat."

Then something else.

"Is that his knee brace?" the sergeant asked Terri, shining her flashlight beam on it.

"Yup."

"Does he normally wear the knee brace?"

"Yup."

Suicide, Barrette thought, standing, staring out into a wooded area directly in front of the car. She pictured Chris parking, finishing up whatever business he had, stepping out, walking into the woods, blowing his brains out.

"It had to be considered because that sort of thing happens," Barrette recalled.

"Will you be opening up the trunk or anything like that?" Terri asked. An autumn chill was in the air. Terri had her arms folded, hugging herself to stay warm.

"Is there any way to open the trunk from the interior?" Barrette asked.

"Yeah."

"Let me see then if I can get in there."

Barrette decided the suspicious activity surrounding Chris Regan's so-called disappearance justified taking out her Slim Jim. This is a long, flat, and flexible metal apparatus cops use to shimmy down a vehicle's window, inside the door, and pop the lock open.

After a few tries, the little button on the car door gave—and set off the alarm, subsequently securing the latch to the trunk.

Inside, they both looked around.

Terri came up with a Post-it note, turned over, on the seat. She picked it up and handed it to Barrette.

The sergeant looked at the note; it appeared to be directions to a house.

424 lft
Stop sign left
Thru 4way stop
Lft on side st to yield sign
Left over creek rt in alley
Brown house

Who writes down directions anymore? Why not GPS the address with a cell phone?

"Listen," Barrette told Terri, "can you make contact

with Chris's kids on Facebook and see if they have had any contact or know where their father is?"

"I can."

It was time to head back to the office and make a few calls, Barrette felt.

Along the way, the sergeant phoned Chief Frizzo and explained what she'd found inside the car. "Handwritten directions, on the front seat of Chris's car. A Post-it note. That and the knee brace and water bottles were about it."

"Directions?" Frizzo asked, curious.

"Yeah," she said, explaining what the Post-it said.

Turned out to be the same directions Frizzo had been given by the deputy she had spoken to earlier that same night: Kelly and Jason Cochran's Caspian house.

8
QUESTIONS

An American flag hangs from a pole off the corner of the Iron River municipal building. The textured, redbrick, four-story structure on the corner of North First Avenue and West Genesee Street in downtown Iron River stands tall in front of three city park benches, its front doors underneath a half-moon-shaped contemporary glass enclosure. City Hall takes up most of the space inside the building, with the IRPD entrance located around the corner, on the east side, the precinct strategically positioned on the lower level. Iron River was once a major mining hub, today relying more on skiing and snowmobiling, hunting, fishing, and biking.

"You wouldn't believe all the crime," said one former resident. "And the drugs. Oh, yeah. The worst types. You betcha. Most of it coming up from Milwaukee."

Late on a Monday evening in October, sitting inside her office, an adult missing-person case gnawing at her, was the last situation Sergeant Cindy Barrette expected to be in. Mondays were not what you would call busy around the IRPD. However, once working as undersheriff earlier in her career, along with serving in various agencies statewide, Barrette was not naive where it pertained to a working law enforcement environment: "Anything can happen at any time."

The only way to exhaust all options when looking into an adult missing-person case is to follow the evidence, while using your investigative instinct and common sense to guide you. Knowing Chris Regan was a military veteran, Barrette phoned the VA hospital in Iron Mountain at seven-eighteen that evening to see if Chris had checked himself in. Or perhaps someone had brought him there for treatment he did not want anyone to know about.

"Let me check," a VA officer said.

Barrette waited.

"Nope, no one under that name is in our *entire* system." Which meant across the entire country, in any VA hospital.

"Thank you."

Barrette entered the official missing person's report, UD-E3, into the two national databases that law enforcement uses. She called Chris Regan's son, Cameron, and his other son, Chris Jr. Both calls went straight to voice mail.

Her next call was to Iron County dispatch. "Get hold of Verizon wireless for me," Barrette said. "See if they can do call-pinging for us."

"I'm on it, Sergeant."

Barrette sat at her desk and thought about what she'd learned over the course of the past several hours. Kelly Cochran, she'd found out from Chief Frizzo, had shown up for work on October 3, several days after an Iron County sheriff's deputy conducted that wellness check. She had since left the job for good, but on that specific day, human resources generalist Laura Sartori had asked Kelly Cochran if she was still worried her husband was going to kill her and himself.

"Sorry, yeah, everything's fine," Kelly had said. She did not seem concerned anymore.

"Okay, then," Sartori responded.

What's more, the Michigan State Police (MSP) had gotten involved in the wellness check and Kelly had contacted the investigating trooper by phone on October 3, the day she returned to work.

"I'm fine," Kelly's voice mail had said. "I appreciate you checking up on me."

Still, something didn't feel right. There appeared to be so much more to that story.

Barrette and Sartori discussed the connection between their missing man and Kelly Cochran. Then hung up.

Sometime later, Barrette heard from dispatch regarding Chris Regan's phone.

"The last time it was used, according to Verizon, was October fourteenth. However, they were unable to locate where, due to the amount of time that has elapsed since."

Barrette stared at the Post-it note she'd taken from Chris's vehicle. It felt significant. Chris Regan was missing. Here was a note with directions to an address. The address and Kelly Cochran meant something to him. This wasn't trumped-up gossip inside a large factory; coworkers whispering in the break room about two people hooking up. Here was a direct connection between Chris and Kelly. Not to mention an indication that the last location Chris Regan seemed to be heading was Kelly Cochran's home.

The IRPD staffed seven full-time officers, including the chief. At one time, the town wanted to disband the entire force and leave patrolling up to the state police and local sheriff's department. But that did not sit well with the majority of taxpayers.

Still, with a department so small, the IRPD relied on outside help whenever it faced a case growing beyond the scope of its own personnel power. So Cindy Barrette contacted the MSP and asked if they could send a trooper to meet her at 66 Lawrence Street in Caspian, Kelly and Jason Cochran's address. The evidence led to this address. Here was the place where, Barrette decided, she could possibly begin to find out where Chris Regan was or what had happened to him. Still, when she thought about it, Chris's car in that park-and-ride lot, those woods around the lot, suicide kept creeping back up into the veteran investigator's mind.

Frizzo reassured Barrette it was a smart move to head over to the Cochran house and ask a few questions.

"Just call me back and let me know how it goes," Frizzo said.

"Okay, then. You bet."

Ten minutes later, Barrette and an MSP trooper were standing on the porch of Jason and Kelly Cochran's modest, run-down country home.

LAWRENCE STREET IN CASPIAN is a rural road: Two-story, country-type Colonial homes built in the 1950s and 1960s, perhaps further back, sit on green lawns, with a few contemporary homes scattered about the area. Pine trees and maples and oaks dot the yards along what is a tarred road with spiderweb cracks, weeds shooting up like exploding fireworks. Kelly and Jason Cochran had no kids. They had been living in Michigan for about ten months. They'd relocated after Kelly found a job in Iron

River at the Ace Hardware. Kelly was the oldest of three siblings. She graduated from Purdue University with a bachelor's in liberal arts. Her majors were psychology and sociology, with a minor in forensics.

Kelly was raised in Hobart, Indiana. "We grew up with a pretty basic upbringing. We raised animals and had a fairly" common life, she said. "That's pretty much it."

In Indiana, Jason and Kelly had been neighbors for what seemed like forever: "I've known him pretty much all my life. Our families talked together. We had cook-outs."

Due to their four-year age difference, Kelly and Jason did not hang out as kids.

"When I turned fifteen, sixteen, we'd sit by bonfires and stuff."

They started officially dating in 2000, after Kelly graduated from high school.

"We hung out a little bit before that, went to some concerts, but nothing really ever intimate. He did have a girlfriend at that time."

By May 2001, they'd ratcheted the relationship up a notch and Kelly said she started "staying over at Jason's house quite a bit." By September 14, 2002, Kelly Gaboyan and Jason Cochran were married. Kelly was twenty.

"The first eight months were great," she explained. Jason "was perfect. . . . He was, like, my soul mate. We could finish each other's sentences. We did a lot . . . um . . . we did *everything* together."

Gradually, however, things changed. After that eight months, Kelly said, the relationship behind closed doors became more abrasive and difficult.

"He would get angrier, easier. There was, like, this second side of him. He still had his good points. He still was 'good,' but there was still a little more to him—this *bad* side."

Kelly described herself as "strong, stubborn, independent, and feisty." From an early age, she learned how to "strive to be independent." Jason, on the other hand, "I don't know if he really liked that [part of me] much. He . . . I really don't think he liked that [independence of mine] at all."

In Caspian, the Cochrans lived in a two-story, dark brown house with white trim, a rotting, ragged handicap wooden ramp leading up to the front door. Trees and overgrown brush hid most of the house from the road. Out back was a fire pit, an old garage with a busted door, some junk and garbage spread about the perimeter of the garage, as well as inside. Tall weeds had grown over and around just about everything. Some attempt had been made to keep up with maintaining the house and yard, but a fruitless effort nonetheless.

Sergeant Cindy Barrette stared at the front of the Cochran house as she and an MSP trooper walked up the wooden ramp. Before reaching the door, the trooper pulled Barrette aside.

"Someone just looked out the upstairs window."

Barrette glanced in that direction and noticed someone was watching them from behind a curtain.

After Barrette knocked on the Cochrans' front door, Jason walked out and greeted them on the porch, the door closing behind him: "Yeah—what do you want?"

Jason Cochran came across as standoffish. His body language—rigid, his chest sticking out—gave away how irritated he was at having two police officers standing on his front porch. At five-nine, 265 pounds, Jason was an obese, but clearly powerful and solid, man.

"Sir, good evening," Barrette said.

"Yeah?"

"You must be Mr. Jason Cochran?"

"I am."

"Is Kelly Cochran your wife, sir?"

"Um, what's this about? Yes, she is. But she ain't home right now. She'll be back in an hour or so."

"Is anyone else inside the home right now, sir?" the MSP trooper asked.

"No."

"Can you tell me where we can find your wife, sir?" Barrette said.

Jason kept looking at the two of them. Eyeing each. He would not say where Kelly was. Then: "If you come back in an hour, she should be home."

Barrette and the trooper looked at each other for a brief moment. Barrette knew Jason Cochran was lying.

Just then, as Barrette contemplated her next move, the front door opened and Kelly walked out.

"Why did you lie to us?" Barrette asked Jason.

Kelly piped in, "Listen, he . . . he just . . . probably thought I was in trouble."

That minor obstruction somewhat settled, Barrette explained she was investigating the disappearance of Christopher Regan, adding, "We were wondering when it was you last had contact with him?"

Jason faded back a little from the group, but stayed in earshot. Kelly stepped forward. She was not in the least bit nervous. One might say she was composed. Barrette was under the impression Kelly wanted to help.

"We had a relationship," Kelly admitted, looking at the sergeant.

"When was the last time you saw him?"

"It was, oh, on or about October fifteenth. I tried calling and texting him."

Barrette kept an eye on Jason, who had no reaction whatsoever to this part of the conversation.

"Did you get in touch with him?"

"No. No answers back. No contact."

"Ma'am," Barrette said, "any indication where Christopher Regan could have gone off to?"

"I think he might have left already for North Carolina. To get down to his new job."

It was hard to tell one way or another how Kelly was feeling about a subject, or get a good read on the thoughts banging around inside her head. Because anything Kelly Cochran talked about was articulated with the same flat effect: an analytical manner or blatant sarcasm. Even monotone. Whether talking about a missing lover or lying to her husband, Kelly had an unemotional sense about her.

Sizing up the situation, knowing what can happen when a love triangle ensues, Barrette came out with it: "Does your husband know about your relationship with Mr. Regan, ma'am?"

Kelly did not hesitate: "He was okay with it."

Now was no time to judge; it was about gathering information. Barrette looked at Jason, who clearly heard what his wife had said.

Besides pushing his glasses up the bridge of his nose and taking a deep breath, the big man revealed zero response.

"We found Mr. Regan's vehicle in Bates at the park-and-ride," Barrette told Kelly. "But he was not with the car."

It might have been a mistake to tell Kelly or Jason where the car was, rather than see if it could be drawn out from them. But as a cop in a fluid situation, you have to roll with what's happening in the moment.

"He loved that car," Kelly said.

"Ma'am?"

"He *loved* that car," Kelly said again.

That one word sent a chill down the back of the sergeant's spine.

Loved.

Past tense. Barrette made note of the grammatical choice Kelly had made, but did not question why she would make it.

Barrette reached inside her front coat pocket, pulled out a business card, handed it to Kelly: "If you have any information about his whereabouts, please contact us."

Kelly took the card and stared at it. "Oh, sure. I will."

Barrette drove back to the office, thinking about the conversation. Something bothered her about Jason Cochran and his wife, beyond Kelly's use of the past tense when describing Chris Regan. For Barrette, it felt as though Jason harbored some sort of deep-seated issue with the situation. It was in his gait, his inflection, the way he seemed to turn his nose to law enforcement. Just a hunch, but there was much more to what was going on over there. The Cochrans (especially Jason) knew more than they had been willing to share with law enforcement.

"Listen," Barrette told Terri O'Donnell over the phone later that night, "do not go back into the apartment, and do not let anyone else inside, please."

"Understood," Terri said.

Barrette tried calling Chris Regan's kids, Chris Jr. and Cameron. She was unable to reach either.

Then she called Chief Frizzo.

"What's up?" Frizzo asked.

"Look, something is really, really wrong here, Chief."

"How so?"

"I don't know, but Kelly Cochran kept referring to our missing man in the past tense. Thought you should know."

Frizzo sighed.

Every internal alarm sounded.

"Let's go ahead and get his car towed in from the park-and-ride then," Frizzo said.

"I'm on it."

9
ANSWERS

MOTHER OF THREE, Laura Frizzo sat down at her kitchen table on October 28, 2014, sipping her first cup of coffee of the new day. It was four-thirty in the morning, Frizzo's regular wake-up time. After some time to herself, she made her son breakfast. Then, same as she did most work-day mornings, Frizzo put pen to paper: *Have a great day! I love you*. Her youngest was fourteen. She needed the boy to wake up every single day before she left that house for work and know that she thought of nothing else besides him, his older siblings, and her two grandkids.

"My world, those kids," Frizzo said.

By six-thirty, Frizzo was on her way out the door. Not a fan of eating breakfast, the chief routinely stopped at the McDonald's in town and ordered her favorite: peppermint mocha. They knew the chief so well, the local chain restaurant actually stashed some of the peppermint mixture during the off-season specifically for Frizzo.

"It was one of the highlights of my morning," she said.

By seven, Frizzo was at the office going through the previous night's work to see where she could be of service. She was more certain than ever that Chris Regan's vanishing act was not going to yield the type of results everyone who loved the man wanted. Frizzo went right to work, determined to find answers for Terri O'Donnell and Chris's family.

"I was supposed to be available twenty-four/seven and there were times I would put in one hundred hours a week," Frizzo said of the job. "Go two weeks without a day off and on one occasion was awake for forty-two hours straight."

Frizzo wasn't complaining, but rather explaining that when you signed up for law enforcement work, you did what was needed, expected, and asked, or you turned in the badge.

The chief searched through the in-house database, but wasn't able to dig up much information about Chris Regan on the local law enforcement network. Main task for Frizzo right then was finding out who Chris Regan was, what he did, where he'd lived, info about family and friends. She needed phone numbers and contact information. People have two sides: the one they display in front of family, friends, and coworkers (and the public), and the one they keep secret.

Striking out on the in-house computer network, Frizzo phoned the local sheriff.

"Yeah, I'll be in Iron River soon."

Waiting for the sheriff to arrive, Frizzo looked at the body-cam videos Cindy Barrette had recorded the previous night while going through Chris's apartment. She also studied the documentation from Chris's doctor found inside that file on the floor Terri O'Donnell had stepped over to first get inside.

Immediately Frizzo noticed Chris's doctor had given him a script for pain pills and he'd just had knee surgery.

And yet, that knee brace was on the front seat of his car?

Looking through the documents further, Frizzo discovered Chris had gotten a letter from his doctor, dated October 14, which explained he'd had knee surgery and any drug screening he'd undergo for his new job would show the pain meds he was on, namely Percocet.

He wanted to prove why that narcotic was in his system, Frizzo knew, putting the letter down. *Why would a guy go through such trouble if he'd planned on suicide?*

Didn't make sense.

Frizzo also considered one nagging issue with regard to the Percocet: Among all those medications inside Chris's apartment, the Percocet was nowhere to be found.

The local sheriff Frizzo had called in for support brought a report on Chris Regan with him to the IRPD. Frizzo now had her hands on Chris's last-known vehicles and addresses, family contact information, any arrests (zero), and so on.

"I need to start talking to people he knows," Frizzo said.

The one plus for Laura Frizzo was that she had nearly two decades behind the badge, the respect of law enforcement agencies all over the state, and personally knew many different experts from various law enforcement fields. When Frizzo ran into a case she felt was growing beyond the small field of full-time officers she had on staff, as this one certainly was beginning to show signs of, the chief leaned on former colleagues and friends.

"Oh, you know it, Chief Frizzo took this case and ran with it," Cindy Barrette said later. "Excellent police officer. I've worked with her for twenty years. She is one of these people who never lets anything drop. I hate to say it, but she's like a hound dog—she does *not* let go."

* * *

LAURA FRIZZO BEGAN her public service career in Grand
Rapids (1991), where she worked as an emergency communications operator at the Grand Rapids PD. Her second daughter was born in 1993. When that child was four
months old, Frizzo put herself through the police academy in Kalamazoo. After graduation, she moved back to
Upper Michigan.

By the time Frizzo was twenty-four, she found herself
twice divorced.

"I married my high-school sweetheart the first time
and left him for this *awesome* [guy], who beat the shit out
of me on a regular basis, so that wasn't going to work out.
After graduating the academy, I was offered and accepted
a job with the Marquette County Sheriff's Department,
but before my start date, I received a job offer from Iron
River Police. Although I would have preferred the job in
Marquette, I took Iron River so that my parents would be
able to help with the kids."

Her first day in Iron River was April 12, 1995. Five
years later, she married again and had a son. That marriage lasted nearly seventeen years.

"The last five years he traveled for work much of the
time and I'd see him once every five weeks. Being alone
changed me, work changed me, so we parted ways. No
doubt I regret many things. But my kids are the greatest
accomplishment of my whole life and they give my life
purpose."

All those years in law enforcement had given Frizzo
access to resources throughout the state of Michigan—
many of whom were going to wind up helping her more
than she knew on this second day of looking into the disappearance of Chris Regan.

* * *

MISSING-PERSON CASES INVOLVE intricate knowledge behind the matrix of cell phone usage and how the telematics of cell phone use works, how cell phones store information, where cell towers are located, and how to obtain pinging information from a particular cell number/tower. Law enforcement can track movements of cell phones if investigators know what information to look for. Most people carry around a personal GPS unit and computer in their pockets, unknowingly recording their movements in life and online. Still, that information is only useful if, as a cop, you can get your hands on it in a timely fashion and understand what it all means.

Later that same morning, October 28, Frizzo met with the MSP to ask for assistance in a case she and her sergeant believed was much more than an adult male making himself disappear. The meds, the messy apartment, the abandoned vehicle, the now-confirmed affair with coworker Kelly Cochran, Kelly's sketchy husband, not to mention a note with directions to the lover's house, all spoke of what could possibly be a deadly love triangle— a jealous husband letting loose and getting rid of a problem.

"We had many directions to go in," Frizzo said. "I needed assistance in preparation of either search warrants or interviews."

The more people she spoke to within Chris Regan's circle, a better picture of his recent life emerged. For example, Frizzo found out Chris did not want anyone to know he was spending time with Kelly Cochran.

"Something happened at work where a comment had been made about their relationship and Chris became very irate," Frizzo said.

This piqued the cop's interest. She wanted to know more about the relationship.

"On a mission" was how Frizzo described her attitude that morning as the case expanded.

Something else bothered the IRPD's lead investigator. Frizzo had called Public Services Incorporated in North Carolina and spoke to the man who had hired Chris. The chief could not overlook the strong possibility that Chris Regan had gotten into an argument with Kelly, and maybe Jason, and decided to take off to North Carolina early. He could always send for his personal belongings. Anger can make decisions for people, Frizzo was fully aware. She wasn't naive, either; she knew that inadvertently left-behind medications, a married girlfriend, a note, and an abandoned vehicle in a park-and-ride could appear to be suspicious, but in today's world, until you had answers to pending questions, what did it actually mean?

"Have you had any communication with Mr. Regan recently?" Frizzo asked Jimmy Torres, Chris's contact person in North Carolina. "We were thinking he might have gone down early to find an apartment or something."

"No," Torres said. "He has not shown up. We were actually wondering what was going on ourselves."

"What do you mean by that?"

"We're surprised and wondering because Chris was so excited and anxious to come down. We've been talking to him and communicating daily, and, suddenly, about two weeks ago, we stopped hearing from him."

The chief paused. Reflected. Nodded in the affirmative on her end of the call.

"We had even discussed internally here that maybe

Chris didn't want the job and was avoiding my calls," Torres continued.

Frizzo confirmed Chris's actual work starting date to be November 10, not November 1. Terri O'Donnell had it wrong. This made his disappearance even more suspicious.

"Thanks," Frizzo said. "If you hear anything, please give us a call."

"Will do, Detective."

Frizzo phoned the lab where Chris was scheduled to get his drug screening for the new job. According to the paperwork found inside that folder on the floor of his apartment, Chris would have gotten that test done already.

"Nope," the lab said. "He never showed up."

Frizzo's next call at ten-fifteen that morning was to Chris's oldest boy, Chris Jr., who described a close relationship with his dad, which they'd recently rekindled after a few years of losing touch.

"We are planning to move to North Carolina together," Chris Jr. said. "He is excited to move and start his new job, but also anxious about everything he has to do before moving."

Frizzo asked when the last time Chris Jr. had spoken to his father.

Chris checked his cell phone.

"October thirteenth, eleven a.m.," he said. "I haven't heard from him since and was beginning to worry."

They discussed whether Chris was suicidal or depressed.

Chris said he never knew his dad to be either.

Hanging up, Chris Jr. stared at his phone.

I'm never going to see Dad again.

10
SOMETHING'S NOT RIGHT

MSP DETECTIVE CHRIS BRACKET was assigned to the Iron Mountain Post in Iron County and became the first state cop invited into the Chris Regan disappearance investigation. Described as a "very nice guy" by a colleague, Bracket was one of those high-school athletes the kids in school looked up to. Incredibly strong and solidly built, Bracket's frame made "him a good tactical guy," said that same colleague.

By request, Bracket and two additional MSP detectives joined Chief Frizzo on October 28 at eleven a.m. for a meeting to delegate work assignments, beyond a discussion about where to take the investigation next. Frizzo put in a call to Iron County prosecuting attorney (PA) Melissa Powell to get a bit of legal context regarding search warrants and interview protocol going into the day. The first interviews the IRPD wished to conduct were with Kelly and Jason Cochran. Start there. Get them—especially the husband—on record with a timeline and details. See where it led.

"A search warrant for the missing person's vehicle or

apartment was not needed," Powell advised. Indeed, under the Community Caretaker Act, suspicion was enough to go into both. "But you might want to consider search warrants for the Cochran vehicles, residence, and phone records."

"Of course. A search warrant for Chris Regan's phone records," Frizzo added, "is pending."

"Good."

Before hanging up, they discussed several additional search warrants Frizzo was thinking about—each of which was in the process of being written.

Powell said to keep her office informed.

As information became available throughout the day, one fact was clear: October 14 was the last day Chris Regan had contacted anyone. After he made various purchases on his credit cards that day, Frizzo found out, there was zero banking activity on any of his accounts and nobody had heard from him again. In addition, Frizzo got hold of CCTV footage from a local gas station dated October 14, between three-thirty and five p.m. Chris Regan's vehicle pulled in, a man fitting Chris's description got out and gassed up, before pulling out and going on his way.

Frizzo made a note: The gas station was located between the park-and-ride and the Cochran house, which, Frizzo Googled, was 4.5 miles.

There's no way he left his car in that lot—unless, Frizzo thought, *unless he jumped into another vehicle with [someone] and took off.*

The other important detail Frizzo sensed was that Jason Cochran, Kelly Cochran, or both, knew more than they were sharing.

As the MSP prepared to reach out to Kelly and Jason Cochran and ask them to voluntarily come into the IRPD for a recorded interview, even though she didn't need it, Frizzo drew up a search warrant for Chris's apartment.

"Look," Frizzo recalled, "I wanted to do those interviews with the Cochrans, but, of course, the 'specialists' want to conduct them. I'm very defensive about my investigations and how they're done. I really didn't want them [the MSP] to do the interviews, but I had to get the search warrants written up immediately."

Priorities.

Meanwhile, word came back from bringing the dogs out to search the fields around the park-and-ride, working under the premise that Chris Regan could have parked and went out into the woods to off himself.

"Nothing," Frizzo was told.

MSP DETECTIVE CHRIS BRACKET, along with a fellow MSP detective, drove to the Cochran house and asked Kelly if she would be willing to come down to the IRPD for an interview.

Kelly said sure.

Jason also agreed.

"Great," Bracket said.

Before they got settled in the interview suite at the IRPD, the MSP personnel decided Chief Frizzo would not be part of the interview process. She would instead monitor the interviews via a CCTV from another room, while typing out search warrants.

Frizzo felt slighted, as if they didn't want her involved in interviewing.

Chris Bracket and MSP detective Jean Belanger sat with Kelly, who appeared relaxed, casual, willing to help, and at ease with the situation.

After a few questions and comments, Bracket, running

the interview, said, "Obviously, we'd like to talk to you about Chris."

"Chris?" Kelly said, as if confused.

It took a few moments for Kelly to admit she and Chris Regan had an intimate relationship and Jason knew about it. But again, it did not seem to faze her in the least. Nor did it feel to either detective as if she was hiding anything.

Then Kelly discussed how Jason was "okay" with the relationships she had with other men. They had an open marriage. Jason was not at all thrilled about her running around town, having sex with random men, but he knew about it, and, as far as Kelly was concerned, he didn't bother her. They were separated and agreed seeing other people was part of that.

Bracket wondered when Kelly saw Chris last.

Kelly mentioned that the IRPD asked the same question the previous night, adding, "Probably two weeks ago from today."

"You saw him? Or talked to him?"

"I talked to him, I think . . . I would say between the twelfth and the fifteenth was the last time I saw him. We had dinner."

Frizzo sat: watching, listening, seething.

Why not follow up with additional questions? What did you have for dinner? Did you cook? Did Chris eat? Did you drink any liquor? Have sex? Details. Lock these two down with details.

Bracket continued asking about the relationship.

Kelly explained that she was "upset" with Chris around the time she last saw him because he had been texting her and calling every day before, but he had suddenly stopped.

"Did you have a falling-out?"

"No," she said, adding how they decided not to have

feelings for each other. They wanted to keep love out of the relationship because Chris was moving. He had asked her to move to North Carolina with him, but she told him Michigan was her home and she wasn't leaving.

Under the assumed pretense of Kelly being the last person to have had contact with Chris, Bracket asked what they did that "last night."

"Ah, we ate. That was pretty much it," Kelly said. She explained Chris generally went to bed around seven-thirty, so she would hang out a little while, watch some television by herself, and then leave.

"You didn't stay over?"

"I never stayed the night."

After being asked, Kelly said the conversation centered on Asheville, Chris's move, how excited he was to be heading south with his son and starting a new job. They also talked dates, Kelly certain it was the fourteenth, the last time she saw Chris; the actual date she believed Chris was moving (November 2); whether Kelly felt Chris suffered from depression (she didn't); and why she believed he was moving (to get away from a "dead-end job" and be with his son).

Bracket asked if they were on good terms.

"We only fought once," Kelly said. Two months back. Someone at work had said something about their relationship. Kelly said she believed certain people at work were badgering Chris about his relationship with her outside the job. And he hated it.

"So, Kelly, what is it you think happened to Chris?"

"I don't know," she said. "I've been texting and calling for the last two weeks."

"You have?"

"You have?" Frizzo said to herself, watching. *That's all you can come up with? "You have!"*

"I've driven by his house a couple of times. I thought maybe he was upset because I didn't want to go to North Carolina, but he would have called me . . ."

Bracket asked if Chris had ever been over to Kelly's house.

"Yes."

"Yes . . . so he knows where it is and everything?"

"Oh, yeah."

"Even way back when you guys first met?"

"No, no. It was probably two months after . . ."

Frizzo thought: *Why would Chris have directions to Kelly's house on the front seat of his car if he had been there before? Why weren't detectives asking this question? Why are they missing all these opportunities?*

In fact, Kelly explained, the last time Chris was out at the house had been three weeks prior, adding, "Twice in the last month."

They established Jason wasn't there whenever Chris stopped over.

Kelly sat and endured questions, when, in truth, she did not have to answer. Forty-five minutes into the interview, she maintained her composure and seemed to have an opinion or answer for any question thrown at her. Bracket and Belanger never pressed too hard on any one issue, opting instead, perhaps, to gather any information Kelly was offering.

The focus, as the interview wound down, turned to Jason and his attitude toward his wife and the marriage—not to mention that he had once wanted to kill her and himself.

Kelly admitted Jason often took off by himself fishing and hunting and she had no idea what he was doing, where he was, or whom he was with. She never considered he'd done something to Chris.

"You're concerned about my safety," Kelly said at one point, after Bracket expressed as much, "but I'm . . . well, *I'm* not."

"You're *not*? . . . Unfortunately, most women aren't."

True to her tough-girl persona, Kelly said, "I'm not most women. And I'm not trying to be. I'm not trying to come off corny or anything. I'm a farm girl."

They talked about the potential of being fooled by a manipulative, violent man who could play games with her mind, and no matter how tough Kelly thought she was, Jason was bigger, stronger, and had weapons in the home.

"I don't think I have ever seen him think more clearer," she said of Jason's recent mind-set.

"Than he is now?" Bracket asked.

"Uh-huh. And, look, he didn't threaten to kill me. Maybe that's the misunderstanding. He told me he had a thought for that. He came to me and told me that. He told me he was severely depressed and he thought about taking his own life. He needed help."

"And he *thought* about taking your life?"

"Yeah."

"That concerns me," Bracket said.

Kelly was asked if she'd mind taking a polygraph. The suggestion distressed her. She'd have to consult with a lawyer before agreeing to it.

During the course of the interview, Kelly mentioned another name—another man at her former job she had been sleeping with. Bracket wrote it down. Then they talked for a few minutes about whether Jason verbally abused her.

She said no.

"Did you ever tell anybody you were a victim of domestic violence?"

"Being hit?" Kelly snapped back. "No. I've never been hit. Never said I was hit."

"How about mentally abused?"

"By Jason?"

"Yeah."

"No."

Bracket and Belanger believed Kelly Cochran was hiding things from them—perhaps how abusive and violent her husband was when they were alone.

Jason Cochran sat outside the interview room, nervous and fidgety. His eyes darting left to right. A bit of sweat beading up on his bald head.

As they concluded the interview, Kelly mentioned how living in Upper Michigan felt like being part of a community; you could actually go to sleep with the doors unlocked or open and not have to worry.

"Did you guys come to Michigan so Jason could use medical marijuana? Is that pretty much why you came here?" Jason claimed the weed helped his back pain and depression.

"No! That was one of the things he tried after being up here a bit. No. We love it up here."

Bracket said they wanted to go back up to Caspian with her and Jason after his interview. They needed clarification as to where Jason hunted and fished, and maybe Kelly could point out some of those areas.

Kelly emerged from the interview room.

Jason stood. Took a deep breath. Pulled up his trousers. Then walked past his wife and in through the same door.

11

A COP'S COP

He's just sleeping," she said.

The three-year-old boy looked up at his stepmother. "Sleeping?"

"Yes."

Laura Kezerle stared at the man lying in the casket. George Robert Sassan, "Bobby" to everyone in the family, had been dressed in his police uniform, hands in white gloves folded over himself, his eyes closed. As they stood looking at Uncle Bobby, Laura's aunt explained to her stepson that his stepfather, Laura's uncle, was taking a nap. He wasn't dead. He hadn't been killed by a fellow peace officer while off-duty. He had closed his eyes and gone off to another place for a while.

Laura was six years old. It was 1975.

Bobby was a handsome man, back when that term carried with it a sense of self-confidence and down-to-earth manners. So much so, Bobby had been featured in several modeling ads for Harley-Davidson motorcycles.

Glendale, Wisconsin, is a small town just outside Milwaukee. A Glendale police officer, Bobby had just turned thirty years old that past May. Hanging out at a friend's bar one night after playing softball, a local pimp walked in and tried to solicit a prostitute drinking at the bar.

This upset Bobby. He grabbed the dude, pulled him down to the floor, and held him in a headlock.

"Call the local [cops]," Bobby said to his wife, who stood nearby, looking on.

As Bobby struggled with the pimp, the off-duty cop drew his weapon.

"When the police arrived," Laura later explained, one of the cops, a white guy, "came in and shot my uncle four times in the back, killing him."

The pimp was black.

"There are many unanswered questions regarding this and it actually was a discussion on the 'Geraldo' show back in the eighties. It's interesting with all the discussion going on today regarding wrongful killings by cops in this country how some think cops target a certain race or whatever . . . but here I am and that's the profession I chose, even after having my uncle shot wrongfully."

Laura Kezerle Frizzo came of age during the '70s in Crystal Falls, Michigan, a small town of fewer than two thousand people, fifteen miles east of Iron River.

"I was the only girl of four kids. My parents are Emil and Linda Kezerle. My dad was raised on a farm, the only boy with four sisters. He grew up in Iron River and the family still owns the two-hundred-acre farm. My mom was born in Chicago and grew up in Milwaukee. . . . Every night there was a big home-cooked meal. We were a vocal family. Loud. Very emotional. My family will tell you I was always stubborn and would never listen or do as I was told."

Part of that adolescent pigheadedness and independence Frizzo carried into adulthood—and, of course, into her police work. An attitude that generally served Frizzo's professional needs well.

ON OCTOBER 28, 2014, late afternoon, after Kelly Cochran was interviewed, Chief Frizzo looked on from the CCTV monitor inside the IRPD and watched as Jason Cochran sauntered into the interview suite. No sooner did Jason settle in and open his mouth for the first time, did Frizzo feel something was off with the guy.

"I'll tell you guys in advance," Jason said without being asked a question, "I see a therapist for high anxiety. I've been institutionalized a little over a month ago where I get, like, really flustered . . . that . . . so . . ."

"Okay," Bracket responded. Then mentioned that if the interview got "too uncomfortable" Jason should ask for a break. Bracket wanted it to be clear that Jason was under no pressure here. They were simply asking questions, having a conversation.

Frizzo listened. Something tugged at her regarding the interview Bracket and Belanger had conducted with Kelly Cochran earlier. Specifically something Kelly had said.

Frizzo repeated it to herself: *"I brought lasagna over for dinner."*

Kelly claimed that on October 14, the last time she saw Chris Regan, she brought lasagna into the apartment for the two of them.

Frizzo went back to the photos Cindy Barrette had taken inside the apartment, paying particular interest to a photo of the kitchen. In front of the stove was a large box. On top of the stove were all sorts of household items. No pans or dirty dishes were in the sink, or cleaned dishes in the washer. In fact, no indication whatsoever existed in the kitchen that Chris had a meal in the apartment in recent days. Every indication, in contrast, spoke to Chris eating takeout on most nights.

As she thought about this while staring at the photos, the monitor caught Frizzo's eye.

Jason Cochran was crying.

No way . . . , Frizzo thought. *Crying?*

Indeed, thirty-six-year-old Jason Cochran was sitting and sobbing like a small child. It felt pathetic. What did he have to cry about?

This guy here, Frizzo knew in that moment, *he is totally involved with Chris's disappearance.*

12
ROCKY ROADS

JASON COCHRAN WAS TIMID. Not, however, in an uncertain or shy way. Jason came across as someone hiding deep, dark secrets. As he explained himself to the MSP, Kelly Cochran's husband said he knew his wife had been seeing other men for the past few months, but didn't know any of the details. He knew Chris Regan, he said, by first name only.

"I wouldn't be able to pick him out of a lineup if I'd seen the guy," Jason claimed.

He told Kelly some time ago he wanted the situation this way because of his high anxiety. For several months leading up to this day, his marriage had been on "rocky roads." He mentioned several "health issues" were to blame. He'd lost a kidney. He had severe back pain and nerve damage and couldn't move around that well. He could not perform sexually.

As Jason spoke, Bracket and Belanger allowed him to say what he wanted without interruption. Jason had no trouble talking, once he got going.

When asked if he believed Chris was the "only one,"

meaning men his wife had been sleeping with, Jason said he knew of one other.

After pausing, thinking more about it, he said there could have been one more.

Jason talked down about himself, placing his position in the household as an unfit husband, always depressed, suicidal, unhealthy. Although he never did, Jason was on the verge of coming out and saying he didn't blame Kelly for stepping out and finding other men.

"Did you ever threaten Kelly?"

"No."

"Did you ever think about taking her life?"

"No, dear God, no. . . ."

Bracket wondered if maybe Jason had given his wife the impression that she should be afraid of him.

"Yeah," he admitted.

They then walked Jason into a discussion about Jason ever meeting Chris. To which, Jason said, "Never physically." He thought he'd seen Chris and Kelly together one time, but couldn't be sure.

"Do you know where he lives?"

"I've seen Kelly's truck . . . [at] an apartment building right there on the main drag. . . . I assume that's where he lives."

"Had you ever been there?"

"I've walked past. . . ."

They asked Jason if he considered Kelly to be "high maintenance."

"Not usually."

Then Bracket asked Jason if he knew why he was being interviewed.

"I, yeah . . . I think so. I know that somebody is missing. I want to guess I was probably the 'jealous husband.'"

"Yeah, yeah," Bracket responded.

Wait, no follow-ups? Frizzo said under her breath at the monitor. She was bewildered by this as she looked on from the other room. *Why are they not pressing him?*

They asked Jason if he'd be willing to take a polygraph.

After saying he had taken a forensic course in college, Jason asked what a polygraph was.

"Lie detector."

Jason stumbled through an explanation as to why he didn't want to. He understood those types of tests to be inaccurate and he wanted to speak with his psychiatrist first, before committing to it. Additionally, he ingested a lot of psychiatric meds on a daily basis, explaining further how one of the pills "helps me to calm the voices I have."

Both detectives chose not to question Jason about his alleged voices, instead opting to ask: "In a delusional state . . . is there *any* chance you could have done something?"

"No. No. I'm . . . uh. Since I've been out of the hospital, I've been like a different person. I don't have any lost time or anything." He explained this further by saying there had been times when, unable to sleep at night, he might be at the dinner table the next day, doze off, and then wake up and realize he had missed an hour of his life. Time he could not account for.

Bracket asked a smart question next: "Do you know how long Chris has been missing?"

"I don't have a clue. . . ."

Bracket wanted to know when Jason learned about Kelly's relationship with Chris.

"July . . . ," Jason said, adding how it had been a text message he found, tipping him off.

Bracket asked if he and Kelly were on Facebook.

They both were, Jason confirmed.

"So, Jason, how long have things been bad?"

It had been two and a half years since his "body went out," Jason answered, blaming his marital problems on his deteriorating health, physically and mentally.

One thing Kelly had mentioned to detectives during her interview was she believed Jason, suspicious she was cheating, might have put a GPS unit on her truck. Detectives thought maybe Jason had ordered it through an online retailer.

After mentioning Amazon, craigslist and eBay, specifically, Bracket asked if either he or Kelly had used those Internet companies to make purchases.

Jason wasn't sure about the others, but Amazon was a site they both had bought items from. Probably "books."

Bracket asked Jason if he and Kelly ever swapped partners with other couples.

"No, not at all. Because of my back," Jason said, "a lot of times I have sexual dysfunction where I don't—even if I wanted to, you know, so much pain, I couldn't—get hard. . . ."

"You ever have girlfriends?"

"No. I never dated outside. Kelly's the only woman I've loved. . . . Like I said, when my body went south, it's like the marriage started going south with it. . . ."

Bracket asked about the previous night. Why had Jason lied about Kelly being home?

Jason gave an "aw-shucks" look, as if embarrassed by his behavior. He said after Barrette and the other officer left, he felt like a "jackass" for lying.

"Is Kelly capable?" Bracket asked at one point, without referring to what.

"I don't think so. I wouldn't see how from her."

"Has she ever been violent?"

"No . . ." Jason explained there was zero abuse in the house, on either part. They fought, yes. They argued heatedly, at times. But that was the extent of it.

"Jason, ah, do you know what happened to Chris?" Bracket asked.

"No, I do not."

"Do you have any inclinations, suspicions, um, suggestions?"

"I don't have a clue, I really don't. . . ."

"Is there any reason your fingerprints or DNA would be in his apartment?"

Although Bracket never clarified if they had found Jason's DNA inside Chris's apartment, Jason's answer would speak volumes. The IRPD had not yet received results back from forensic testing and had not finished processing the scene.

"No, none whatsoever."

"In his vehicle?"

"No," Jason said. He went quiet for a moment, obviously thinking about something. "The only way I think maybe my fingerprints would be anywhere," Jason continued, "would be Kelly in his apartment and took something from our house to his house. Otherwise, there should be no reason whatsoever."

Jason asked about his medical marijuana plants and a few additional "nonrelated" questions pertaining to the amount of plants he could legally have inside his house. Then he asked for a business card. It felt like he was being helpful and wanted to make himself available.

Thirty minutes after they started, Bracket and Belanger were done with Jason.

* * *

LAURA FRIZZO WAS PUZZLED by the interview—if not completely bowled over. She saw so many holes in Jason's account of his life, she was eager to dig in and pick it all apart.

MSP detective Jean Belanger walked up to Frizzo after Jason and Kelly left. According to Frizzo, the MSP detective said, "I don't think he's capable."

"Huh?" Frizzo was stunned by this conclusion.

"Yeah, I do not think these people are involved," Belanger added.

"Wait a minute. Are you kidding me right now?" Frizzo said, looking at the detective.

Bracket and Belanger left.

13

THE OTHER MAN

THREE MSP DETECTIVES, Jean Belanger, Chris Bracket, and Russ Larson, each from a different post in and around Iron County, sat with Kelly Cochran's most recent lover on the afternoon of October 28. It was Kelly herself who'd given Belanger and Bracket his name.

All he knew about the situation, Tim Huntley (pseudonym) explained after Bracket asked, "was that my ex-supervisor, I guess, Chris Regan, has been filed as a missing person."

"Okay," Bracket said.

When Tim Huntley first arrived at Lake Shore to begin work on September 3, 2014, he was excited and thrilled to be employed by one of Iron County's largest companies. "Assembly," Tim later said. "Military assembly." It was an intense and complicated job, but could also be rewarding.

Chris Regan was Tim's team leader, though they knew each other only from nodding hellos in passing during working hours. They never mingled outside of that professional environment.

During her interview with the MSP, Kelly had given Tim's name as someone she'd been having an affair with, but had since cut it off. The investigation, in this early stage, was dictated by information. Cops followed names and places.

Tim Huntley was next in line.

"We ended up talking to . . . um, Kelly . . . Kelly . . . Cochran," Bracket explained to Tim, having trouble finding her surname on his notepad.

"I didn't know her last name," Tim said.

Just after his first day on the job, Tim ran into Kelly outside, in a designated smoking area employees frequented on break. Though they worked in different departments, Tim and Kelly happened to be having a cigarette at the same time one morning and started chatting.

"Separated," Kelly had said. "My husband and I are separated. I'm going to be filing for a divorce soon."

Single, living with his brother and sister-in-law, Tim liked what he saw. Kelly came across edgy and independent. She spoke her mind. Although he hardly knew her, Tim admired Kelly's liberated resolve. The strength she had to end what she described as an unstable marriage and start a new life on her own impressed him. He viewed meeting her as the start of a friendship.

Soon they were meeting at the smoking area every day.

"Here's my cell," Kelly had said one morning. "Call or text me anytime."

Tim had a certain edginess about him, too. He liked to wear skullcaps, dark clothing. He was proud of the various tattoos he had gotten over the years.

Kelly could relate.

In his midthirties, Tim and Kelly were close in age.

They both liked to party. Worked at the same place. Shared similar tastes in food and music. The one little detail Kelly left out of their early conversations as they got to know each other was that she was still seeing Chris Regan, Tim's team leader. But it wasn't long before Tim found out through the workplace grapevine that something was going on between Chris and Kelly. So he asked her.

"Ah, I had a relationship with Chris prior to you starting work here," Kelly told Tim one day in late September.

"Okay. You still seeing him?"

Kelly said she was not. "We had seen each other for a while, but not anymore. He still contacts me, though." Tim felt Kelly was annoyed by Chris still contacting her. She made it appear as if it bothered her that Chris was still pursuing a relationship, even though she had told him it was over.

Tim made a point of saying that if she was still seeing Chris, he wanted no part of it. He knew she still lived at home with her husband, with whom she claimed to be divorcing. Having Chris in the picture on top of Jason felt like too much.

"It's done," Kelly reassured Tim. "Promise."

Not believing her, Tim stopped talking to Kelly.

AS TIM HUNTLEY AND the three MSP detectives sat in Bracket's vehicle and discussed his relationship with Kelly, Tim said he had never met or seen Kelly's husband.

"I went over there once," Tim explained. Meaning the Cochran house. Kelly had painted a solemn portrait of the marriage and had told Tim that Jason was gone, out of the house, staying with friends or family. "She said that, like, for the past how many years it was, that . . . she wanted [the divorce] to be completed. The story I got from her was he didn't want to tell his folks down in Indiana. . . . She said the marriage had been done for years."

The interview had a casual, conversational tone. Tim started out quite nervous, but soon fell into the ebb and flow of the questioning, which indicated a desire to help any way he could.

"Did she ever say anything about seeing anyone else, or whatever?" Bracket asked.

"Yes," Tim said.

"Who was that?"

"So, um, she kept mentioning a 'friend' or 'friends.'"

It was never black or white with Kelly, Tim went on to note. He called Kelly the "elusive type—I kind of got that vibe."

One of the places Tim and Kelly met after work was Wildwood Lake, just east of Iron River, off U.S. Highway 2, in Bates Township. As their friendship progressed, Kelly told Tim one day, "Meet me at the park-and-ride. We can go from there."

According to one report, *[Tim] and Kelly would text and then meet up after work for a few beers. They would go several places, including the "spot" near Wildwood Lake. You would get to the spot by turning south at the road just in front of the park and ride in Bates Township.*

They'd talk. Hike. Find a secluded area near the lake. Have sex. Then go back to their private lives.

Tim gave the MSP detectives his cell phone, which still had several text threads he and Kelly had exchanged.

"Did you communicate through text and phone calls?"

"She never really talked on the phone," Tim said. "It was like a couple of texts." They'd go back and forth for a bit, but then Kelly would up and "disappear for, like, days" without warning.

Tim found this strange.

Chris Regan came up in the discussion. The MSP wanted to know what Tim thought of him. Was there any type of rivalry between him and Chris for Kelly's affection? On paper, the oldest motive could be placed among Kelly, Chris, and Tim.

"Oh, gosh, no. [Chris and I] liked each other. We got along great at work."

Tim was asked what he thought had happened to Chris.

"He was here one day . . . then gone. Just me personally, I kind of got the feeling, okay, then, well, he's not here, um, Kelly's being elusive. I don't know who this mysterious 'friend' is I've heard about lately, so I don't know."

Jean Belanger interrupted: "Could she be talking about her husband?" The question was in reference to Tim mentioning Kelly had been referring to a "friend" in several of her recent texts.

Just the previous week, Tim added, he'd received what became the last text from Kelly. On October 24, after Tim sent her a text asking what was going on, Kelly responded: **Can I call you in a few? Just to let you know, I had to help a friend with a huge problem.**

Tim was flustered by the timing.

You talk to me and then you're gone for a few days.

And that was it. He did not hear from her again.

That text was quite a bit more secretive and terse than most from the past, Tim told the MSP. On October 5, 2014, at five thirty-one p.m., Kelly had sent Tim a wink-face emoji. By then, she was not working at Lake Shore any longer—she'd been fired, actually, and walked out of the building by Laura Sartori after not producing the paperwork to support a medical leave she claimed was for a shoulder injury.

I need out for a bit, Kelly texted a few minutes later on that early October evening. By "out," she meant her house. **I'm climbing the walls.**

Hah, yeah, I bet, Tim texted back.

Meet me somewhere?

Where at?

Name it.

Well, we could meet at the spot and go from there.

Ok, see ya soon.

Nothing too late though. I've enjoyed catching up on my sleep.

Whatever, old man :P

Yep.

Later that night, early into the next morning, after they'd met and had sex, Kelly was texting by eighteen minutes after midnight: **And I think I'm ok getting hurt for a chance at knowing you. Just being real. Guess it takes a twelve-pack.**

Tim didn't answer right away. At five in the morning, he finally sent Kelly a response: **Wow . . . I should have gone to bed earlier.**

Hope your day goes quick and painless, Kelly answered at eight-ten in the morning. Then, with nothing said for about twelve hours, she texted at eight forty-two p.m.: **Hope all is ok with u.**

Tim did not respond. The following morning, October 7, 2014, at eleven-twenty, **How's that shoulder?** Tim texted.

Kelly had told Tim she'd injured her shoulder long ago in a car accident and needed an operation to right it.

Sore, but better, thanks. Just no arm wrestling.

No surgery? Lol.

He recommended it. I just don't want to do the surgery again now.

After a few additional pleasantries, Kelly asked Tim if he had plans that night. To which Tim said nothing currently.

I need a smile, she texted.

:)

Not exactly what I meant, Kelly came back with.

Oh oh . . . :) Well, what were you thinking?

Anything to get me out of this house.

Kelly explained that she was "cooped up" in the house all the time now since being out of work. Tim said it didn't sound half bad, being holed up in a house, adding that "Netflix and wine" made a "good combo."

Well, if you decide to go out and play, text me :) Kelly wrote.

OK. See, I'm tired . . . I feel like we went out last night.

Kelly waited almost an hour before answering: **Oh boy. I was hoping to wear u out tonight.**

One of these days we rent a room in town and just have fun.

A half hour went by. No response.

Guess you don't like that idea, Tim texted.

I do! Kelly responded fifteen minutes later.

For a girl who wants to get out of the house you sure are busy, Tim texted. **Nope?????**

They wound up meeting and getting hammered. The following morning, Tim texted at six-ten, saying he slept through his alarm. By eleven, Kelly still had not yet responded. But sometime later, she asked if he was on break. She wanted to know if he'd had any problems after waking up late.

A little, Tim texted.

Kelly wanted to know what.

Tim said he should know better; it was all his fault for getting drunk and staying out too late.

Kelly said it was her fault: **Since I kidnapped you. ;)**

Tim said he hit a deer on the way into work that morning and his sister-in-law, with whom he lived, was "bitching to me about dirt on the floor."

After a few unimportant questions, Tim said he was home alone and resting up from a long night and even longer day.

Kelly texted back: **U left a lot of bruises on my back :) must have been a good night.**

:)

Hope ur night is awesome, Kelly texted.

I'm still tired so hopefully sleep soon, Tim texted back.

For the next several days and throughout the weekend of October 11 and 12, Kelly and Tim texted occasionally. Kelly asked Tim to grab her tool bag from work and meet her somewhere with it. She'd left it behind when she was walked out of the building. By late in the day on Sunday, October 12, Kelly was talking about taking a walk together near the lake. She wanted to meet "at the carpool lot by the spot"—Wildwood Lake. It was four-ten when she wondered if maybe it was too late in the day. To which, Tim said it wasn't, but he needed to shower first.

By seven-seventeen p.m., they were done, both back home, and texting again.

The next day, October 13, Kelly waited until four thirty-three p.m. before asking Tim how his day had been.

Tim mentioned he had laundry to do. He needed something to eat. How tired he was.

Kelly responded: **poor thing.**

That was the end of their conversation. The night

passed. Tuesday, October 14, came. Tim woke up, checked his phone.

He had not heard from Kelly.

Tim went about his business. Thought nothing of Kelly not responding to his texts. She'd done it before. She'd go a "couple of days" without communicating, and then "she'd come back and then text me and then I wouldn't hear from her again," he said. But this day felt different. Something was going on with her. She had been hot and heavy and wanting to meet up and have sex, texting frequently over the past two weeks.

Then, suddenly, on October 14, silence.

14
TRUTH AND CONSEQUENCES

As Tim Huntley sat and spoke to three MSP detectives about Kelly Cochran on October 28, 2014, he painted a vague image of a woman prone to, at best, exaggerating the truth—at worst, pathological lying. Tim explained how people would ask Kelly questions about how she'd hurt her shoulder, and if five people asked, each would get a different answer.

Detectives wanted to know if Tim could add any insight into Kelly's marriage. Like had she ever discussed what went on behind closed doors?

"Yeah," Tim said. Kelly once referred to her marriage "for the past three years as being like she's been wanting out." She claimed Jason was "in need of treatment and that he refuses. . . . She said she got to a certain point where she [could] not sit around and watch somebody die, that [Jason] was aggressive with her and would push her around . . . and that he was threatening her."

Quite a different scenario than Kelly had portrayed with the same set of detectives earlier that day.

The topic of money came up. Detective Bracket

floated a hypothetical: Was Kelly perhaps broke and using Tim as someone to hang around with because he had money to spend on her?

Not a chance, Tim said. For one, he was not basking in the sun rays of financial freedom by any means. Second, Kelly claimed to have a brother in Indiana whom she'd helped with a business and they were making upward of six thousand dollars per week.

"According to her."

Bracket asked Tim if he could save those texts from Kelly, screenshot and e-mail to the MSP.

Tim asked, when did Chris's disappearance become a missing person's case?

"Look, we have no reason *not* to believe you," Bracket said, "but we tell everyone, if there is something on your mind, there's *something* she might have said, and it's kind of back here [in your mind]"—he pointed at himself, gesturing an overlooked thought—"and you're not sure if you want to say something, just make sure you get it out *now*. Because if we find out something down the road, you don't want to be part of—"

That comment made Tim anxious. Interrupting, he said, "No, and, well, okay, then . . ."

"And I'm saying that if you're holding *anything* back . . ."

"Yeah, okay . . . she *has* seemed kind of different."

"From a certain date, did she seem different? Or was she always?"

"I don't know. From, like, day one, she was kind of, like, well, she kept to herself and didn't want to say too much about what's going on."

Tim shared a story of a night they spent together in early October. Kelly talked about how she'd gotten "into a wreck—that she went down to Indiana randomly, like, on . . . like, kind of on a whim, on a weekend, since she'd been out of work. She said she'd gotten into a car wreck and her 'friend' was in pretty bad shape. They had driven down there, and it almost seemed like they were driving back in the middle of the night [when the accident happened]."

"When was this?" Bracket wondered. However cryptic the story sounded to Tim, it had the potential to provide answers. "Roughly? Do you remember when that would have happened?"

Tim could not think of the exact date, but was certain it was after she had been fired.

"Did she *ever* say who this 'friend' was?"

"She *never* told me who the friend was."

"It would always be 'a friend'?" Bracket asked.

Tim looked through his texts to see if he could recall when, precisely, she had brought up this so-called "friend." He thought it started out as a text conversation and they finished talking about it in person.

Searching through his phone, Tim guessed the conversation started just before October 5.

MSP detective Jean Belanger, quiet and nearly invisible throughout most of the interview, piped in: "I have to ask a question, and it's probably going to be kind of embarrassing, but, um, was there anything unusual, strange, or did you have any unusual sexual encounters with her?"

Tim paused. "Um . . . I wouldn't say that it's . . . I mean—nothing, like, out of the ordinary. She had talked about, like . . ."

"Was she wanting multiple partners?" Belanger wondered.

"I knew that she was, like, what you would call, like, the kinkier type . . . whatever, that's what she alluded to. But it was never . . ."

"Did she suggest something like that?"

"Nothing with multiple people that I can remember."

Belanger explained how the MSP recently "discovered" Kelly had had multiple relationships going on at the same time and they were trying to find out anything unusual about each one. It was part of their investigation, the detective suggested, which could "help us find Chris."

Tim explained how Chris's toolbox was there in work one day, but gone the next, and everyone wondered what had happened. He said not many people on the shop floor liked Chris because of the changes he was implementing as team leader.

As Tim spoke, Detective Belanger asked, "Do *you* know what happened to Chris?"

"I have *no* idea what happened to Chris," Tim snapped back, offended by the insinuation.

"You don't know if he up and left town, someone hurt him, or he's being held, or something crazy?"

"You know," Tim said, "I remember my coworker . . . he kind of—like I said, the rumor mill flies in that place—but Chris would be on his cell phone texting or calling and everyone assumed he was trying to get hold of [Kelly] . . . and, you know, it is what it is, I don't care. Whatever. I do not care."

Tim mentioned a discussion he'd had with a coworker one afternoon. After Chris stopped showing up for work, Tim told his coworker it seemed "kind of odd," Chris just disappearing.

Tim's coworker had said, "Well, you know, maybe a jealous husband got to him?"

Bracket said, "So you can kind of see where you fit into the puzzle?"

"Yeah, I understand that."

"We ask everyone," Bracket added, "but what if we wanted a polygraph from you to see if your information was up to par—"

Before Bracket could finish, Tim said, "Absolutely!"

"And what if the polygraph operator asked, 'Do you have any involvement with Chris being missing?'"

"No!"

"'Do you know what happened to Chris?'"

"No!"

Tim wondered about the polygraph being accurate. "I know what the truth is . . ."

Belanger said, "You know the truth, *do* you? So what *is* the truth?"

"For me, the truth is I had nothing to do with him disappearing."

15
EXCLUSION

THE ONLY OPTION MSP detectives had at this point, after talking to Tim Huntley, was to see if Kelly and Jason would answer additional questions. Chris Bracket and Tom Rajala approached the couple on Halloween.

"Hi, Kelly, how are you?" Bracket said after Kelly opened the door.

"Cold," she answered.

"Cold?"

"Yeah," Kelly said, hugging herself, rubbing her biceps.

"Do you remember me? I'm Chris."

"Yeah."

Bracket introduced Rajala. Explained that he was from the MSP's Calumet Post.

As they stood on the Cochran porch and talked, Kelly and Jason's dogs barked incessantly. Kelly said she needed to quiet them down before she could come out.

That situation under control, Kelly sat inside Bracket's MSP cruiser, rubbing her hands together, trying to stay warm, the heater blowing warm air on her.

Bracket mentioned new information had come up and they needed to clarify a few facts—namely, the dates October 14 and 15. The detective called those dates "important" within the scope of the investigation. He mentioned how it would help if Kelly could tell them where she was, what she was doing, and if she'd had contact with Chris on either of those days. The idea was to get Kelly and Jason pinned down to specific narratives.

"So, if you, basically, in your *own* words, kind of tell us what, from morning to night, everything you remember what you did on the fourteenth?"

Kelly didn't seem to have a problem answering. She began by explaining how being out of work made her days run all together: "Honestly, there's not much I do during the day, except for when I've been doing little projects at home. If the dates are right, I believe we were going to dinner"—she was referencing herself and Chris—"Ah, we were planning on *doing* dinner."

Kelly was certain the last time she saw Chris Regan was October 13, a Monday. They had dinner at his place. She knew this because she recalled discussing a drug-screening test for his new job he was scheduled to take in "two days," on October 15.

Yet, after a lengthy conversation, with Bracket mentioning several appointments Kelly said she'd had, Kelly clarified it must have been October 14 when they had their last dinner together.

"Lasagna," she said. She'd made it. "Every day is a Saturday" when you're out of work, Kelly added, trying to reason her confusion.

Bracket wanted details: what she did that night while inside the apartment, what Chris did, where Kelly parked, what time she arrived, what time she left.

Kelly said Chris played on his laptop while she cooked.

They ate. Made small talk. Chris retired about eight. Kelly, out of respect for her husband, never stayed the night at Chris's. She left soon after Chris went to bed.

She never saw him again.

As she spoke, it became clear why the oven did not appear to have been used. Kelly said she had brought the prepared, fully cooked food over and reheated it in the microwave.

Bracket wanted to know what Kelly did after leaving Chris's apartment.

"I'm not one hundred percent sure I came home. . . ." But then, after thinking about it, "Probably tended to the dogs, took them out. Settled in for the night." She liked to play solitaire on the computer. After she had dinner with her lover and went home and played computer games, Kelly explained, her husband was out, likely "walking or fishing." But he did come home at some point. She just wasn't sure if he was there when she walked in or he arrived shortly afterward.

Mr. Invisible, apparently.

"I will be honest with you," Kelly said next.

Bracket and Rajala looked at her.

"After I talked to him, after you guys questioned Jason, you guys told him he was the primary suspect and asked him if he killed Chris or did something with him?"

"We never said—" Bracket tried to say.

"Well, I was offended," Kelly interrupted. "*He* was offended!" Kelly stepped away from her usual stoic demeanor; she seemed irritated now. "So, I mean, if it's something about my husband, I *know* my husband. I'm not going to answer any questions about him because of the way he was questioned or how he was questioned."

Bracket noted to himself that Kelly's attitude changed

completely after a bit of pressure was applied. Kelly was now aggressive and abrasive.

Rajala tried to talk their way out of the situation best he could by saying they asked every source the same questions and were not pointing fingers or singling anyone out. Just gathering facts.

To that, Kelly said what truly bothered her was she did not think anything had happened to Chris. "Chris is a private person. He doesn't make enemies. Like I said, he had run-ins with guys at work, but not something that somebody's going to kidnap him."

They went back to the night, October 14, and wanted additional details.

Kelly pushed back. She claimed she did not have a good memory and didn't want to give the wrong impression.

CHIEF FRIZZO HAD UNCOVERED a piece of information that did not make much sense. An Amazon.com search warrant she had filed came through. The chief had asked for any transactions Chris Regan might have conducted on the site during the month of October. When Frizzo received the printout, sitting at her desk, studying it, the date October 28 popped out.

"I noticed Chris had a charge on his bank statement come through on October 28, 2014."

That date did not gel with the October 14 or October 15 date everyone was certain Chris had disappeared.

"Obviously," Frizzo said, "this date is *after* he went missing."

The chief believed someone could be using Chris Regan's bank card.

* * *

KELLY COCHRAN CONTINUED TALKING to Bracket and Rajala inside Bracket's car parked in front of her house. Kelly seemed more nervous than she had been—which, in and of itself, became a red flag.

As they continued, Kelly talked about how she thought Chris might have been using Match.com to meet women.

Bracket appreciated that information, then asked when Kelly had first reached out to Chris after leaving his apartment on October 14.

She texted Chris the following day, but never got a response. Because that was odd, Kelly added, she drove by his apartment.

"He always calls me back. Or, if he doesn't call, he will text me. And if there's a problem, he'll say 'fuck off'. . . ."

Kelly considered that Chris must have needed space, so she left it alone after not hearing from him. She texted a few times, drove by once more, and that was it.

The one important fact clear from this conversation was that Kelly believed she saw Chris's car parked in the lot of his apartment complex on October 15. On that day, in fact, after not hearing from him, Kelly knocked on his door.

"When he didn't answer, I went in—'cause I have keys."

She thought the apartment looked "in more disarray" than it had when she'd left, so she "guessed" he had done additional packing for the move.

After that day, Kelly said she never went back.

Not hearing from him, however, "pissed" her off. It was unlike him. Chris would always return texts or calls.

They talked for another ten minutes about Chris Regan's habits. Detectives tried to pin Kelly down as to what time she went back there, looking through his apartment by herself, but all she could recall was "later in the day."

AS FRIZZO CONTINUED STUDYING Chris Regan's Amazon records, she figured out the issue. Chris had ordered a book from Amazon, which wasn't in stock at the time. So, when the book became available, Amazon shipped it. His card had been billed on the date the book shipped.

16

INCLUSION

Detectives Rajala and Bracket managed to get Jason Cochran to sit for a second interview on the same day, October 31, 2014, inside Bracket's cruiser. Jason seemed different. Admittedly, he'd been suffering from "high anxiety" and felt "flustered" since that first interview at the IRPD.

Jason reiterated that he knew Chris by name only, adding how he'd felt deeply depressed lately. Regarding the extramarital affairs Kelly was involved in, Jason said he "didn't want to know about" them, so he didn't ask questions. Lately, though, things with Kelly had been better.

"She's been home a lot more."

Since getting out of the psych hospital in late September, Jason said, he'd felt suicidal, but had made some "positive changes" in his life. The marijuana he grew and smoked helped.

The tone Jason expressed was one of a guy who wanted to help. Jason said he was in a lot of physical pain, probably the current weather front affecting his sciatica nerve.

They talked fishing. Jason liked to fish for bass and trout at "the [Caspian] Pit," a body of water located about six hundred feet from the Cochran home. Standing by the pit, Jason could see what was going on back at the house. He said with all his health problems, it was a good place to sit and think. He could "hobble" there and back on most days without any problem.

Bracket focused on October 14. What had Jason done that day? Had anything in particular stood out in his memory?

"No," Jason said. He guessed he'd gone fishing, or for a walk. Maybe he went across the street to visit the neighbor, a guy he hung out with from time to time. Other than that, he couldn't recall anything more.

Bracket asked if Jason was truly "okay" with the various extramarital relationships Kelly had with other men.

He was getting the help he needed and hoped his wife would one day see the light and completely come back to him.

Bracket floated a hypothetical, making it clear they weren't accusing Jason of a crime, but trying to look at every scenario possible. The detective mentioned how he and his colleagues could see that perhaps Jason would be "relieved" if Chris Regan was out of the picture and it was "over" between Chris and his wife. He wanted to know if Jason understood this dilemma they faced as investigators.

Jason agreed he was relieved. "But I'm really hoping he shows up because I, this, um . . . is just kind of awkward, or whatever. I never met the guy. And I *don't* know anything about him. . . ."

Rajala asked if Jason hunted.

He hadn't since moving to Michigan.

"So you have a rifle—a shotgun?"

"Shotgun. It's a twelve-gauge. Single-shot."

"That's the only firearm you have?"

"The only *gun* I have."

For the next five minutes, they talked about the various potential hunting/walking/fishing locales Jason frequented around the Cochrans' Lawrence Street property.

Bracket asked Jason if they could take a look at his phone.

"It's in the house."

Bracket said they'd like him to go inside and get it.

Jason got out of the car. He had Kelly open the door because the dogs were wild and the possibility of them biting was high.

They went back and forth about the dogs and what to do. Jason seemed offended they had asked for his phone and made a point of not really wanting to go into the house and retrieve it.

Rajala explained that the MSP and IRPD were doing everything they could to find Chris Regan, and if part of the investigation offended anyone, that was just too damn bad.

Jason said nothing.

Bracket posed a potential situation where a person might be tied up inside someone's house and they, as police, had to weigh the possibility here and check it out.

"Ah . . . ," Jason said, understanding now where they were going with wanting his phone.

"Would you let us look to see if [Chris] is tied up inside your house?" Rajala asked. "A walk-through really quick, just to see if he's in there? To see if he's sitting in a chair with duct tape over his mouth?"

"Aha!"

"That's where I am going with this."

"Right. I can assure you he's not inside the house or anything. And I've, I really don't want to let you guys inside the house to search. . . . I know he's not in the house."

Rajala mentioned the main reason for the visit: "Right, so look. But we have a warrant to search inside your house, okay? To get that phone. . . . Now, if the phone is in there, we need to go get it."

EARLIER THAT SAME DAY, Chief Frizzo had spoken to Bracket. She made a point to tell him they needed to get inside the Cochran house and take a careful look.

"Nose around," Frizzo encouraged. "See what you can find. I am curious if you see any cement blocks lying around. Things like that."

Bracket said he'd see what they could find out.

JASON ULTIMATELY ALLOWED RAJALA and Bracket into the house after Kelly got the dog situation under control. What choice did he have, after all?

The detectives took a quick look around.

Jason located his phone and handed it over.

Finding nothing out of the ordinary, after Jason gave up his phone, "We appreciate it," Bracket told him. "I know it's an inconvenience with your phone. But we will try to get it back as soon as we can."

Frizzo contacted Bracket later, after he and Rajala left.

"The Cochrans were cooperative and let us walk through the house."

"And?"

"Nothing. No cement blocks."

17
QUACK-QUACK

IT WAS LATE OCTOBER. Jason sat at the dining table inside the Cochran house, an empty spiral-bound notebook in front of him. On the top of the first page, he wrote, *why*. Underneath it, a title: *Where Monsters Hide*. Each word was printed in jumbled and messy adolescent script.

Under the title, Jason sketched out a projection of a novel outline. He wrote how a person *cannot truly love without knowing hate*. From there, he wrote about how *monsters have predators*. He then applied the nature versus nurture argument, noting how "some" monsters were "born" and some were "made," before concluding *monsters have no idea their* [sic] *monsters at all*.

As the outline continued, Jason mentioned how monsters put on a face for the world—for the general public and family. Then he described a *scent and look* evil has, completing the thought with how only true *evil recognizes evil*.

Ending the first of what would be seventeen pages, Jason explained his theory that a predator can at times be the prey, and the prey can at times be the predator.

"He wrote a book," Kelly later explained. "I lived with him." She laughed. "The book is about him. He was trying to make himself the good guy in the book when, in the end, he was really the bad guy."

According to Kelly, Jason's outline was a riff on *Dexter*. In *Dexter,* the Showtime series, a forensic blood specialist working for the police is, at night, roaming through town murdering those people in society he believes are bad: pedophiles, drug pushers, abusers.

"Jason was making the call on who is the bad guy," Kelly added. "And you can't. We're all human. You cannot pick and choose who the bad guys are."

On the second page of the outline, Jason wrote *first chapter* underneath the title. Then introduced his main character, someone named *Jason Quack-Quack*. "Uncle Quack-Quack" was a nickname, his mother-in-law later said, that Jason's nieces and nephews called him, for reasons she did not know.

"It was just a name the kids had given him," Kelly reiterated, "nothing more."

Kelly noted that Jason was "very awkward and weird around kids." He did not know how to act. Not in an abusive, creepy way; rather, more shyness and feeling uncomfortable. Kelly had dreamed of having kids.

"I did. Just not with him. I knew there was something wrong with Jason. I had seen things from the start with him. When we were first married. Things with animals and, eventually, the way he was with me. And it got worse."

In a series of bullet points, Jason described his character, the Jason *the world see's* [sic], within what is a *normal life.* His list included: *married, no kids, always in pain, halfway to crippled, not quite middle age, angry at life, has own hit list, superhero "shoes."*

Over the door of the house where fictional Jason lived was a wooden sign: *if your* [sic] *not invited your* [sic] *not welcome—enter at your own risk.*

Page three, the second chapter outline, focused on Jason's family life. His character was *argumentative, beats wife, scares children, blows what little money the family has on booze and stupidity.*

The third chapter was more of the same. Jason Cochran, Kelly's husband, talked about how Jason, his fictional alter ego, *squanders other people's money* to feed his own narcissistic lifestyle. This Jason was a *womanizer* who thinks he is *god's gift to humanity.*

Chapter four began to paint a picture of a darker Jason (the character), a *child molester.* This Jason had just been released from prison after a second bid for harming kids in a sexual manner. But jail had not done anything to deter the character from immediately searching for other victims. At some point in the book, Jason Cochran wrote, he wanted to see *this character "stumped,"* as he termed it, which meant *tied to a tree* and then covered with honey so fire ants could kill and consume.

Chapter five had one word scrawled on the page: *Rapist.* No further explanation.

Six ventured into the territory of Jason the character coming from a family of killers. Jason's kin *works the traveling carnival while searching for their victims.*

Chapter seven introduced a new, unnamed character, a *sex worker, stripper.* She was going to be *disence infested* [sic], meaning "disease infected." She was a *homewrecker,* and by the end of the book, she would have *two victims* under her belt.

The next chapter introduced *the politician,* with one note attached: *monsters come in many shapes.*

The Priest was written across the heading of chapter

nine. Jason wanted this person to be from the Jehovah's Witnesses or the Church of Latter-day Saints.

Chapter ten was simply *The Sadist*. The remainder of the page was blank.

Chapter eleven—or a new chapter one, as Jason Cochran had not yet decided if this was the beginning of what he called Part B—had just a title: *That Smell.*

The smell Jason referred to was a *scent all living things [emit] when afraid,* as if fear had an odor. This idea would be a major theme throughout the second half of the book. Jason talked about how, within *the natural world,* the hunted person could *smell when the hunter [was] close.* He reckoned it to be human instinct in its purest form. He referenced a rabbit smelling the nearby fox, and how the hair stood up on your arms or neck when fear struck. He called it *the tingle* and the *holy spirit feeling.*

Chapter twelve began to lay out a few plot points. Jason (the writer) talked about a *14 year old boy* who was *home alone.* It was four days before Easter. His parents were at work. Two missionaries—*Jehovah* [sic] *Witnesses, [but] not really evil*—arrived and knocked on the door. He referred to the missionaries as *evil behind the ruse of God or religion.*

As Jason sat on this day and wrote an outline, it appeared he had smoked some of that weed from the basement. He would write a word, but not have the thought completely drawn out in his mind, before scribbling it out. He did this repeatedly. He'd start a word and trail off, not completing it.

Chapter thirteen was a half-thought-out attempt. He talked about a *DUI* who would be captured, not mentioning what DUI stood for.

Fourteen: *Captured, pays.*

Fifteen was blank.

Then came the conclusion: *quacks-quacks tingle—monsters know the smell of other monsters.* He repeated the sign over the door phrase found on the fictional home.

Then, for the conclusion, Kelly Cochran's husband wrote, *Wife saves the day.*

Jason Cochran described the denouement as a family cookout at the house. Everyone was enjoying the day; guests mingled and talked. *No one heard the car pull into the driveway,* Jason wrote, before warning, in a scribble of words, *the hunted can smell,* with two additional words crossed out—*the hunter.*

In the end, *quack-quack excuses himself,* and the outline ended.

Kelly said Jason had actually written and completed this book, though no one reported finding it. She also called her husband "a typical psychopath." Jason had a dark side he could hide from the public and those who knew him best.

Although the writing in the outline spoke of a person not very well educated, someone who had trouble maintaining a well-balanced, healthy line of thought, Kelly said her husband was "very smart," adding, "We were both too smart for our own good."

Jason's writing spoke to the contrary, however. What was Kelly getting at by calling Jason "genius-smart"?

"He was, like, mad-science smart. His writing, in a grammatical sense, no way."

As an example, Kelly explained that Jason was into mixing chemicals. Not, for instance, cooking meth in the house—but actual harmful chemicals.

"He had some major things planned out," she said, referring to Jason's obsession with chemicals and mass murder. "Crazy things."

One was to poison Michigan's water supply.

No one else around the guy had seen this side. Therefore, not a lot of people had bad things to say about him. Kelly contended that this was indicative of Jason "putting on a good show" for everyone. He was an expert at playing stupid. Being that country bumpkin. The guy who seemed to be a bit slow and passive.

Jason's back injuries, moreover, were a ruse. Videos the MSP had extracted from Kelly's cell phone—which Frizzo would find later—show the two of them, in September 2014, out at a waterfall deep in the woods, alone. They came across like two lovers out for a day in nature. They talked respectfully to each other. And what's more, Jason is seen in the videos at one point jumping from rock to rock and walking around without any difficulty.

"Clearly," Frizzo said, "when I viewed that, I could see this is not a man in any physical pain that would preclude him from doing . . . well, *anything*."

18
FRUSTRATION

Laura Frizzo made a decision to take control of an investigation she believed was heading off the rails. She did not want certain MSP detectives on the team assembled to look into the disappearance of Chris Regan. Frizzo couldn't see how these particular cops were moving the needle of the investigation any closer to finding Chris Regan. She called the local MSP lieutenant and explained she wanted Jean Belanger, for one, off the case. It was not personal. Frizzo had years of practical experience interviewing witnesses and suspects, digging knee-deep into intricate investigations. She did not want anyone to disturb the momentum she felt was heading in a specific direction: Jason Cochran.

"I'm sorry," Frizzo explained. "But if someone's mind is closed already, come on."

The lieutenant sent another MSP detective the following day.

The guy, Frizzo said, played the dominant male role of trying to take over.

"How many times have you been to [suspect-interview-training school]?" he asked Frizzo (according to her) shortly after coming aboard.

"Never," Frizzo said.

This was no way to create what should be an optimal environment in order to find Chris Regan. It wasn't about making friends, being the top cop who solved the case. For Frizzo, bringing a guy home to his family and/or finding the people responsible for making him disappear was what mattered.

One of the last things Jean Belanger did in the case was to call Chris Reagan's ex-wife, who no longer lived in Michigan.

Chris's ex explained she and Chris had been married for twenty-eight years. The divorce was finalized in 2010. Since that time, she said, "I've had little to no contact with him."

Three months after their divorce, she added, "Chris remarried." That marriage didn't last. She wasn't sure how long, exactly, but he divorced again, reconnected with Terri O'Donnell, and moved from Suttons Bay, a small town on the east side of Lake Michigan, to Iron River.

" 'Bout all I can tell you," she concluded.

"Do you know where your ex-husband might be, ma'am?" Jean Belanger asked.

"I have no idea."

"Do you think Chris is someone who would not want to be found?"

"I'm not sure what he is capable of," the ex-wife answered. "We grew apart. . . ."

According to Belanger's reading of Chris's ex, she seemed "genuinely concerned" about Chris and "his welfare."

* * *

OVER THE NEXT SEVERAL DAYS, into early November, Laura Frizzo wrestled leadership of the investigation. She'd developed strong feelings that Jason Cochran was aware of what had happened to Chris Regan. Frizzo could not shake the "jealous husband" theory.

With that, Frizzo took her theories and findings into all MSP meetings, telling the team they were ignoring "every indication" that Jason Cochran was involved.

The room would go quiet. Then, according to Frizzo, she'd be ridiculed and belittled about having "tunnel vision."

"Me? *I* am the one with tunnel vision! Are you kidding me right now?" Frizzo snapped one day.

Part of it, Frizzo believed, came from her "being the only woman" at the table. "All these men on one side, me on the other. They cannot be *that* stupid, I'd think when my Cochran theories were shot down. They had to be ignoring it because the someone bringing it to them—who doesn't have as much 'training' as them and was putting it together—is a woman, and their egos wouldn't allow it."

Interviewing suspects and witnesses was not something one could sit in a classroom and learn, Frizzo felt. It came from hands-on experience of doing it and making mistakes. She respected the MSP and understood their role in the hierarchy of police work in the state of Michigan. But nobody knew the people of Iron River better than the local cops—and nobody was going to convince Frizzo that her ideas and instincts were off. She felt certain: Kelly, Jason, or both, knew where Chris Regan was and what had happened to him.

She was not going to let go.

Days like the one spent in that explosive meeting, Frizzo explained, along with the forthcoming holiday season, led to the MSP casually dropping out of the case and leaving a majority of the investigation in the hands of the IRPD.

Just as well, Frizzo thought.

"That should have been done a long time ago," Melissa Powell, the local prosecutor, told Frizzo, after she and Frizzo initiated frequent meetings and discussions about where to take the case next.

Frizzo wanted to search the Cochran house and sit down for a formal interview with Jason and Kelly Cochran— something she had not yet done. Not inside her cruiser, on the Cochrans' stoop, casually talking, playing cat and mouse. Rather, a shine-a-light-in-your-face interrogation inside the IRPD's interview suite, with Frizzo at the helm, cranking up pressure.

Time to find out what they knew.

"Let's do it," Melissa Powell encouraged.

19

THE UNEXPECTED

A LOCAL WOMAN CALLED the IRPD on November 5, 2014, after a news story broke about Chris Regan's disappearance.

Betsy Roy (pseudonym) was the nosey next-door neighbor, looking out her windows and doors from behind the blinds, eager for something in town to happen so she could gossip. After giving the officer her name, Betsy said she lived near the park-and-ride in Bates Township, where the missing man's car had been found.

"My husband and I, we noticed a large amount of crow activity in the woods near the park-and-ride over the past few days. And yesterday, in fact, I saw an eagle in the same area."

The implication was that the birds had been circling a body.

The officer thanked the woman and turned over the lead to the IRPD. Not thinking it would amount to much, Frizzo asked the MSP to take another look in those woods with the K9s.

On the same day, an IRPD investigator contacted a

coworker of Kelly's at Lake Shore. The guy's name had been given to the MSP by Tim Huntley.

After being asked, the man repeated a conversation he'd had with another coworker, who had said something "strange" to him recently, especially in light of Chris Regan's vanishing act.

"What was it?" the IRPD officer asked.

"He said, 'Isn't it strange that Jason Cochran went to Indiana during the time, or shortly after, Chris went missing?'"

"Was there anything else?"

The source hesitated. Then: "This guy knows something about the disappearance—he's good friends with Kelly."

The officer took down the name and said someone would contact him for an interview.

Then a woman by the name of Gladys Ryder (pseudonym) came forward. She called into the IRPD and, after saying she wanted to remain anonymous, explained she might have important information about the disappearance mentioned on the local news. Gladys had lived about five miles outside Iron River for the past three years with her former boyfriend, Joe Speck (pseudonym).

"I'm no longer with Joe, but we stay in touch."

"Did your ex know Chris Regan?"

"He did." She explained that Joe and Chris had once worked together years ago in a town upstate. Some sort of retail business.

"What is it you're concerned about?"

"Joe has been saying some rather strange things about Chris I think you need to know."

"What is it, ma'am?"

"Look, I am a bit reluctant to speak with the police because I don't really trust you."

After being reassured that the IRPD was on a mission to collect information and find a missing man, nothing more, Gladys felt more at ease and told a story.

A few months back, she had found out some "things" about her boyfriend.

"He'd been going on those . . . dating sites. I found out he was also meeting up with [certain people] down in that Iron River area. They'd often meet at different locations and then leave together." She listed several places, one being the Bates park-and-ride. "When I saw on the news that the missing man's car was left there, it reminded me of some strange behavior on Joe's part one night when we passed by the same park-and-ride."

"What was that?"

"He would always stare at the lot as we drove by."

"When was the last time you drove by the lot with Joe?"

"Oh, about October second or third. It's just weird," she continued, "because Joe would make comments regarding how strange it is that a guy he once worked with is missing—he would bring it up at odd times."

Nervous about coming forward with the information, Gladys said she was done for now and hung up.

A day later, she called back.

"I've been talking to Joe recently. He's been telling me how he's catching these mice in his house and then explaining in graphic detail how he is torturing and killing them, throwing them against trees and drowning them. He knows I am an animal lover and he is trying to get to me. He smokes a lot of marijuana and is always telling me, 'Nobody knows the *real* me.' Hitler is one of his heroes and he has all sorts of guns, other weapons, and knives, inside his house." Gladys became overwhelmed by emotion for a moment before continuing, adding how she would often eavesdrop on conversations Joe had with a friend—she gave the IRPD the man's name—regarding how "easy it would be to kill someone and get rid of the body around here. He likes to burn things, too, and had a burn pit near his house in the woods."

One specific incident at Joe's house, not too long ago, Gladys said, had caused her great concern.

"What's that?"

"The last time I was at his house, I noticed several white bags of lye inside the house. I asked him what they were for and he said, 'My garden.'"

"Okay . . ."

"Yeah, well, Joe does not *have* a garden. Never did."

Lots of people use lye; yet not many would apply the chemical to garden soil. Lye is generally used for making soap and detergent, or processing natural gas and gasoline, papermaking, neutralizing acids, and perhaps even to process soft drinks and chemically peel fruits and vegetables. Lye can also be used for making grits, bagels, and lutefisk (a fermented Scandinavian delicacy, which most who try it for the first time find repulsive).

Beyond all of that, however, lye has been currently used for what some call "green funerals." Instead of opting for cremation or regular burial by embalming and casket, the corpse is dissolved in lye and the "resultant slurry," as it is called, is discarded in a specific location.

The detective asked if there was anything else.

"I found two computers at his house and they contain . . . pornography that includes Joe in the videos. They were recorded inside Joe's house, for sure. I found them without him knowing."

That didn't sound like anything beyond consensual sex between consenting adults. Unless there was something illegal going on within the context of the videos, what was the big deal? Gladys sounded more appalled than concerned.

Then a bombshell: "I spoke to Joe on the phone near the third week of October. It was the last time we talked."

"What did he say?"

Gladys hesitated. Then: "That he killed a . . . guy."

PART 2

BUTTERFLIES

20

PINK METAL

NOVEMBER 10, 2014, WAS ONE of those early winter days in Upper Michigan holding residents hostage, confining most indoors. The snow fell steadily—wet, heavy, slushy stuff sticking to everything like flour. Chief Laura Frizzo was alone, driving, the wipers slapping loudly back and forth, ice and snow caking up on the corners of the windshield.

Frizzo was frustrated with the MSP and how Jason and Kelly Cochran had been handled during interviews. MSP detectives had investigated and believed Chris wanted to disappear, or he'd committed suicide and his body would—or would not—be found someday.

"There's nothing there," the MSP told Frizzo when she broached the notion of the Cochrans needing more scrutiny. "We can't allot any more resources to this case if you feel that you want to keep pursuing Jason and Kelly Cochran."

Frizzo could do nothing more than throw up her hands.

"You need more evidence if you want us to assist with traveling and collecting DNA. We just cannot do it."

Frizzo had requested the MSP's help in the investigation, to begin with, and here she was now, hopeless and irritated they did not want to support her. Over the past week or so, Frizzo had spent hours watching the MSP interviews with Kelly and Jason, becoming more irate and annoyed by the lack of follow-up.

"That's a red flag!" she'd shouted at the monitor more than once.

"If I had been doing those initial interviews," Frizzo said later, "and this is just me, I mean, but I would have had a *lot* more follow-up questions."

Kelly's injury, for one. When Kelly talked about her shoulder and the accident she was allegedly involved in, she was clearly lying. Otherwise, she would have had a clear-cut explanation. Her account would never change. Add to that what Tim Huntley had said about Kelly having different stories. At least, Frizzo felt, there needed to be some sort of investigation into the accident itself to confirm what she'd said.

"If I was in that room and she was talking about this injury," Frizzo added, "I would say, 'Tell me more about it. Who were you with? Where were you going? Where did the accident actually happen?' And none of those questions were asked."

Staring at the monitor, watching Kelly talk about her injury, Frizzo had thought, *I know this is a lie. I know it didn't happen that way*.

The injury was significant. Had Kelly hurt herself during a fight with Jason? Maybe a confrontation with Chris Regan? What if Kelly killed Chris—had she injured her shoulder during the course of that crime or covering it up?

Kelly should be pressed on the issue.

And what about Jason? Frizzo considered. During his interviews with the MSP, Jason had talked about walking into town, a three-mile journey one way, and just happening upon Chris Regan's apartment, recognizing his and Kelly's truck parked in the lot near a truck with a canoe strapped on top. He had just happened to "realize" it must have been "this Chris guy's" apartment.

What the hell?

Had anyone considered that Jason was complaining about his back and other injuries, which he claimed had kept him confined to home for the most part, and yet here he was walking back and forth into town? And just *happened* to run into his and Kelly's truck?

"And they don't follow up with any questions," Frizzo explained. "Incredible. Why don't they ask him what would lead him to walk in the direction of Kelly's boyfriend's apartment, anyway? He had said clearly, several times, where he preferred to walk. That route was in the total opposite direction. He would have had no reason to walk three or four blocks west, in another direction. And if he did, let him tell *us* about it. But nobody asks."

The chief felt a definite connection between the Cochrans and Chris Regan's disappearance. MSP detectives did not want to believe one or both could have been involved.

It was time, Frizzo decided, to crank the vise closed on these two and see what they had to say.

TURNING ONTO LAWRENCE STREET in Caspian, Frizzo drove slowly. The road had not yet been plowed. Conditions were slick, with a fresh, however thin, layer of snow covering everything. Under different circumstances, Frizzo would have appreciated the beauty of it all.

Frizzo parked in front of the Cochran house. She took her time walking up the wooden ramp, being careful not to slip. Her plan was to get Jason into the IRPD first. Sit him down, alone. Something indicated—or perhaps just a detective's instinct—that this would be the last time the chief got a legit crack at the two of them. Kelly did not want anyone in law enforcement to be alone with Jason. Frizzo had to tread lightly. A door slammed in her face would only prove to be another roadblock she'd have to jump.

She controls him, Frizzo told herself. *She's the strength. She's the mastermind in the family. She tells him what to do. Whatever it is he did, Jason was under* her *direction.*

When she'd shared this theory with MSP colleagues, however, according to Frizzo's recollection, she was told: "You're way off base. You do not know what you're talking about."

The chief strode from her car to the door. She was dressed in her IRPD black fatigues, duty belt strapped to her waist, with her 9mm Glock 17 holstered, and a pink Ruger .380 fastened (hidden) to her ankle. She wore a bulky winter jacket with a ruglike furry collar and heavy black boots. Sewn into the outer biceps of her coat sleeve was the IRPD emblem of a gold eagle, its wings spread, and a red, white, and blue flag with five stars covering its body.

Knocking on the Cochrans' door, Kelly and Jason's dogs started barking.

Kelly had a cigarette in her mouth and wore a blue hoodie. She seemed surprised and flustered after opening the door to the chief of police.

"Hi, Kelly. I'm Chief Laura Frizzo, with the Iron River Police."

They shook hands.

Frizzo asked Kelly to put the dogs somewhere so she could come in for a brief chat.

Kelly beckoned Frizzo into a foyer area, which was closed off from the rest of the house. Frizzo stood for a moment as Kelly grabbed the dogs and told Jason, who belatedly stepped into the picture, to put them upstairs in one of the spare rooms. The door leading into the house had what appeared to be a hole just off center, duct tape covering it. Looked like someone punched a fist through the door from the inside.

Frizzo stood in the kitchen. Kelly scrambled around, picking things up, not really making eye contact. She was off her game, for sure. Fidgety, like a woman whose house was a mess and company had stopped by uninvited.

"You want to just have [Jason] come in here, too?" Frizzo said, giving the visit a more serious, professional tone.

Jason appeared. He and Kelly sat down on the living-room couch. Frizzo stood in front of them, a piece of paper in her hand.

The chief explained she had spent the weekend reviewing the MSP's investigation. In light of everything Kelly and Jason had told detectives thus far, she wanted to know if they had any issue coming into the IRPD to sit and talk. Clear up a few things that seemed to be—although she never said as much—nagging at the seasoned investigator.

"Again?" Kelly asked, discouraged. Both Kelly and Jason looked stunned. Shoulders dropped, jaws hanging. *Why in the world are we being summoned into the IRPD again?*

"Yeah," Frizzo said, almost apologetically.

"And that is in regard to the same thing?" Kelly asked.

"Yes," Frizzo said, reiterating her point of having several questions and "follow-up" to do. "You have only one vehicle, right? So I was wondering if one of you would be willing to come down with me now, and the other come down in about a half hour?"

Jason and Kelly took a moment.

"So?" Frizzo asked.

Jason agreed to go first.

Kelly Cochran's husband stood, stared at Frizzo momentarily, before stepping out of the room to get dressed.

21

CAT AND MICE

WITH ONE HAND ON the steering wheel, Laura Frizzo pulled a Marlboro Light out of her front breast pocket and popped it into her mouth.

"You mind if I smoke, Jason?"

"No, go right ahead." Jason spoke with a soft, slow, upper-Midwestern inflection, a bit of Canadian influence there.

Frizzo fired up her butt and cracked the driver's-side window.

The drive to the IRPD from the Cochran house was slow because of the storm. Frizzo and Jason chitchatted about everyday things. Fishing. Hunting. The landscape. Weather. Jason even mentioned where he generally took his walks as they drove by a trail leading to "the pit" area, noting what type of fish—small and largemouth bass, trout, northern pike—he put his line into the water, hoping to catch.

At five minutes before noon, Jason sat inside the IRPD's interview suite, a small, nondescript, whitewashed room. Jason had his arms in front of himself on his lap. He wore

large-framed glasses, a gray T-shirt, his white-and-gray
goatee neatly trimmed. Kelly Cochran's husband seemed
rattled and anxious, his face and head Valentine's Day
red, his body movements fidgety.

Frizzo made him wait for ten minutes before walking
in, carrying a yellow legal pad of questions. She sat down
at a round table, opposite Jason. Although the chief was
friendly, Laura Frizzo felt Jason Cochran knew what had
happened to Chris Regan, either because he was involved
and Kelly was protecting him, or participated in the crime
under Kelly's direction.

With a strong belief that truth is immutable and one
does not have to recall it, Frizzo had a difficult time shaking
the fact that Jason had staked claim to several (different)
versions of the same events during his MSP interviews.
Many of which did not add up.

"He'd changed just a few minor details," Frizzo recalled.

Which was where the truth lived. In between those
minor inconsistencies—that blurred area.

The chief reintroduced herself. Then: "Like I said, I
have reviewed the interviews you had with the detectives.
And I did some checking with other witnesses. So I just
wanted to go over a few things with you."

Jason looked at the investigator. He took a long, hard
swallow, before nodding nervously in the affirmative, letting the chief know he understood.

"It's my understanding you moved here from Indiana?"
Frizzo asked.

"Yes."

"And how long did you live in Indiana?"

"Ah, my whole life."

Prompted by the chief, Jason laid out the same narrative he'd dictated the past few weeks while MSP investigators were poking around, asking questions: how he and Kelly met, how he was once arrested on a warrant for not showing up in court on a medical debt, how he knew about his wife's infidelities. He explained they'd been separated the past several months, though still lived in the same house, along with how he'd been dealing with physical and mental issues since moving to Michigan that past February.

As Jason described his current medical crisis, he painted a picture of a man who could barely get out of his own way, someone who once had kidney cancer on top of a host of back issues. He repeated that he was unable to work, which had been devastating, he said, to his overall demeanor and attitude about life.

"I really do miss working . . . it gave me a feeling of purpose."

Regarding the strain on their marriage, Jason blamed himself, saying he couldn't have sex because of the stress it put on his back. He took Flexeril for it, but the drug had only helped so much.

They discussed Kelly's schedule while employed at Oldenburg. Kelly punched out around three-thirty p.m. every weekday. She'd walk through the door. Change. Then claim she had "errands" to run or friends to see, before leaving. She wouldn't return home until eight or nine on those nights. Jason knew she was going out to see men.

"In July, it was two times a week," Jason explained, adding that he'd often question Kelly when she came home: "What were you doing?"

"I don't want to talk about it," Kelly would respond. "You're just being nosey."

"I picked up her phone one day and saw a message from a guy named 'Ken,'" Jason told Frizzo. "The message said something about 'a date.'"

"Why would you have to go out with other men and not me?" Jason had asked his wife.

"Ken took it the wrong way," Kelly had said, minimizing the message. "We're just friends."

Regardless, Jason added, this episode made him sad. He recalled crying that night after she left. He knew what was going on, but couldn't do anything to stop it. The impression Jason gave, without coming out and saying as much, was that he didn't feel like a "real man." He could not perform the duties a husband should, and this convinced him to allow Kelly her time to go out and get what she needed elsewhere.

"It wasn't long after that we started discussing divorce."

Pressed for a time frame by Frizzo, Jason dated this period "July"—the same week he saw the Ken message. Jason realized "she was seeing *other* men, too," noting he found the names "Chris" and "Curtis" on her phone. So he confronted Kelly about it. But she wrote it off, saying, "You have nothing to worry about."

In August, Kelly went to Jason and, he said, she talked about being "close to divorce."

"I'm just staying with you because you cannot take care of yourself, physically or financially," Kelly had told her husband.

"I had withdrawn from friends and family by then," Jason told Frizzo. "I was really depressed."

By September, Jason was having trouble sleeping and eating. He'd lost forty-five pounds in forty days.

"I was crying all the time. I thought frequently about how to kill myself. I planned to walk out into traffic or walk off a bridge. But couldn't think of a large enough bridge in walking distance from the house. I did actually walk into traffic a few times."

As the depression grew more intense, and he told Kelly how he was feeling, Kelly admitted she was seeing other men, which only intensified his feelings of worthlessness.

"I had racing thoughts in my head, which were yelling the whole time. I had to go to the hospital."

By then, Kelly was going out "four or five times" weekly. They had stopped communicating. Jason claimed he'd be dead now if he hadn't gone to the hospital.

"I told Kelly I wanted to kill myself."

"Did you also tell her you wanted to kill *her*?"

"No," Jason insisted.

Kelly visited him only once while he was in a hospital psych ward. Doctors prescribed Zoloft, Zyprexa, and lorazepam. Heavy-duty psychiatric drugs. The combination of drugs helped Jason build self-esteem and feel better. When he returned home, Kelly was still running around, but Jason said he could deal with it in a healthy manner.

As Frizzo listened, she kept track of the dates. Jason talked about his time in the hospital beginning "on or about September eighteenth." He returned home five days later. After being released, Jason told the chief, he felt less affected by his surroundings and Kelly leaving every night of the week, unquestionably seeing other men. Yet, Frizzo knew he was lying: After all, Kelly had told her boss at Oldenburg days after Jason's release from the hospital that Jason had threatened to kill her.

"Were you going over to the neighbor's for bonfires?" Frizzo asked.

"Yes, I was."

That neighbor, David Saylor, a guy Jason's age, lived up

the road. Frizzo had spoken to Saylor and his grandmother, with whom David lived. Whenever Jason felt "low," he'd pop over to talk to David or his grandmother. They'd cheer him up. Make him feel better.

"Kelly and I were starting to talk, too, near this time," Jason said. "We were eating dinner together once in a while."

So, Frizzo thought, staring at Jason Cochran, *at the same time Chris Regan goes missing, here they are getting along a little better. . . .*

22

NIGHT WORK

IT WAS STRANGE WHEN he later thought about it: the noises. The banging and sanding and sawing. In the middle of the night. Two, three, four hours of power tools running for three nights in a row.

Who remodels their home when the rest of the world is sleeping?

"Like eleven o'clock, all the way up to three in the morning," David Saylor later said. This would have been, he guessed, in October. Definitely near October 14, David was certain, but no later than that.

"Sawing and sanding," David told Frizzo.

David met Jason near the end of September 2014, Kelly a few weeks later. David, along with his uncle, Todd, lived with their grandmother. David and Jason ran into each other outside one day, hit it off, and started hanging out "every day," David recalled. Kelly was never around much. David would see her from time to time, but not for long periods of time. Kelly was in a constant hurry to be anywhere but by her husband's side.

"Jason told David Saylor not to trust me because I was

having relationships with other men," Kelly later explained.

Jason would stop over, or David would stop by the Cochran house. They'd play cards or roll dice. There were times, David said, when he and Jason were kicking it and Jason would abruptly blurt out that he needed to sleep. It seemed a strange way to act, David thought.

At other times, Jason would stop what he was doing and suddenly announce that he needed to go for a walk.

Always alone.

He'd be gone two hours or more.

David was in the Cochran house one afternoon. He looked toward the stairs leading up toward the second floor.

"What are you doing up there?" David asked a day after hearing those noises. They were in the Cochran living room.

"Remodeling," Jason said. "I couldn't sleep. I was working on the stairs, refinishing them."

Funny thing, David later told Frizzo, "I never saw him either bring in construction materials or bring out anything to indicate construction work."

Besides, the house had been remodeled upstairs before the Cochrans had moved in—and those stairs Jason said he refinished?

David glanced at them.

No work had been done.

23

VOICES CARRY

CHIEF LAURA FRIZZO STARED at Jason Cochran. He squirmed in his chair. Fiddled with his hands. Looked down, to the side, hardly ever making eye contact. When he did look in Frizzo's direction to answer a question, Jason seemed unsure of what he was saying—as if he knew he could not lie to this investigator and get away with it.

Frizzo moved on to the subject of Kelly's truck parked at the apartment complex where Chris Regan lived. She asked how Jason just so happened to stumble upon it while out walking one afternoon. Seemed like an incredible coincidence.

Jason mentioned "ending up on the M-189" and how he'd always had great vision. He happened to look to his right as he walked by the apartment. Lo and behold, there it was, in front of him.

Ah, just like that, you say. I don't think so, Frizzo thought, watching Jason twist in his chair.

Jason said he spied the truck with the kayak on it, put it together that Kelly had once said she and this guy Chris went kayaking together. It all made sense in the moment.

"And how long ago was this?" Frizzo wondered.

"Oh, a month and a half ago, maybe."

The chief asked, why had Jason walked down that specific road? Frizzo reminded him that he'd maintained there were only certain places he would—and could—walk to from his home. And that direction, where Chris's apartment building was in town, had never been part of those discussions.

"So now you're changing that," Frizzo suggested. "I've actually seen [closed-circuit security] video of you walking *around* the apartment."

Was Jason stalking his wife and her lover?

After a conversation regarding where Jason walked, and how it was actually in the opposite direction of Chris Regan's residence, Jason had no explanation.

Frizzo moved on.

She wanted to know what he said to Kelly that night when she got home. According to Jason, he now had solid proof she was inside another man's apartment. He had seen the truck. Had Jason called his wife out when she walked through the door?

"I didn't say anything to her," Jason claimed. "I didn't want to know."

The weak link, Frizzo told herself. While sitting, listening to Jason lie, Frizzo felt Kelly was the puppeteer, in total control of this man.

"Even though I have to check out all possibilities, and I never lose sight of that," Frizzo said later, "there is no doubt in my mind—at this moment of *that* interview— that these two people are involved in Chris Regan's disappearance. She is the mastermind. Whatever Jason did, he did under *her* direction."

It was one thing to theorize, quite another to prove.

Especially, Frizzo knew, without a body, a crime scene, or any tangible evidence.

Frizzo asked Jason if they had ever talked about Chris Regan's disappearance. Chris was a guy Kelly dated. Someone Jason admittedly wanted out of the picture. What were they saying about him inside the Cochran house?

"We don't talk about it," Jason said.

"You don't talk about it?"

"I don't want to hear about it."

"This is a guy she's had contact with since July. He's missing. And you do not want to *talk* about it?"

"I don't want to know. I thought he would come home after a few days. I'm hoping he comes home soon so this will all be behind us. . . ."

Frizzo asked Jason about his anger.

Jason said it was "different" before and after his hospital stay.

"I was suffering from delusions. I do not remember threatening Kelly. I was seeing people who weren't there. I was having trouble . . . hearing voices."

Frizzo wondered about the voices.

"They were telling me to kill myself—that everyone would be better off without me around. . . . The urges would get very strong at times."

Jason teared up as he talked about his parents in relation to his possible suicide. He would never want to put them through losing a child. He felt like a disappointment.

"Nonstop," he said of the voices. "Every day—before going into the hospital."

The chief asked Jason his thoughts about taking a polygraph.

Jason babbled on about his medications and how he would need to okay it with a doctor first.

He paused.

Silence.

Then, thinking it through: "I've changed my mind. Why *should* I? It's not something I want to do."

"It's just a tool to determine if you're being honest."

"I feel I am being harassed."

Ignoring that, turning the tables, Frizzo said: "It's a great tool for someone who is innocent."

Frizzo could sense Jason was getting anxious and wanted to end the interview. She mentioned how the sequence of events since Jason had been released from the hospital, on top of the discrepancies in some of what he had told investigators, made it appear as if he had things to hide. She was doing her job, trying to clear up any confusion. And a polygraph, the chief reiterated, would help in that regard.

"I'll take that into consideration," Jason said.

Yeah, right.

Frizzo stood, walked out of the room. When she got to her desk later on, thinking about it, she recognized several areas in which Jason did not want to go. He'd changed the subject several times. Totally avoided certain topics.

All red flags.

"I also knew," Frizzo concluded, "that *that* particular interview was likely the last time I would speak to him in this manner."

24
DETAILS

KELLY COCHRAN WAS FULLY prepared, Frizzo could tell a few moments after entering the interview suite and looking at her. Kelly had her game face on. She knew how to sit in the chair. How to focus her demeanor for a police interview. How to come across as the suspect being unfairly accused of a felonious crime. She was composed. She understood, completely, the complexities of being seen as the suspect, as opposed to a witness.

"She knew just how far to take you," Frizzo said later. "Kelly would take you to a certain point and no further."

Frizzo needed to change that. However, the chief had to be careful. As a cop, one ran the risk whenever involved in the meticulous scrutiny of a suspect that cherry-picking and finding whatever it is you're looking for might force you to miss important information. Frizzo also knew that without a body, without some sort of clear evidence of involvement, all Kelly had to do was answer the chief's questions and withstand the pressure. She could then walk out and not look back. In the scope of the investigation, what did Frizzo actually have on Kelly or Jason other than a gut feeling and a few inconsistent stories?

Another concern was the certainty that she was only going to get one last chance under these confined, controlled conditions. Kelly would not likely sit down again within the four walls of the IRPD to talk about her missing boyfriend and extramarital affairs.

After Kelly gave Frizzo the dates of them moving into the state, when she started working, and when she was "terminated," Frizzo brought up Kelly's shoulder. This was important to the chief. A potential answer to Chris's disappearance lurked within this so-called "accident."

"It's an old injury," Kelly said. "A car accident years ago I reinjured in an accident [recently]."

"Where?"

"Probably Wisconsin."

"*Probably* Wisconsin?" Frizzo stressed.

"I don't know."

"When?"

"September twenty-sixth or twenty-seventh. I do not know."

"Who was driving?"

"A guy named Mike. But I don't know his last name."

"How do you know him?"

"He was going to pick up a vehicle. I met him through friends."

"Which friends?"

"What do you mean?" Kelly asked.

"Who connected you? How do you know him?"

"Actually, I cannot remember."

"Is there any record of the accident, Kelly?"

"The police came, there was another vehicle involved. . . . We were in a pickup truck. Green. A Dodge,

I think. The accident happened as we were coming back. Mike had to switch vehicles in Green Bay. I have no idea why he had to pick up the vehicle. I have no idea where he lives, in Iron River or . . . I haven't seen him since the accident."

"Where'd you guys meet up to go on the trip?"

"He picked me up at my house."

"Where did the accident happen?"

"Another vehicle ran into the driver's side of the vehicle I was in and it was like on U.S. 141 somewhere."

Vague, Frizzo thought, staring at Kelly. *Details that cannot be checked out with any sort of comprehensive investigative examination. She's lying.*

Frizzo stared at Kelly.

Where, the chief considered, *should I take this interview next?*

WHEN SPEAKING TO HER, Kelly Marie Cochran can sometimes come across as an intelligent, well-spoken, well-educated woman. She "hates TV, personally." Instead, Kelly explained, she opts for reading authors such as "Voltaire, Patterson, Dickens, Shakespeare." She loves "poetry, history, psychology, medical studies, and forensic books."

At least, that is one side of this complicated, aloof, guarded woman.

"You have to understand Kelly," Laura Frizzo later said. "She is well-rehearsed. She was definitely prepared with her body language, how to sit in the chair during this particular interview, her eye contact with me. When I spoke to her that day, November tenth, something told me this was not the first time—I mean, like, the first time this has happened. I always thought, from the *very* beginning, that Jason was starting to have psychological issues when he did because he wasn't as strong mentally as Kelly—and the things they had done together were starting to catch up with him."

Frizzo believed Jason had done "heinous things for his wife," and because of that, his mind was unraveling.

Was he in the midst of a psychological breakdown?

Kelly, by contrast, was settling in, enjoying the ride. Able to conduct herself in a seemingly rational, calm, unremorseful manner, even after what Frizzo was about to discover were the most horrific things imaginable that one human being could do to another.

Jason's biggest fear, Frizzo had recognized while interviewing him, which could be utilized at some point, was getting caught, going to jail, letting his family down.

"Her thought process was completely different," Frizzo added. "She thought, 'I'm never going to get caught. I'm too good at this. I'm smarter than you and everyone around you.' Where Kelly does *not* have a conscience, Jason, well, he struggles because he *has* a conscience."

Frizzo was describing, at least with Kelly, the psychological wiring of a serial killer. Remorselessness, narcissism, grandiose thinking, glib superficial charm, impulsiveness, a shallow affect. The pathological foundation and framework of a psychopath capable of the worst.

PART OF WHAT MOTIVATES Kelly, she explained in a series of letters and conversations, is a desire to "study people and pick apart their brains." It fascinated her to think "what the brain is capable of."

Kelly used the word *surprisingly*—strangely enough—as a qualifier, before saying, "Surprisingly, I *like* animals."

Surprisingly, I like animals.

What was Kelly implying? Was she trying to crush the

common cliché that a majority of serial killers torture and maim animals?

"Yes," Kelly said during a telephone interview. "Serial killers generally dislike animals and torture them. I *like* animals, that's what I'm saying." She laughed.

And Jason?

"My husband *hated* animals. . . ."

Kelly claimed she endured an "impossible marriage." At first, she did not elaborate. She simplified it: "I was told that a psychopath and sociopath could not live together and carry on for over thirteen years."

Asked later what role she played within that logic, Kelly replied: "The sociopath. Jason was the psychopath."

Jason Cochran's wife was someone, Kelly went on to explain, who "seeks out answers for everything." Although, she added, she understood "some things were meant not to have an answer."

This particular letter, one of many over the course of one year, was signed, *Sincerely, Awesome*.[2]

CHIEF FRIZZO DECIDED TO stay on point—the accident—as that November 10, 2014, interview carried on. After, that is, Kelly explained how she'd torn a tendon in her shoulder long ago and the recent accident likely reinjured it.

"Would you mind if I asked what doctor you saw?"

"Is that necessary?" Kelly snapped back.

"It is not."

The fact that she wouldn't answer such a basic question was significant and all Frizzo needed to hear.

2. This section is from letters and telephone interview between Kelly Cochran and author.

Kelly talked about being fired from her job.

"Tell me about the issues you were going through with Jason at the time."

"Do I need to?"

Frizzo encouraged Kelly to explain.

"He had severe depression. He went into the hospital. They diagnosed him and then released him with treatment."

The straightforwardness of her answers was telling in and of itself.

Lies are not easy to recall.

"Your employer and other people at Oldenburg told us that you were saying he was going to hurt you. Have you seen a change in that anger since he's been released from hospital?"

"I've noticed the anger is gone. He is tired all the time, though."

"Do you think he could ever carry out on those threats you told others at your work about?"

"I was never really afraid of him. . . . He didn't really get to that point"—severe depression—"until the end of July, after he lost a close friend on his birthday."

"When did he threaten to kill you and then kill himself?"

"He threatened suicide."

"Yeah, but he threatened to take you with him. . . ."

"He would have *never* taken me with him."

"When had he made the threat, Kelly?"

"Just before going into hospital."

"Did he mention anything about hearing voices in his head to you?"

"He said he 'thought' he heard voices in his head, but he never went into detail about it."

Frizzo noticed the underlying theme within every word Kelly uttered: *Are we done yet? This is really starting to annoy me.* Her answers were contrived, thought out and constructed around what information she believed the chief had.

"She was cocky and arrogant," Frizzo said later. "Very sure of herself and very irritated with me for bothering her with all of this."

Frizzo looked for the opportunity to inject Chris Regan into the conversation. Kelly's answers to the questions Frizzo asked about Chris and her relationship with him were what mattered most. What Kelly had to say regarding times, dates, what they did, the last time she saw and spoke to Chris, was going to determine Frizzo's next move.

Reiterating the subject of Jason and his mental disabilities and status, Kelly said, "I never planned on leaving my husband."

As Frizzo listened, she knew this to be a blatant lie. In looking through Kelly's cell phone—after the MSP collected hers and Jason's phones under that warrant—Frizzo read texts Kelly had sent to her sister while Jason was hospitalized. "And she told her sister that Jason has been acting crazy bad lately. She told her that she was going to drive an hour to the hospital to break things off with Jason and that she had a breakfast date in the morning. Come to find out, she had breakfast at Chris's apartment the following morning."

But Kelly never mentioned it. Why not tell an investigator looking into the disappearance of your boyfriend these important details about interaction with him? Why hide anything? Why wasn't Kelly interested in helping the chief find Chris Regan?

"How do you think it made Jason feel when he got out of the hospital, came home, you were still seeing these other men?"

"It would have bothered him," Kelly said, adding that when Jason finished his "treatment plan," he was a "different person." She saw a marked change.

"Then how could you continue seeing other men, knowing what it would do to him?"

"They were relationships I already had." She hesitated. Looked away. "I love Chris. I wound up telling Jason about the extent of the relationship with Chris."

More contradictory information.

"Jason told me that the two of you never discussed those details because Jason didn't *want* to know."

Kelly said nothing.

Frizzo asked for details about the affair.

She and Chris met at work, Kelly said. Started a more intimate relationship about a month after (same as she'd told the MSP). "We'd go on walks at Lake Ottawa. Go see the loons at Iron Lake. Go hiking. His knee would bother him, though. He liked to hike, ride his bike, or just relax."

"Had Chris ever been at your house?"

"Maybe two occasions," Kelly said.

"When?"

"The last time was, oh, maybe a month ago. Or before that. The last time I was at his place was the day after we had dinner together and he didn't return my texts. He was supposed to go for his drug-screening test the following morning."

A date would be helpful, but Kelly said she was having trouble. She'd talked it through with the MSP detectives, who "were trying to help me figure out a date, but it's hard to remember."

Focusing on a timeline, Frizzo asked Kelly to think about the day and what they did.

Kelly recalled bringing lasagna over to Chris's. She arrived at about "four or five p.m. He was sitting in his chair. . . ." She'd brought the meal over on a plate and used the microwave to reheat it, never mentioning that large box in the kitchen in front of the oven and microwave.

Frizzo asked about the texts Kelly said she'd sent to Chris the following day.

"I sent him a text and he didn't respond. I told him I hoped he was feeling better."

Chris's text to Kelly on October 13, Frizzo knew, had said he was "over that illness and no longer sick."

Another—however small—contradiction.

As they talked about that last night Kelly claimed to have seen Chris, Frizzo stuck to specifics. For example, Kelly said she made garlic bread in a skillet on the stove. But Frizzo knew the stove had not been used, hence several household items left on top. In addition, no skillet was found in the sink.

"Did you wash any of the pans—I don't recall seeing any evidence of lasagna for dinner left in the apartment. . . ."

"I brought it on a plate, washed the plates, took them home."

Chris's sink, Frizzo knew, was full of clean plastic containers he was washing and boxing up. No one, far as she could tell, had used the sink in some time.

Kelly never mentioned this.

Discussing their overall relationship, Kelly put herself into a hole. In her October 28 interview with the MSP, Kelly said she had never been inside Chris Regan's truck and he owned only one kayak. Now, here, she told Frizzo she'd gone hiking and kayaking with Chris in his truck and that he had two kayaks.

"We spent most of our time indoors," Kelly said. "Watching movies and having sex."

Frizzo stared at Kelly.

Without being asked, Kelly said they didn't have sex on that last night she saw him.

"We did have sex the time before that, but I cannot remember when it was."

25
TROUBLED LIFE, TROUBLED WIFE

From the time Kelly Cochran was a teenager, her mother later explained, "I had issues with her doing drugs." There came a point when Melanie Gaboyan decided she'd put up with so much of her daughter's misbehavior, insubordination, and drug use that she instituted what Melanie described as a "tough love" policy. She believed she could only reach Kelly this way.

"When she was eighteen, I had to kick her out of the house." Kelly and her friends routinely showed up "totally obliterated." Melanie had "three kids to raise." The last thing she wanted was for Kelly and her druggie friends to corrupt the other children.

Melanie, at fifty-eight, worked customer service at Home Depot. She wore brown-framed glasses against gray-streaked, brown hair, parted in the middle, cut just above her shoulders. She carried a Midwestern, motherly charm: pudgy cheeks, thin lips, large frame. Melanie had a sympathetic sincerity in her manner. She'd obviously given her daughter—maybe throughout their entire lives— repeated chances, probably overlooking the truth because she wanted her daughter to thrive. Once asked, Melanie said, "I would absolutely do anything for my daughter."

Not long after instituting that attitude of tough love, Kelly's grandmother, Melanie's mother, died. Melanie felt depressed and lonely. During an admittedly vulnerable moment in her life, she told Kelly she could return home.

"But listen," Melanie warned, "I cannot have that around here. You can come home, only under the condition that I can drug-test you anytime I want. If you refuse, you'll have to leave."

Kelly agreed.

Then Jason, living next door, moved in. Jason and Kelly were dating seriously by then and talking marriage. According to Kelly, "Jason was very violent" right away. She spoke of one particular day when she watched Jason place a litter of kittens into a burlap sack and beat the kittens until they were dead.

"That was before we even got married. I'm no cat fan, but I like animals. I like animals better than people most of the time."

If you ask Melanie, her daughter's behavior had gotten "worse" as time passed. So bad, in fact, Melanie tried convincing Kelly she needed rehab.

Kelly wanted nothing to do with it.

"My parents are amazing," Kelly said later. "Been married almost four decades. Loving parents. Always supportive. Not the type of parents"—she smiled while adding this—"that you would expect to have a child like me."

Kelly described herself as someone "always meant to be 'out there,' a free spirit. A social loner. Independent."

Melanie saw that familiar pattern emerge all over again, but this time it came with a fast-paced, downward progression. Kelly was older. She was more set on not listening to anyone but herself. As a teen, Kelly dealt with her mother's "rules" by running away from home, living on the streets, doing drugs and drinking. Caught, she'd stop using for a while, agree to mandated counseling, but then start the process all over again, once the pressure was off. Throughout this time, she'd been picked up and sent to a girls' home.

"I put myself into the girls' home," Kelly said later.

"You need to quit that!" Melanie would tell her daughter. Kelly's mother was scared for her child. She could see Kelly's drug use escalating as each year passed. Not necessarily a situation where a teen decided to experiment with weed, graduated to snorting Ecstasy and cocaine, while hanging in the woods with friends and a six-pack of wine coolers. Kelly was using hard-core opiates—or, as she herself said, "Anything I could find."

"I'm not on anything, Mom!" Kelly snapped back.

Melanie could tell when Kelly was high. They'd be eating dinner. Melanie would look over and, shaking her head in frustration and fear, watch as her daughter nodded out, "falling asleep in her food."

KELLY COCHRAN WOULD TALK about this period of her life—a young teen abusing drugs and falling in love with Jason—as an evolving, ascending rocket she had boarded without necessarily knowing how fast she was going. She sketched herself as a scared, abused woman, living with a man she had known most of her life—a tyrant, intimidating and controlling her. Because of this pressure from her new husband, not to mention the anxiety of what he *might* do, Kelly said, abusing drugs became an easy and convenient way to numb the emotional pain. But she never considered that she could end the relationship and not marry the guy.

"With Jason, I knew him all my life," Kelly said. "He had a pretty normal upbringing, his parents normal people. Good people."

Kelly said she was so close to Jason, she missed a lot.

"I feel like there was a split in him." Not multiple personalities, but two different people. "Just the way that he looked at me, the threats, some of what he did. Me waking up and him standing over me with a gas can. The look in his eyes." There was a time, she added, she saw the "man I had fallen in love with. At other points, there was somebody completely different." Kelly said she knew of no traumatic events in Jason's life besides the loss of his best friend in high school, which had devastated and changed him. "I don't know if that was traumatic enough to split him—to me, it's not."

Something that bothered Kelly was Jason's "sexual preference."

"I knew his secrets. In order for him to get off, he had to inflict pain. Choking, beating. I mean, the reason he had girlfriends, and why I was okay with it, because it gave me a break—a little reprieve for me."

After they wed, living in Indiana as a couple, moving out of Kelly's parents' house, Kelly said, "Jason tried to tighten the reins even more. I guess that's the best way to say it. He would monitor most things I did. It wasn't as bad at the start as it was the last four or five years."

"In the beginning, it was verbal abuse," she explained. "I think that was the worst, at the beginning." As the marriage became static and mundane, even bourgeois, she claimed, Jason began to "push and shove" her around. "I mean, he got mad. We had some times where we'd yell at each other. . . . There were a lot of times where he'd grab me, push me, shove, and it just got worse."

Based on Kelly's version, one had to consider if Jason had suffered from mental issues all his life, or had he developed the condition during the course of their marriage?

"I want to say . . . yes," Kelly explained, regarding Jason's mental status. "But, on the other hand, I think I was a little bit too close. It is my *belief* that I think he had some issues."

In 2007, when things between them were volatile, they decided to separate.

"I'll kill you!" Kelly claimed Jason screamed at her routinely, giving one reason why she felt compelled to consider leaving.

"If I ever wanted a divorce . . . he wasn't going to let me go. He had thrown stuff. Slammed doors. Broke things . . ."

Later, while talking through—if true—traumatizing events for anyone, strangely, Kelly recalled many of these anecdotes with a half smile on her face. She sat with one leg crossed over the other, her arms folded on her knees. She never looked away. She'd shrug her shoulders once in a while out of nervousness, perhaps in contrast or even disagreement with what she was talking about. At least from her body language, Kelly Cochran seemingly wanted to give the *impression* she was scared.

26

CHAOS REIGNS

CHIEF FRIZZO AND KELLY COCHRAN stared at each other. To say that Kelly was contentious that day, Frizzo later explained, would be an understatement. Kelly was irate and upset, far beyond the point of being deliberately devious.

Kelly mentioned what a "worrier" Jason had become since they'd moved into town.

"Jason told me," Frizzo said in response, "that he hasn't gotten angry *once* since coming out of the hospital."

"He doesn't really show his anger toward me. We shout at each other. We both call each other names. I am sure he's called me a slut, and whatnot."

"Has he ever thrown things at you when he's angry?"

"Not in the house."

Frizzo asked for a second time about Chris Regan and the last time Kelly saw him.

Kelly explained that lasagna meal again. How she texted Chris the following day and, with no response, took a ride over to his apartment. She let herself in with keys Chris had given her.

"It looked like he had started packing—like leaving cabinets open. That job meant everything to him. I was weirded out, actually, by the way the apartment looked when I went back. I am surprised he didn't make his drug test. He wanted his son with him in North Carolina. They had some bet that whoever arrived there first had to buy dinner."

The chief brought up the subject of text messages as the interview seemed to come to a natural end. Frizzo had gone through most of the phone records by then: Chris's, Kelly's, and Jason's. While conducting a tedious, careful examination of calls, Frizzo discovered an interesting set of facts, one of which Kelly needed to explain.

Frizzo found communication between Chris's cell phone and Kelly's cell phone on October 13, arguably the day before Chris went missing. Nothing of particular interest, essentially. But the next day, October 14, at three fifty-seven p.m., Chris texted Kelly's phone. Chris was "probably" getting gas at the fuel station near his apartment (that CCTV video). Kelly did not respond to that text. Yet, about a half hour later, at four-thirty p.m., someone sent a message from Jason's cell phone to Chris Regan's cell phone.

Chris responded to it.

After that, a phone call was placed from Chris's phone to Jason's phone.

Seven minutes.

At five twenty-five p.m., about an hour later, "one final text message," Frizzo explained, occurred "from Chris Regan's phone to Jason Cochran's phone."

Why would Jason be communicating with Chris Regan on the day Chris allegedly went missing? Frizzo wanted Kelly's thoughts.

"He wouldn't be," Kelly responded. "If anyone was

using or texting from that phone to Chris, it would have been me."

She explained that whenever her phone wasn't working, she'd use Jason's.

"But you're going to text him *while* you're with him?" Frizzo asked. The chief had established this with a time-line from Kelly. According to the times she had given the MSP, Kelly would have been at Chris's apartment then.

Kelly became perturbed by the push back. "Yes . . . ," she said. Then stopped herself. "Wait. What do you mean?"

"What was Chris wearing the last time you saw him?" Frizzo asked, changing the subject.

"I think he was wearing his Keen boots and jeans."

Kelly was done.

Frizzo stood and thought about the cell phone calls. She knew from her investigation that Kelly's phone had texted Chris's phone on October 15, 16, and 17, but not at any time after that. What's more: Kelly's phone never called Chris's phone at any time *after* October 14. And yet, she had told the MSP she "called and texted him for two weeks straight."

NOT LONG AFTER THAT INTERVIEW, Chief Laura Frizzo sat in her office. An MSP detective popped in.

"You got a minute, Chief?"

"Yes? Can I help you?" By now, Frizzo was done with the MSP. To her, they were looking at only one side of the coin. Frizzo was taking the reins and running with the case in the direction she believed it should go.

"Listen, Kelly called us," the MSP detective said. "She doesn't want to talk to you anymore. Why don't you just sit back and allow us to do this. You have too much on your plate, as it is."

"What the f . . ." was all Frizzo could say.

"She says someone is following her, and, look, we . . ."

"*What* are you talking about?"

"I'm getting ready to head out on Thanksgiving break," the MSP detective said. "I am not going to be thinking about this case while I'm gone."

"Well, hey, that is your choice—but I am!" Frizzo said.

The conversation ended with Frizzo more fired up than ever about Kelly Cochran. All Kelly did with that phone call was draw more attention to herself.

"I had to be the voice for Chris Regan, the victim in this case," Frizzo concluded. "Because it was clear to me that no one else was."

27
THE DARK SIDE

After Jason Cochran stopped working, Kelly Cochran explained to me, their relationship took on an even darker form than had existed previously throughout their lives.

"His issue was his back," she said. "It . . . caused him not to be able to work. He wasn't able to do anything. He was an invalid."

Jason couldn't move around much outside, especially. By that point, he'd filed for disability.

This made Jason even more miserable, Kelly added.

"Things got worse because . . . he was angry. He was jealous. I was always leaving the house, every day, working seven days a week. He became *very* jealous. *Very* angry. There was times when he threatened me. . . ."

Kelly spoke of a day when they lived on Mississippi Street, in Hobart, Indiana. It was 2008. Jason was in a rotten mood all the time. According to Kelly, he owned a "thirty-aught-six," referring to the bullet, a .30-06 Springfield shotgun cartridge with a soft tip.

"Anytime we had guns in the house, they were loaded.

We had a fight. At this time, there were no other relationships. I wasn't seeing anybody. He put the gun to my head. We were screaming and yelling."

They argued back and forth. Yelled. Screamed.

"I'm gonna do it!" Jason said, per Kelly's recollections.

"Go ahead. . . ."

Without warning, Jason pulled the trigger.

"I don't know if I was necessarily scared, I'm sure I was, but here he had a gun to my head and he pulled the trigger. Gun wasn't loaded *that* time. It was the only time the gun *wasn't* loaded."

If Kelly's walking-on-eggshells marriage was so volatile, brittle, violent, and dysfunctional, why hang around to see what the guy was going to do next? Why not move on? Get a divorce? According to Kelly, this sort of violence in the house had been going on ever since she'd started living with Jason.

Kelly talked about being raised in a family where parents stayed married. "I was taught that you worked it out. If something was broke, you fixed it. . . . Nothing is easy. If it were easy, there wouldn't be a divorce rate like there is."

Kelly thought moving to Michigan would help. Although it was mostly Jason's idea from the start, Kelly supported it because she believed the relocation might do the marriage some good.

However, nothing positive happened after they got settled in Michigan. Jason became even "more jealous" and "had no intention of going to work."

Kelly didn't start a job for two months.

"I was in no hurry. We had money saved up."

Her first job in Michigan was at Ace Hardware in Iron River. She worked the cash register. Stocked shelves.

Made keys. From there, she went to work at Mr. T's Restaurant, serving tables. Two part-time jobs took up most of her time.

Jason stayed at home. Took walks. Fished. Smoked and grew weed. Made friends with the neighbors. Played games for hours and hours on Facebook every day, while eating and smoking.

Applying at Oldenburg, Kelly said, gave her the possibility of doing what she loved: "Building things, making and fixing things."

She stopped using drugs for a time so she could pass the screening.

"The last time I had used anything was probably six weeks prior to the test and that was marijuana."

Working so much, she spent less time around Jason. Their problems seemed to dissipate because they rarely saw each other. This opened up an opportunity to seek out men for sex and companionship.

By the end of June 2014, Kelly was working forty to sixty hours per week at Oldenburg; her shift was five a.m. to three p.m. Mr. T's fired her because (she first said) she kept calling in sick. She quit the hardware store. She was unable to maintain three jobs simultaneously.

According to Kelly, meeting Chris Regan just happened.

"I first met him on the day of my interview. He was one of six that did the hiring—that was the first time. I would see him in passing." Military assembly, where Chris was team leader, was located "right behind electrical assembly," the department where Kelly worked. They would stop when passing each other.

"Hi, how are you?"

"I'm fine," Kelly would say, smiling, sensing a spark.

"We would make small talk. We ended up talking more, I'd say, in June."

They planned—and blew off—several dates before hooking up.

"I was married. I was trying to . . . I knew it was wrong to be dating someone at work. I felt uncomfortable. Some of the things with my relationship at home made things worse."

After making plans and not meeting, Kelly considered that the flirting would not turn into anything more than a mutual crush. While she was at the car wash one day, vacuuming out her truck, Chris called.

"Hey! Nice to hear from you," Kelly said.

"Yeah, sorry about not being able to meet up."

"We talked for, I'd say, forty-five minutes to an hour."

By the end of the conversation, they finally had a plan in place to go on a date.

"Tomorrow?" Kelly said.

"Hiking?" Chris sounded excited.

Kelly suggested a nearby lake.

When she started dating Chris, Kelly later said, "me and Jason were separated. We were living together, but we were separated. . . . We both agreed on [the separation]. But he wasn't moving out. I ended up putting a lock on my phone. Jason wasn't going back home [to Indiana]. He wasn't going to show his parents he'd given up. . . . Things were getting rough at home. The . . . aggression was getting worse."

Jason would go through her phone any chance he could; this forced Kelly to change the password continually.

"We were separated and agreed on seeing other people."

That first date with Chris at the end of June went well.

"We met at a local lake."

They drove separately. Parked in a lot by the trail. Went hiking.

Afterward, they sat on a picnic bench. Talked. This "led into more intimate actions," Kelly recalled.

They had sex that day. That one date led to seeing each other three times a week, after work, at night. Within a few weeks, it was four to five times a week.

According to Kelly, they got along "really well. We respected each other's privacy. A lot of the guys at work would give Chris hell. We'd been seen talking together. It was friendly. We'd never be intimate or anything like that at work. Never show affection. But we did joke around and talk. . . . Some of the guys said, we know you're dating her, we know you have a relationship. He got upset because he was a supervisor there."

Not long after that, Chris sent Kelly a text.

"He was mad. Really pissed."

He didn't want anyone at work to know. He didn't want to lose his job.

Kelly claimed she said "sorry" and took the fall.

Chris ultimately admitted to the guys at work that he was having an affair with Kelly, but only because they wouldn't leave him alone about it.

On most nights they got together, Kelly cooked dinner. They'd hang out at Chris's apartment.

"We'd eat. We'd have sex. We'd talk. We'd watch movies."

Then, one day, Chris stopped calling or texting.

Kelly didn't understand. According to her, she thought it had to be because she didn't want to take off with him to North Carolina. She said Chris had asked numerous times and she was clear she would not leave Michigan.

"There is no way that my father," Chris Regan Jr. later said, "wanted her to move there with us. Absolutely, that is false and one of her lies."

MANY REPORTED THAT JASON COCHRAN did not have an angry bone in him. Beyond his *Where Monsters Hide* outline, former friends and relatives said Jason's demons were private. He didn't stomp around, red-faced, full of rage. Yet, as Chief Frizzo dug into Jason's life as part of her investigation, a different picture emerged.

One source told a rather chilling tale. One day, Jason had explained to this man: "I was driving and was pulled over by a female cop." Jason had a look of indifference about him. Like he had no feeling one way or another about it.

"The whole time the cop was at my window," Jason continued, "I was visualizing chopping her into pieces with the hatchet I kept under the seat."

This same source further claimed Jason was "very racist and talked about tapping into the water source and adding some chemical that would wipe out a huge area of blacks."

Another source told the chief Jason once explained that he "knew how to get rid of a body so only the teeth remained."

When Frizzo heard this, one thought entered her mind: Finding Chris Regan was going to be one of the most complex tasks of her career. She needed guidance. A source no one else had access to. And she had no idea then, of course, that it would be Christopher Regan Sr. himself.

28
PIECES

FRIZZO NEEDED A BREAK. Not a rest. Extra sleep would be nice, obviously—but it wasn't time for that right now. Instead, Frizzo needed some sort of boost to get her over the hump of questioning the Cochrans and the opportunity to search their house. There was something inside that house. Frizzo could feel it.

For weeks, Frizzo had been trying to speak with Jason's mother, Mary Cochran. She'd left messages. Tried phoning the residence at different times. No one ever picked up or called back.

On November 19, as Frizzo left yet another voice message, a woman came on the line.

"Yes . . . hello?"

"Mrs. Cochran, this is Chief Laura Frizzo from the Iron River Police Department in Michigan."

"Yes . . . okay."

Frizzo explained—without giving away too much—why she was calling.

"Yes, yes. I am Jason's mother."

"When was the last time you spoke to your son, ma'am?"

"Just this past weekend. He called me from his cell phone."

"Has Jason come to visit you [in Indiana] over the past couple of weeks?"

"No, no. I don't think so."

"What about during the month of October?"

"Oh, yes. October," Mary Cochran said. She recalled the visit specifically, without hesitancy.

"Do you know if it was early in the month or later?"

"I would say, around the second week. I think it was a Thursday. He stayed for the weekend."

Specifics, Frizzo noted. A Thursday, the second week of October, October 9. If Jason had stayed the weekend, that would have pushed it to October 10, 11, and 12. That made Jason available to be back home on October 14 and 15.

"Thanks," Frizzo said. "You've been helpful."

Frizzo got Jason's phone cleared from evidence. She decided, strategically, to drive it back to him. This would allow her to feel the two of them out, see where they were at, maybe get another crack at asking a few questions. The chief's evidence pointed in no other direction. Her colleagues at the MSP might have disagreed, but Frizzo was following the bread crumbs, trying to exclude the Cochrans. But everything she found included them.

It was four o'clock when Frizzo and another officer arrived at the Cochrans' Caspian home.

"Here's your phone, Jason," Frizzo said after the big man answered the door.

Frizzo was hoping to be invited in, but that wasn't going to happen.

"Can I get Chris Regan's keys to his apartment from you, Kelly?" Kelly had come out of the house and into the foyer, where they all stood. The last thing Frizzo needed was Kelly and Jason Cochran having access to Chris Regan's apartment. Moreover, based on that monotonous, time-consuming review of the text messages among the three phones, Frizzo realized Chris Regan had never actually given Kelly keys to his apartment.

Kelly disappeared into the blackness of the house. Frizzo waited.

"Here," Kelly said when she returned, handing over the keys.

"Jason, hey, was wondering when you last visited your parents in Indiana?" Frizzo tossed out in a casual manner, as if she'd just thought of it.

"August," Jason said.

"Not in October?" Frizzo responded. She mentioned how she'd just spoken to his mother and she claimed it was the second week of October.

"No. Look, my mother takes medications for rheumatoid arthritis and it affects her memory."

"Well, she seemed to recall speaking to you over the last weekend, so I think her memory might be all right, Jason." To Kelly: "And how was it *you* got hold of these keys?"

"Chris gave them to me about two months ago."

The impromptu interview was done. Clearly, Kelly was uncomfortable and did not want her husband saying anything more. Even clearer, she was finished talking.

Frizzo and her colleague walked back to their vehicle as Jason closed the door. Before getting in, looking over the roof of the car, staring at the Cochran house, Frizzo said, "They are lying to us."

BY DECEMBER, AFTER THE Thanksgiving holiday break, that same MSP detective stood again in Frizzo's office.

"Look, back off. You need to let it go. If you don't, they are not going to cooperate anymore."

Kelly had called the MSP to complain about Frizzo harassing them.

"Are you kidding me?" Frizzo snapped back.

"You're going down the wrong trail!"

Frizzo was beyond frustrated. The evidence pointed toward the Cochrans. No one else. She'd gone through the phone records. Conducted interviews. Spent countless hours reading every piece of paper associated with the case. The Cochrans lied about small things. This was a problem. Murderers don't get caught in big lies; they make their mistakes telling seemingly insignificant lies they easily forget.

"Chris Regan had financial problems and other issues," the detective told the chief, according to Frizzo's remembrance. "And he just wanted to disappear. . . ."

"I don't know what records you're looking at—but, um, he was *not* behind on any bill. He's got a pension from the military coming in. He's living in an apartment, working full-time. All his bills are paid up. He is very organized."

The detective dropped his head into his hands. "He disappeared because he wanted to, or he killed himself."

"No, no, no," Frizzo said.

Frizzo was not giving up. She knew the Cochrans had answers. She needed to find that missing piece to get them back into the station under a warrant.

29

HOME LIFE

THE SUBJECT OF PETS had always been a focal point whenever Kelly Cochran talked about Jason's violent tendencies. Kelly and Jason had bought a dog right after they married. A feisty little thing. It liked to get into the garbage. Nothing would deter the pooch from knocking the garbage over whenever they left the house. One afternoon, the Cochrans arrived home to find the dog had spread the garbage all over the floor.

Jason walked in, stopped in his tracks, looked around.

"He became infuriated and beat her," Kelly claimed.

Then Jason "put [the dog] inside the garbage can and beat her while she was inside . . . and then put the lid on it."

A few years later, there was a cat "in heat" and she kept coming around the house, Kelly said.

"I guess it was bothering him. He ended up drowning the cat in a . . . [swimming] pool."

She told this same story two different ways: The second, later version had the cat bothering them one afternoon while they were putting in a swimming pool for a client.

Oddly, Kelly showed no emotion as she talked about

these brutal, violent episodes of animal cruelty. She described intensely graphic scenes of cruelty in a flat tone, without any emotion.

For every story Jason's spouse told of his punishing, maniacal behavior, there was a friend or relative of Jason's to counter the claim. They testified that throughout his life, Jason had never shown any animosity, hatred, or anger toward animals or people. In most testimonials, Jason was a gentle giant. Sure, he'd gotten mad once in a while, but nothing to the extent of Kelly's claims.

One former friend spoke of Jason's family having lots of farm animals. "Jason's mom was really good about taking my daughter around to pet the horses and things, and it was a great time." Jason was usually there. He appeared happy, this same friend added. Calm. There was nothing about his behavior then, or at any other time, to indicate Jason was—or could become—violent or fly off into a rage.

However, that didn't mean it wasn't there.

"There was no one at all who described Jason as violent or abusive, to us," Laura Frizzo later said.

Furthermore, when one reads through the available text history between Jason and Kelly, there was not a single instance where Jason spoke to his wife in a threatening manner. Additionally, Kelly never came across in responding texts as a woman in fear of her husband. To the contrary, her attitude proved she was the aggressor. And Jason's replies to those same texts showed a man who was ridiculed and told what to do by a domineering spouse.

When they moved to Michigan, Kelly made no effort to keep it secret that she was stepping out. Jason begged for her to come home after work and not spend the night with other men. His texts were pleading and passive, maybe pathetic. Never threatening.

Kelly would turn around and tell him that his jealousy had "better end."

I'm sick of you going through my shit!

They lived in Caspian under a dynamic that Kelly mandated, maintained, and controlled. She was out running around all day and night (after she stopped working full-time), monopolizing their only vehicle, with Jason trapped in the house, playing video games, smoking weed, overeating, taking walks, and napping.

"You have to understand, Jason is not from Michigan," Frizzo later said, speaking of that period before and after Chris Regan went missing. "He's living six and a half hours from where he's raised and his family is. She is . . . doing whatever she wants. He's trapped inside. And his wife, who he has done all these things to show and prove his love to, is belittling him constantly—and there's nothing he can do about it."

"You better knock this shit off," Kelly would scream, pointing at Jason whenever he started looking into her life and asking questions.

"You're right, baby, I'm sorry. I don't know what I'm doing."

In Jason's home computer, during the summer and fall of 2014, he was Googling phrases such as *How to stop being a jealous husband*. It got to the point where Jason once told Kelly: "You will continue to fuck me over and I will continue to love you, anyway."

ABUSING ANIMALS, BEING VIOLENT toward the neighborhood cats and your own dog, is one dark side of human behavior. But Kelly also claimed Jason exhibited these cruel and psychotic behaviors around people, too.

"He's threatened quite a few. One would be a friend of

mine. . . . He had threatened [this guy] a couple of times, but I witnessed one."

Kelly had what she deemed a "friendship relationship" with this man. Entirely platonic.

"Jason did not want me to talk to him. We went sky-diving together and he was pretty jealous of that. [Jason] threatened him and said he would kill him if he didn't leave me alone."

When they moved into the Lawrence Street house in Caspian, Michigan, in January 2014, those same linger-ing "issues" from Indiana followed. According to Kelly, it was Jason's decision to move to Michigan. There was no talking him out of it. She said Jason "picked the state because he was able to grow marijuana and smoke mari-juana legally [in Michigan]. He grew it at home in Indiana, but it was legal up [there]. I believe there are other reasons, but I cannot be sure of those."

"Look, Jason and Kelly had lots of farmland in Indiana and could have grown all the weed he wanted without ever being caught," one Indiana law enforcement officer said. "That is not the reason they left Indiana. They were running from something."

"Jason was running from his own demons and his own mistakes," Kelly said later about the sudden move. "There were a lot of things he was running from and, at the end, he just stopped talking to me about it all. A lot of it was to isolate me, though. He had seen the independence that I had started. My independence made him crazy. He tried to stifle every bit of it that I had."

Jason found a few homes on craigslist and sent Kelly up to Michigan to meet with a real estate agent. She soon found the Caspian house and bought it.

Nothing changed, Kelly proclaimed. They were still fighting. Jason was smoking more weed than ever, and she was beginning to branch out and meet new men. It was a time, Kelly believed, when she leaned heavily on drugs just to get through the day.

"I've used drugs a lot. There really wasn't one certain kind of drug I used. When things got bad, I started using pills a lot. I was depressed a lot and took a lot of pills. I have experimented with just about any kind of drug you can think of."

Chief Frizzo became interested in Jason's back pain. The videos Frizzo viewed of Kelly and Jason frolicking around a waterfall in September 2014 proved to the chief there was perhaps a lot more about Jason Cochran they needed to learn.

"He had some pain," Kelly said. "But any man who can . . . lug a two-hundred-pound man . . . around and do the other things he did, is quite capable in body and mind, so . . . no. I never considered him disabled. I think he, I don't know . . . I think he, um, he sought more attention for his injuries than he needed."

The reason Jason wanted to move to Michigan, Kelly claimed later, had nothing to do with a change of pace and the opportunities Michigan offered for Jason to grow his own weed legally. Jason, Kelly concluded, was feeling the heat back home. He'd done too much in Indiana. He needed to leave the state before authorities caught on.

"He killed multiple people in Indiana," Kelly told me during a telephone interview in 2017. "He also wanted to get me away from my family so he could control me easier."

30
NEW BLOOD

IN HIS YOUNGER DAYS, Mike Neiger had a rugged, out-doorsy look to him. Salt-and-pepper, thick, mountain-man beard; red cheeks from windburn; small, curious eyes. Born in Petoskey, Michigan, which is part of the shoreline in Little Traverse Bay, on the very northern tip of the state, south of Lake Michigan's Beaver Island, Neiger spent twenty-five years with the MSP. First as a road trooper. Then a long stint in forensics.

Neiger was sixty-one years old when he and Frizzo first met. Neiger explained to Frizzo that he had recently retired from the MSP, where he had spent the final ten years of his career as a forensic specialist. Since retirement, he'd started a company, Michigan Backcountry Search and Rescue (MibSAR), which allowed him to volunteer his time in "select cases" throughout the Upper Peninsula, Lower Michigan, and certain locales in Canada. His main course of investigation was missing-person cold cases and unsolved homicides.

"Evidence collection, direction and assistance, missing-person flyers . . . and tracking services for possible deceased bodies," Neiger explained.

"A tracker?"

Neiger said his services were free. He sent Frizzo references. What a considerate gesture, especially when Frizzo could clearly use any help she could get.

Skeptical at first, based mostly on her fractured relationship with the MSP, Frizzo called a few of those referrals, and Neiger was given high marks all around.

It was November 13, 2014. Frizzo went to have a look at Chris Regan's Hyundai Genesis. Neiger's expertise could help in that regard.

Neiger had a comforting, fatherly look about him. The beard was gone. A receding hairline might have made him appear to be getting on in years, but he was actually in better shape than most men thirty years younger, spending six days a week training, as he put it, "muscularly and aerobically."

Chris Regan's leased vehicle was scheduled to be returned to the car company soon, Frizzo found out. She needed to get into it and have a look. The MSP had already done a once-over, but at this point in the investigation, Frizzo double-checked everything, if for no other reason than to get a feel for the evidence herself. She'd found a report where the car had been swabbed, yet the steering wheel had been missed.

The only item of importance they were able to find inside Chris Regan's car was a knitted hat. Frizzo hoped she would someday need a DNA sample from Chris Regan and the hat proved to be loaded with hairs.

The other important task at hand was a second search of Chris's apartment. Frizzo touched base with Chris Regan Jr. and found out he was on his way into town to clean out his father's apartment. She needed to get in there beforehand. The MSP and IRPD had done a cursory check of Chris's residence, but Frizzo knew an investigator with Mike Neiger's experience and expertise could give her a closer forensic look. There was an answer there, Frizzo felt. She just had to find it.

The search warrant came in on November 24, 2014.

"The purpose, really, for me going in there, again, was to try and collect some type of items that might contain DNA for down-the-road comparison purposes."

They bagged and tagged "a flossing device, a toothbrush, a bicycle helmet, gloves, another knitted hat."

Mike Neiger walked around the apartment carefully. He studied each of the rooms with an eagle's eye for detail. He advised Frizzo to take the drain trap from the bathroom and the kitchen sink, common areas for DNA from blood and hairs to congregate.

"I identified some prints of interest, too," Neiger said.

"Anything else?"

"Yeah, come in here."

They walked into the bedroom. "Look at that." Neiger pointed to the bedsheets. "That spot could be blood."

Frizzo could feel the case moving somewhere.

Momentum—that was all she'd ever wanted.

AS FRIZZO WAITED, FOCUSING on what stone to overturn next, the phone company came through in locating text messages between Chris Regan and Kelly Cochran on October 13, 2014. This find had the potential to be big. It had taken a while, but they were able to go back into computer records and extract the actual messages. Most cellphone users think they can delete texts completely. However, the cellular phone companies, for no particular reason, save and file them. Most of the time, the texts are deleted after a few weeks, but these particular days in question were available.

Sitting at home, Frizzo opened the file and read. It gave her a great overview of the casual banter between Kelly and Chris in those days just before Chris was last heard from.

Sure wish I knew if you were okay or not? Please let me know, OK? I hope you are, Chris texted one day near his disappearance. He had not heard from Kelly in twenty-four hours. He was wondering what was going on. They had made tentative plans to hang out in an earlier exchange, but Kelly was AWOL.

OMG, don't hate me. Lost contacts. I did get you a gift on my trip.

Kelly told Chris she had been away. Frizzo had learned through investigative work that it was Kelly who had actually gone to Indiana on October 9. It was not Jason, as Jason's mother had reported to the chief. Neighbors in Indiana would later confirm this.

"Kelly told Chris Regan she had gotten him a gift in Indiana while she was gone," Frizzo explained. "She told him on October thirteenth (when he asked her to stop by) that she couldn't give him the gift until the next day, the fourteenth. . . . I believe one hundred percent that Kelly went to Indiana to retrieve the gun [that would be used] to kill Chris Regan."

Kelly told Chris she'd had trouble with her phone—the reason for her silence.

I was going to stop by your place but figured you wouldn't hear me knock, Kelly texted.

Come over tonight, Chris texted. **Got some juicy gossip to share.** He ended the text with a smiley face.

Kelly said she couldn't give him his gift until the following day, October 14, asking, **Is tomorrow better?**

I thought you fell off the earth. I would not have heard. I sleep sound now. OK, how come? Chris texted.

I have been a bit sick and crabby. That's why.

So? I am sick too. You could use a hug and some kind words. See you at 5.

I feel like my head is in a vise.

Poor girl. Maybe you will feel a little better tomorrow. Sound better? Chris texted.

I'm hoping. This sucks. You OK? Kelly replied.

I'll survive. Glad to get the cold thing over. You better? Lucky you. Mine dragged on for a week almost.

As they continued texting, Chris advised Kelly: Drink liquids, take a multivitamin, eat food, and bundle up and watch television.

Kelly responded that when she was ill, she always drank her fluids, especially water. She added that TV made her "lazy," so she wasn't going to lounge around, zoning out.

That's the idea, dork. Rest.

I'm trying. That's not easy for me.

Good night, Chris texted.

Sleep well. See you tomorrow.

I can't wait. I've missed you. Sorry to be so cheezy [sic].

31

LISTEN AND LEARN

IRPD POLICE CHIEF LAURA FRIZZO needed to get into the Cochran house under a search warrant. Besides the comforting feeling of knocking on the door, slapping that piece of paper against Kelly's chest and telling her to get out of the way, Frizzo wanted answers. If she could go through each room, turn over every piece of furniture and look behind every picture, dig in the garbage, sift through every square inch of that house, the chief was certain she'd uncover a clue to the whereabouts of Chris Regan. Without telling anyone, Frizzo felt she'd connected on a spiritual level with Chris Regan. She believed his presence was driving and guiding her. It was hard to explain. But he was there. Pushing her in different directions. Not voices in her head, or some sort of spiritual apparition, but a pull, an instinctual grip. It was indicating that something bigger than just the chief was involved.

"It would be almost two years, you have to understand," Frizzo explained. "I imagined what my reaction might be when, or even if, I ever found him. It was always such a roller-coaster ride. One day, I'd have no doubt whatsoever that I would find Chris Regan. The next, well, I'd feel hopeless."

This day was an in-between one. Frizzo knew she had enough for a warrant, she just needed to lay it all out, present it to the prosecutor and get it signed off.

The more Frizzo looked into the minor details Kelly had given her and the MSP during interviews, the clearer it was that Kelly was manipulating the truth. As she went through the interviews the MSP had conducted with Tim Huntley, Frizzo saw that the park-and-ride in Bates Township was the place where Tim and Kelly often met before a sexual rendezvous. Tim was certain of this, so Frizzo went back through her last interview with Kelly. Kelly claimed to have no idea where the park-and-ride was located.

This detail could not have been a simple, overlooked fact. In other words, it was not something that one would forget. Unless it was significant.

Even more compelling were the phone records and texts coming in under warrants the IRPD and the MSP's technical investigations unit had filed weeks ago. The deeper Frizzo looked into communication among the three parties' phones—Chris and Kelly, Jason and Kelly, Jason and Chris—it was clear that a search warrant for the house was needed fast.

Between May 15, 2014, through October 13, 2014, a 151-day period, Kelly Cochran's phone sent and received a total of 5,434 text messages, an average of 35.9 per day. Voice calls from and to Kelly's phone number during that same period came in at 3,604, a daily average of 23.8.

Just numbers, really. Yet Frizzo was astonished by the data after comparing the numbers to those of Jason and Chris's phones.

The second significant date range was October 10,

2014, through October 25, 2014. Focused on Kelly's phone, there had been 506 total text messages sent and received, or 31.6 per day. Voice calls came in a bit less, 19.8 for a daily average.

Until she took into consideration why the daily average was different, slight as it was, Frizzo could have never known that such a small (percentage) number would be so significant to her investigation. When the chief looked at October 15, 2014, specifically, an anomaly jumped out: zero text messages on that day were sent or received, with only one phone call made from Kelly's phone, at ten-fourteen p.m. The previous day, October 14, Chris Regan had texted Kelly's phone at three fifty-seven p.m., but she did not respond. Yet, Jason's phone texted Chris Regan's phone at four-eleven p.m., and Chris's phone texted Jason's phone back. Just after that, Chris's phone made a seven-minute voice call to Jason's phone. The last text logged on that day took place at five twenty-five p.m.

Chris's phone to Jason's phone.

An incredible find lurked within the muck of all that data. Frizzo realized at eight fifty-seven p.m., Kelly's phone called Chris Regan's phone—something that had not happened all day—for a duration of one second.

"I would never have even caught this call without a thorough phone records investigation," Frizzo later remarked. "This call didn't show up on Chris's cell records—only Kelly's. Which was explained to me by the tech person from Verizon that because of the short duration, one second, it didn't register on *his* incoming records. Thankfully, though, it was caught on *her* outgoing calls."

Why a one-second phone call from Kelly's phone to Chris's phone on that day?

Frizzo believed Kelly was scrambling around her house trying to find Chris's phone.

"I knew when I found this in the phone records that it meant Chris was dead by this time, and most likely shortly before she had made the call to his phone. She was desperate to find it before he was reported missing and someone was able to ping the location of his phone."

There was more.

On the following day, October 15, a few text messages flowed to and from Kelly's phone, Kelly and Jason's phone, and a third, unknown, number. With this information, Frizzo knew for certain Kelly's phone had been working fine. There had been nothing wrong with it, as Kelly had claimed during her interviews. Why would she give the excuse that her phone was broken for why she used Jason's phone to contact Chris Regan's phone, when it was clearly working? Why lie about such a seemingly insignificant fact?

Because it was important.

In addition to the information about Kelly's phone, Jason's phone unraveled another thread, which proved to be even more compelling. Jason's phone came in, on average, during a period between October 10 through October 31, with 19.6 text messages per day. Voice calls during that same span of time were eight per day. For October 15, in particular, same as Kelly's phone, that number dropped significantly to four total communications: two incoming voice calls, two outgoing text messages.

During the twenty-two-day period in October, when Frizzo had a chance to look closely at the communications per day for Jason and Kelly, they averaged 4.7 per day, eight days with zero communications. Between October 15 and 16, there were no communications; and between

October 26 through 31, zero again. On October 12, however, nine communications were exchanged between Kelly and Jason. The next day, October 13, thirty. On October 14, the first five communications of the day were between Jason's and Kelly's phones. During this same period of time, October 14 and 15, four communications passed between Chris Regan's phone and Jason's phone, texts and voice calls. The final contact of that day came in at five twenty-six p.m., a text, initiated by Chris's phone to Jason's. The following morning, at eight twenty-one, one outgoing text went from Jason's phone to Chris Regan's phone.

Then an entire day passed without any communication—that is, before a text message at five thirty-two p.m. was sent from Jason's to Chris's phone.

Interesting data. But what had it actually proved to the chief?

One had to go backward in time in order to see how important this data was within the scope of Frizzo's investigation. Jason's phone records from May 2014 to October 2014 proved that silence between the phones meant only one thing: the end of Chris Regan's life.

First, during that period of time, May 1, 2014, through October 13, 2014, 918 voice calls were placed to and from Jason's phone. Yet not *one* of them had been made to or from Chris Regan's number.

Additionally, 1,490 text messages were sent to and from Jason's phone. But again, not *one* of them to or from Chris Regan's number.

Even more alarming: All of these communications had bounced off cell towers near the Cochrans' house in Caspian. Every last one of them—including Chris Regan's phone.

Why was Chris Regan's phone bouncing off cell towers near the Cochran house on a night Kelly had said she spent with him at his apartment—the last time anyone had seen or heard from the guy?

Frizzo sat back. Thought about it: *Someone lured the guy over to the Cochran house. He showed up. Never left the place alive.*

Then this: During that time period *before* October 14, 2014, most of the text messages between Jason and Kelly were abrasive and even sometimes degrading on Kelly's part, with Jason coming across desperate to spend time with his wife and win her love. Then, suddenly, after that October 14 date (which Frizzo now believed was the last day of Chris Regan's life), Kelly and Jason were exchanging gushy texts like new lovers, with Kelly referring to Jason as "handsome" and begging him to "fuck me" all the time.

32

SIGNED, SEALED, DELIVERED

FRIZZO SAT DOWN WITH Iron County prosecuting attorney, University of Tulsa College of Law graduate, Melissa Powell, on February 27, 2015. Since October 2014, although she had been involved in other cases, Frizzo put her focus on finding Chris Regan and arresting those responsible for his death. Over the past two months, the chief had utilized every resource she could. The next step in that sequence was for Frizzo to get inside the Cochran house and—maybe more important—onto the Cochran property and commence a meticulous search. By this time, Frizzo knew Kelly and Chris were likely never inside his apartment together on that last night he had been heard from. All the evidence pointed to the contrary: Chris Regan had driven to the Cochran house, was murdered there, with his car being later dropped off at the park-and-ride in Bates Township. The Post-it note with directions to Kelly's house, which was found on the front seat of Chris Regan's car, was one of the most important factors that convinced the chief. Whoever had dumped his car had failed to dispose of this clue.

The chief sat with PA Melissa Powell and talked through what information she had for a search warrant. Frizzo couldn't help but think that this stage of the cat-and-mouse game she'd been playing with Kelly Cochran was going to end at 66 Lawrence Street. One needed probable cause, Frizzo understood, before a magistrate would consider a warrant. Proving probable cause in a murder investigation where law enforcement did not have a body was challenging, to say the least. The MSP contended all along that without a body, Chris Regan was an adult missing person who had likely disappeared on his own.

Frizzo, of course, had never believed that—all of the evidence she'd discovered supported the contrary.

"Let's hear it," Powell said. She sat back at her desk. Took out a yellow legal pad.

Melissa Powell was an attractive woman with aqua-blue eyes, sandy-blond hair, and an unforced smile. She had a reassuring air about her, especially how she operated inside a courtroom. Yet, behind her subtle charm, Powell was a tough prosecutor, who delivered justice within her county in the old-fashioned way. She made sure she didn't take on prosecutions to assuage a cop's ego, for a personal vendetta, or for political gain. She simply wanted scum off the street. And you did that as a prosecutor by presenting evidence that a jury could not overlook. If Powell prosecuted Kelly and Jason Cochran for the murder of Chris Regan, the PA was going to present the most ironclad case she could build. No corners would be cut; no endless rabbit holes or suspects overlooked because a local cop had blinders on.

Frizzo laid out a long list of investigatory facts she'd compiled since October 27, 2014, when Terri O'Donnell parked in front of the IRPD and reported Chris missing.

The chief believed all of it was strong evidence that established the validity of a search warrant.

One by one, she rattled off her most promising leads: the affair between Kelly and Chris, Kelly skipping out of work with her injured shoulder as an excuse, the wellness check on Kelly after she'd reported her husband wanted to kill her, and Jason Cochran's anger about the affair and how he had discovered text messages between Kelly and Chris and other men.

She further listed how Kelly explained in all of her interviews that she'd spent the better part of the evening of October 14 at Chris's apartment, but phone records proved otherwise. The chief emphasized how Kelly had been unable to explain with any logical reasoning why she would be texting with Chris from her husband's phone at times when she was supposed to be there, inside Chris's apartment, sitting across from him on the couch.

Additionally, Frizzo had recently recovered a video of the Cochrans' white truck. It showed the truck traveling eastbound first, then westbound, away from Chris's apartment. This occurred during a time frame when Kelly claimed to be inside the apartment with Chris.

The chief also brought up the "voices" Jason heard inside his head. She mentioned a text proving Kelly never had keys to Chris's apartment—she likely took them from Chris. Plus, Chris's keys were still missing, and several neighbors reported that Kelly would have to bang on Chris's door to get in. Chris would sometimes leave a rug in between the door so Kelly could get into the building.

"I think they might be looking to take off," Frizzo told the prosecutor.

"Why would you say that?"

"Kelly has been listing furniture for sale online."

The prosecutor nodded affirmatively. She understood the urgency of Frizzo's plea.

"I've also been contacted by a private investigator who is looking into Chris Regan's disappearance. He came into the station and told me—very respectfully—that he did not want to interfere with anything we had going on and said he would keep me in the loop as to what he was working on."

"That should not affect your case . . . and any information he receives should be turned over to you."

"Okay. I'll work on this warrant and e-mail it when I'm done," Frizzo said.

The final note Frizzo made on a list of forty-eight summarized facts, included in her warrant, summed up the chief's case: "I believe that these listed investigative discoveries show that Christopher Regan's last destination was to 66 Lawrence Street, Caspian."

The paper and electronic trail of Chris's life ended there.

33
EXECUTION

At eight-thirty a.m. on March 5, 2015, Chief Frizzo took a ride over to Kelly and Jason Cochran's Caspian home. Frizzo was looking to stir up the waters a bit. Her search warrant was done. She'd expected it to come through soon. Fearing they were preparing to run, Frizzo wanted to keep tabs on Kelly and Jason.

"Kelly, hey, I have some things I'd like you to have a look at—I think they're Chris's. Can you come down to the station for me?"

Kelly seemed taken aback, but agreed.

They drove separate vehicles.

Frizzo wanted to monitor Kelly's reaction to seeing something they had in evidence. She also wanted to rattle Kelly a bit, let Kelly and her husband know she wasn't going away.

Frizzo displayed the yellow Post-it with directions to the Cochran house, which had been found inside Chris's vehicle.

"Have a look at this," Frizzo said, placing the plastic bag that held the Post-it onto a table in front of Kelly.

Kelly stared. Went quiet.

"You recognize that handwriting—do you think it's Chris's?" Frizzo asked, staring at Kelly, gauging her body language.

Kelly shook her head. "I am unable to say for sure."

Frizzo pulled out a pair of biking gloves the IRPD found outside Chris's apartment in January.

"Those his?"

"Cannot say for sure, but they do look like something he would wear."

As they talked, a *ding* sounded. Kelly took out a TracFone from her purse and stared at the screen.

After reading the text, she said, "Why didn't you tell me two detectives were going to talk to Jason while I was here?" It felt to Kelly as if Frizzo had pulled a sleight-of-hand trick.

"I didn't know anything about two detectives going over there to speak with Jason, Kelly. Detectives working this case are not even in town at this time."

Not long after, two people walked into the IRPD; a man named Jackson Roper (pseudonym) and a woman. They were private investigators, Roper explained, working on the case. They had just come from talking to Jason at the Cochran house.

"He wouldn't allow us in or talk to us," Roper told Frizzo. "Can we talk to Kelly—she's here, right?"

"I'll check with her."

Kelly agreed, so Frizzo gave them an interview suite.

After the discussion between Kelly and the two PIs, Frizzo approached Kelly.

"Can I come over to your house and talk to you about a few things, Kelly?"

"That's fine." Kelly just wanted to go home.

"I'll be right over."

Kelly left. Frizzo sat down with the PIs.

By that time, around ten-thirty in the morning, Stephanie Brule, a prosecuting attorney standing in for Melissa Powell, who was out of town on business, called to say the warrant was well done. She encouraged Frizzo to get it "sworn" in front of the magistrate.

The PIs would not relate exactly what they had spoken to Kelly about. Still, "Jason was angry with us for being there at the house."

"I have a search warrant prepared and I'm thinking of executing it today," Frizzo told them.

"You think I could assist in that?" Roper asked.

"I'll check with the prosecutor, but maybe you can be part of it—as long as you don't touch anything, you know."

"I think they might be a flight risk," Roper said. He did not complete his thought with a specific reason, but warned Frizzo there was the chance the Cochrans were going to run.

Frizzo thought about something her administrative assistant, Wendy Otto-Shimun, had recently uncovered: Kelly had added herself as a member of an online group searching for "Homes to Rent in Middle Tennessee."

"Well, thanks for the info," Frizzo said. "I'll let you know about the search. I don't see a problem."

"You betcha."

Roper and his partner left.

Chief Frizzo spent a lot of time talking on the phone and exchanging e-mails about the case with Jackson Roper. So she felt completely confident in his ability and did not see him as some sort of bogus Hollywood-type sleuth. Jackson Roper was actually a retired law enforcement officer with nearly thirty years on the job.

She called the prosecutor and filled her in on what was a parallel investigation, essentially, telling her Roper could help and she could use all the eyes and ears she could get at this stage.

"Extra eyes and theories are never a bad thing," Frizzo commented later. "I don't need to claim all the glory to anything. The best investigator is a team player and realizes every player helps bring forth a victory. The prosecutor's office allowed [Roper] to be present, with the understanding that he touches nothing and is there only to observe and assist."

"You're cleared to come," Frizzo explained to Roper.

The chief gathered her troops. It was time to head over to the Cochran house and take that place apart.

34

BARE NAKED LADIES

SHE WAS WITH SEVERAL friends. They'd decided a road trip was in order. Kelly and her girlfriends piled into "this huge Ford Econoline" van and headed out to a local lake.

As they trekked down the road, singing to the radio, laughing at each other's jokes, the weed burned hot and the drinks flowed cold.

When they arrived at the lake, one of them made a suggestion: "Let's strip down naked."

"Hell, yeah" echoed throughout the van.

Clothes flew in the air as they all ran toward the water. They frolicked and swam like adolescent schoolgirls on the first day of summer break. Laughing and splashing, yelling and screaming, Kelly looked up toward the parking lot.

"Cops," she said.

With that, she realized she'd lost the keys to the van in the water.

Panic.

"Shit!"

The cops took off from the parking lot and the girls

went back to the van to try and figure out how they were going to get home.

One of the girls called her father.

And he taught us how to hot-wire the van over the phone, Kelly wrote.

Years later, Kelly would tell this story to a pen pal. It arose during a discussion—via letters—over the idea of marriage. At this time, both were incarcerated. The man had written to Kelly after seeing an article about her in *Rolling Stone* magazine. After introducing himself, they exchanged several letters, which turned into a quasi-romantic relationship, subsequently becoming sexually explicit and deeply personal. The man was much more of a writer than Kelly. He'd send twelve-, thirteen-, fourteen-, or even fifteen-page letters detailing his life and the life he wanted with Kelly.

In her girls'-day-at-the-lake letter, Kelly talked about her life with Jason. She spoke of her marriage as if it had been a fairy tale gone bad. *I married the boy next door,* she wrote. She'd meant that literally, not as a description of Jason. *I thought it would be perfect.* But, of course, it wasn't. From the earliest days of the marriage, she had tried, she wrote, *[to] do everything to make him happy and to feel love.* Fairly early into the union, she felt that Jason wasn't "capable" of love. This was the hardest part of the relationship for her to "understand." She couldn't wrap her mind around the idea that some people were not able to love their fellow human beings.

Kelly described how she should have run at the first sign of Jason's unloving, violent tendencies, but she didn't, obviously. *By then, it was too late,* she wrote. (Although Kelly failed to say when all of this actually occurred.) Something she never mentioned to the IRPD or MSP: she felt Jason "wasn't going to let" her go.

There were "many times" throughout the marriage when she "begged" Jason to let her go and grant her a divorce.

Jason made his stance clear: *"I will kill you if you try to get away."*

Marriage, Kelly concluded, *is horrifying to me.*

In letters to her parents, Kelly talked about the marriage as if she lived a daily existence under the fear and anxiety that Jason would kill her. She described him as a Svengali-like figure, thumping around the house, intimidating her with his stares, threatening her, letting her know she was forever trapped. There was no way out.

Her parents wrote during this same period, asking Kelly why she never asked for help. How come she never pulled them aside and whispered that Jason was a raging, controlling maniac who was probably going to kill her someday?

I thought I knew the answer to this . . . , Kelly wrote. Contradicting what she would say to her pen pal, Kelly said she had not become scared of Jason until October 2014: *after seeing him do everything he did. [He] would have found a way to . . . kill me.* She talked about how strong she used to be (emotionally), but now she saw herself as "weak." She talked about how Jason had taken much from her: *I blame myself for staying.*

At this point, they slept in separate rooms. She'd wake up and there he was: *Standing over me, staring with this hollow look in his eyes . . . [Jason] had two sides to him, but maybe one with just good acting ability.*

Answering her parents' question specifically, Kelly said she was scared of what Jason would do if she left.

To her.

To them.

To anyone she knew.

She was scared of "failing" at her marriage, before writing how she once believed: *[I] could save him from himself.*

These were strange and inconsistent comments. Because if Kelly was so terrified of what Jason might do (to her or to anyone in her family, especially), why would she risk being caught cheating on him? It didn't make sense. She portrayed herself as the terrified wife, a woman in constant fear, wondering if her husband would kill her at any moment.

CHIEF FRIZZO FOUND TWO VIDEOS on Kelly's phone contradicting everything she had said in these series of letters. There they were hanging out at a waterfall. Jason smoking a joint, playfully standing on the rocks, smiling for Kelly. And Kelly, talking to him casually, lovingly. Jason reciprocating. The videos portray Jason as a calm, charming guy who is having a nice day in nature with his wife.

"Jason Cochran is the victim here, too," Laura Frizzo said later. "That much became clear to me as we began to unpack the horror that happened to Christopher Regan."

35

PREMONITION

IN LATE FEBRUARY, Laura Frizzo was talking to one of her high-school girlfriends, who'd just happened to be in town for a few days. Of course, the subject taking up most of Frizzo's mind was Chris Regan's disappearance. On March 4, Frizzo's girlfriend called her. She was taking off and wanted to say good-bye.

"Listen, Laura, I have a good friend who's a psychic."

"I . . ."

"I know, I know. But I spoke with her. She'd like to talk to you about Chris to see if she gets anything from the conversation."

Frizzo's friend gave her the psychic's name and number.

"We'll see. Thanks," Frizzo said.

Could it hurt?

Later that day, the chief found herself doing something she never thought she would do: sitting down with a psychic. There was no mistaking that Frizzo had experienced spiritual moments regarding Chris Regan's presence in her life, as if he were guiding her in some way. She could not deny how deep the connection between her and this missing man, whom she had never met, had become.

As she listened to the psychic talk about Chris Regan and the case, Frizzo felt a tickle of folly. What was she doing? Relying on a stranger to tell her what happened to her victim? Or simply passing time until that break came through?

It was not a visit to lead the investigator in any particular direction. Frizzo knew the search warrant was going to be sworn any day now and she was anxious. She needed to keep her mind occupied, but also focused.

Walking out of the psychic's, Frizzo took a moment inside her car to reflect. She took a breath, lighting a cigarette.

Exhaling, the chief was taken by one specific thing the psychic had said.

"She told me that she felt Chris was hit with something on the back of his head—possibly a baseball bat."

Sure, anyone could have taken an educated guess at that, and, within reason, gotten close. But what Laura Frizzo was about to find would convince her that there was an ethereal force working alongside her, something she could not explain.

36
BLOOD AND AMMO

CHIEF LAURA FRIZZO AND colleagues rolled up on the Cochran house in Caspian in early March, 2015, at eleven fifty-one a.m. one morning. Jackson Roper, the PI Frizzo had been talking to, stood by, waiting for the opportunity to help where he could.

Kelly answered the door after the chief rapped on it with force, making it clear this was not a social call.

"This is a search warrant for the residence, property, outbuildings, and vehicles. The lab is on the way," Frizzo explained. "Once they get here, you cannot stay inside the residence."

Frizzo found Kelly to be "emotionless"—that stoic, blank affect she had all but mastered by this point. Though Kelly seemed to understand the serious turn her life and Jason's had taken, she did not seem rattled by the notion that the police were there to collect murder evidence.

"Where is Jason?" Frizzo asked.

"Upstairs. Sleeping."

"Go wake him up. You cannot be here while the warrant is processed and executed. Can you go to a neighbor's or friend's?"

Kelly yelled, "Jason! Jason!"

The big man came down the stairs and stood behind his wife. Disheveled, he said nothing.

Frizzo mentioned the dogs. Get them secured somewhere so the troops could trickle in and dig. Then: "Maybe you and Jason want to sit in a patrol car to stay warm—'cause it's pretty darn cold out there today."

They agreed.

As she walked into the foyer of the Cochran house, just beyond that ramp leading up to the door, Frizzo noted the door into the kitchen and the hole in the center of it. Next to the door, on the inside of the house, a wooden baseball bat leaned against the wall. Frizzo felt the bat had been placed strategically there for some reason.

Seeing the bat, Frizzo looked up. On the ceiling above the bat, she noticed a spatter pattern of some sort, which the PIs had told Frizzo to look for.

Gotta be blood.

"It had been cleaned, I could tell. But you could still see the staining where it started and widened as you went into the dining room."

Luminol, the chief thought. *The entire area needs to be sprayed.*

Taking a moment, feeling as though she was standing on the spot where Chris Regan entered the house and someone smashed him over the head with that bat, Frizzo felt a tingle. That damn psychic and her baseball bat premonition.

Before they stepped out of the house, Frizzo asked Kelly and Jason about weapons in the house.

"There's a gun under the entertainment center," Kelly said. She pointed.

"You and Jason, sit down on the couch."

Not a request.

Frizzo walked over to the entertainment center. Looked, spotted, then picked up a Blue Steel .22-caliber revolver, fully loaded, tucked inside a canvas holster.

A bat and gun? Kind of armed to the teeth here.

One of the MSP troopers who had walked through the house "to make sure it was safe" came across a twelve-gauge shotgun upstairs. Unloaded. Inside a case.

Beyond those weapons, no others.

The Cochrans had stopped using their iPhones by this point, which the IRPD had forensically searched, downloaded, and given back to them. Frizzo and her team found two TracFones they were now using. Burners. An Alcatel and Huawei. *Wired* magazine had once rated these phones, based on the notion that the user was concerned with being "targeted for confiscation and search," as the perfect choices if one wanted to avoid "leaving a trace of your phone activity." In fact, one could "wipe clean and destroy" these burners "without much thought."

Before Kelly and Jason left the house to sit inside a cruiser, Frizzo looked around the living and dining rooms. She noticed a few household items that had an odd air about the way they were positioned.

"That couch is pulled out at a strange angle," Frizzo said to Kelly. Looking at her, Frizzo noticed Kelly had blue paint on the cuticles of her fingernails.

"Um, well, I've been doing a lot of rearranging. We've been painting, too."

"Look, you cannot stay in here. You're both free to leave and go anywhere you want. You just cannot stay inside the house."

After the Cochrans left, Frizzo walked into the living

room. She slid the couch back to what appeared to be its natural position in the room.

Bleach spots were on the carpet beneath where the couch had been moved.

"I want those," Frizzo noted, pointing down.

As forensic investigators walked in and out, the search picked up pace. Jackson Roper joined Frizzo. More eyes. More experience. Frizzo had felt she was in this alone. No one else believed her. It was comforting to share her theories with Jackson and have him at least consider different possibilities.

Roper and Frizzo had a short chat in the kitchen. While they talked, the PI pointed to the ceiling.

"See that?"

Frizzo looked up.

"It was my partner who actually saw this," Roper said.

MSP lab technicians and forensic investigators spent the better part of eight hours going through every inch of "the west side" of the Cochran house.

As luminol was sprayed around areas of the kitchen, ceiling, and living room, Frizzo recalled, "There was lots of reaction to it."

Which meant blood, cleaning solution, or a mixture of both had been present at one time in those areas of the house.

Why would there be blood on the ceiling?

Frizzo stood in the kitchen. Put a hand to her chin. Thought to herself what might have transpired in the spot where she stood: *Chris walks in. Gets hit with the bat and falls to the floor. He tries to get to the back door to get away. . . .*

She had always assumed that before the last night of his life, Chris Regan had never been to the Cochran house.

It would have been easy for him to walk in and be blind-sided.

Frizzo was outside when one of the technicians called her back in.

"Look."

They stood and stared at the ceiling where luminol had been sprayed.

It lit up.

"We're taking those tiles back to the lab for more testing."

In total, the MSP removed twelve ceiling tiles from the house for further testing and DNA comparison. Positive reaction from luminol was noted on the ceiling in that one area above where the bat was found lying against the wall, on the carpeting in the living and dining rooms, and the entryway door hinges and one screw on the doorknob. They found no traces with luminol tests inside the Cochrans' truck or inside the garage.

As Frizzo searched the house, she came across various types of ammunition for guns that they were unable to locate in the house.

"The biggest find of that day," Frizzo recalled later, "would have to be the twenty-two-caliber revolver, because I felt we may at some point be able to link this weapon to another murder, if not Chris's. The ammunition I found for weapons they didn't have in the house immediately made me wonder where the guns were. I thought instantly they had disposed of these weapons somewhere along the way." That is, between Indiana and Michigan, when the Cochrans moved into the area. "So we needed to hang on to those to see if, down the road, we could link them to other homicides where this ammo would have been used."

The ammo for a .38 was off-brand. Not your typical-caliber bullets, Frizzo noted.

"Interestingly, this unique ammo (same caliber) was used for an unsolved homicide in Merrillville, a neighboring town to Hobart, where the Cochrans had moved from two months before relocating to Michigan. I had my secretary surf the Web for any unsolved murders in Northwest Indiana around the time they moved to Michigan. This murder happened in their hometown. A witness described a white SUV vehicle leaving the area around the time of the homicide. What did the Cochrans drive? A white Ford, extended-cab pickup."

As the search wrapped up and Frizzo was walking around, she walked over to "two huge rolls of plastic commonly used to insulate windows." She stood a moment and stared.

"There was so much of it."

Why would someone need all that plastic?

NICHOLAS GRABOWSKI, A TWENTY-SIX-YEAR law enforcement veteran, sat with Kelly and Jason inside his cruiser as the search continued into early afternoon. The Cochrans had sat with Grabowski for thirty minutes before taking off. After the Cochrans left, Grabowski found Frizzo. He thought maybe they had gone over to a neighbor's house, but wasn't sure. Still, he wanted to share the conversation, brief as it was.

"What's up?" Frizzo asked.

"So Kelly says to me while we're talking inside the car, 'If you guys find blood in the house on the carpeting, it's from my female dog coming into heat.'"

The chief shook her head in disbelief. A bit of anxiety

bubbled up as Frizzo began to think about Kelly and Jason taking off.

"Thanks, Nick."

The dog, Frizzo knew, because Kelly had told her not long ago, was fourteen years old. A menstrual cycle was highly unlikely.

"Did Jason say anything?" Frizzo wondered.

"Jason didn't say much, but he did ask me if there was anything interesting that I've done, careerwise. Kelly then said, 'We watch a lot of crime shows and we're really interested in that kind of stuff.' I told them, 'I once worked a serial killer case in Highland Park.'"

"What was their response?"

"They asked me no other questions after that."

"What was their demeanor?"

"They were *real* quiet. Didn't say a word after that comment."

"Thanks."

It was close to quarter to six in the evening, the search moving along, Frizzo a bit perplexed as to why the MSP was only focusing on the west side of the house and seemingly uninterested—in her view—with any other section. As Frizzo wandered about the front of the house, a man, angry and excited, who had walked out of a home nearby, stepped into the yard and approached her.

"You people need to clean up this neighborhood! You have no idea half of what goes on here"—he pointed at the Cochran house—"and over there . . ." He pointed at another home down the block.

"Sir . . . sir . . . ," Frizzo said. "Calm down, please."

"Well, you need to clean this place up."

"Sir, has a detective been over to your residence to speak with you?"

"No one."

"Can I talk to you then, right now?"

"No, I don't think that would be a good idea. I've been drinking."

"What about tomorrow?"

"Yes, thank you."

He walked away.

37

NEIGHBORS

WHEN TODD SAYLOR WALKED through the door of his grandmother's Lawrence Street house on the night of March 5, 2015, Jason and Kelly were inside, sitting, talking to Todd's grandmother and nephew, David Saylor. There had been quite the stir in the neighborhood throughout that day and night. The idea of cops trekking in and out of the Cochran house, MSP lab techs and crime scene investigators (CSIs) milling about, tagging brown paper and plastic bags of household items, was alarming for this quiet community.

"Hey," Todd said. "What's up?"

Kelly was in the middle of a conversation with David.

"If anything happens, call my mother," Kelly was saying as Todd sat down. She handed David a phone number.

Todd looked at Jason, who didn't say much. His face turned rose red as he started to sweat.

Staring at Jason, it was clear to Todd that his neighbor and friend was agitated and nervous and confounded by the day's events.

"He got really quiet," Todd later said. "He is a quiet

guy, anyway. But he likes to talk. He likes to laugh and stuff like that. But not that night."

Paranoid was the way to describe how Jason Cochran was feeling.

"They're coming back," Jason finally said.

"What? Who?"

"The cops."

THE ERRATIC AND ADMITTEDLY alcohol-fueled neighbor from the previous night called Frizzo the next day. He apologized for his behavior. He now wanted to talk about his neighbors, the Cochrans.

"I'm sorry about last night. I'm just frustrated."

"I understand," Frizzo responded.

"We're all tired of the activity around that house," he explained, mentioning another house in the neighborhood, too. "There's always people coming and going."

"Has anyone talked to you about whether or not you've seen particular vehicles around the Cochrans' house back in October, last year?"

"Never been asked about that or anything."

"Can you tell me anything about the Cochrans?"

"Well, I can say that she injured or broke her arm in early October—I was speaking with another neighbor about it and we just assumed the husband had broken her arm."

"What makes you say that?"

"This other neighbor, name's Gary Wernholm, said he also suspected it based on his observations of the relationship."

"You ever see an SUV-type vehicle over there?"

"Not that I can recall."

Before they hung up, the man mentioned that the

Cochrans had a fire pit in the back of the house. He said something about a "burn barrel," as he described it.

"A what?"

"Like a fifty-five-gallon drum they burned things in."

Frizzo said she'd be back in touch.

Hanging up, Frizzo went to her list of items retrieved under the warrant.

No burn barrel.

RETIRED, GARY WERNHOLM HAD LIVED on Lawrence Street in Caspian for thirty years; his house located across the street from the Cochrans' home, kitty-cornered. When Frizzo caught up to him that same week, Wernholm explained he had not much associated with the Cochrans, but he did have a conversation with Kelly the previous October. It was an incident he could recall vividly.

It was mid-October, to be exact. A particularly warm fall day in Upper Michigan. Wernholm had opened the windows in his house because it was such a nice day. "You know, air things out a bit." But as he sat in his living room, the wind blowing in, a putrid, dreadfully foul odor wafted across the street and filled his house.

"What in the name of . . ."

Wernholm looked out his front door.

"Smoke?"

The Cochrans had a fire going inside that barrel.

"Like something I never smelled before," Wernholm said. "Just awful."

Wernholm walked out of his house, across the street. He could now see smoke billowing in ribbons from the Cochrans' backyard. A thick, heavy smoke.

As he thought about it while crossing the street, getting closer to the smell, Wernholm recalled how he had

Air force veteran Christopher Regan Sr. was an avid hiker and cyclist. When the 53-year-old went missing in October 2014, friends and family grew increasingly concerned that foul play was involved. *(Photos Courtesy of Christopher Regan Jr.)*

When the Iron River Police Department went into Chris Regan's apartment, his belongings appeared to be in the middle of being packed for a planned move to Asheville, North Carolina. *(Photo Courtesy of the Iron County Prosecuting Attorney's Office)*

Suspicion arose when law enforcement learned that Chris Regan had left behind his prescribed heart medication. *(Photo Courtesy of the Iron County Prosecuting Attorney's Office)*

Chris Regan's ex-girlfriend, Terri O'Donnell, reported him missing. Terri checked Chris's phone for contact information as his apartment was being searched for clues as to his whereabouts. *(Photo Courtesy of the Iron County Prosecuting Attorney's Office)*

All of the household items in these photos convinced Chief Laura Frizzo, as she dug in and questioned those closest to Chris Regan, that the last person to have seen him had been lying to her. *(Photos Courtesy of the Iron County Prosecuting Attorney's Office)*

A reddish stain in the bathtub of Chris Regan's apartment caught the eye of law enforcement. *(Photo Courtesy of the Iron County Prosecuting Attorney's Office)*

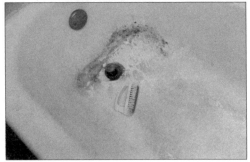

Laura Frizzo was the first woman to be named police chief in Upper Michigan.
(Photo Courtesy of Wendy Otto Shimun)

Laura Frizzo faced continued opposition from some colleagues pressuring her to stifle her instincts. Laura promised herself, however, she would not stop until she found answers.
(Photo Courtesy of Mollie Holebecke)

The Iron River Police Department became the epicenter of the investigation into Chris Regan's disappearance. *(Photo Courtesy of the Author)*

Jason Cochran, a 36-year-old Indiana native who had recently found out his wife, Kelly Cochran, was having an affair with Chris Regan, became an early suspect. *(Photo Courtesy of the Iron County Prosecuting Attorney's Office)*

Jason Cochran smiles for his wife. Kelly later said Cochran was violent and suffered severe mental health issues during their 13-year marriage. *(Photo Courtesy of Kelly Cochran)*

Kelly loved to take selfies. The 34-year-old said she lived under the anxiety of being killed if she walked out on her "rocky" marriage. *(Photo Courtesy of Kelly Cochran)*

The back of Jason and Kelly Cochran's Caspian, Michigan, home—where a fire was reported by neighbors one night, and a foul odor filled the neighborhood. *(Photo Courtesy of the Iron County Prosecuting Attorney's Office)*

These computer-generated images, designed by the Iron County Prosecuting Attorney's Office, depict Kelly Cochran's version of what happened on the night her husband, Jason, shot Chris Regan in the head. *(Photos Courtesy of the Iron County Prosecuting Attorney's Office)*

This burn barrel was recovered from the Caspian Pit (a body of water located about 600 feet from the Cochran house) in April 2015.
(Photos Courtesy of the Iron County Prosecuting Attorney's Office)

After divers pulled the burn barrel out of the water, it was clear to Chief Laura Frizzo someone went to great lengths to hide it, submerging the barrel with a clothesline (matching the one formerly attached to the Cochran garage) tied to cinder blocks. *(Photos Courtesy of the Iron County Prosecuting Attorney's Office)*

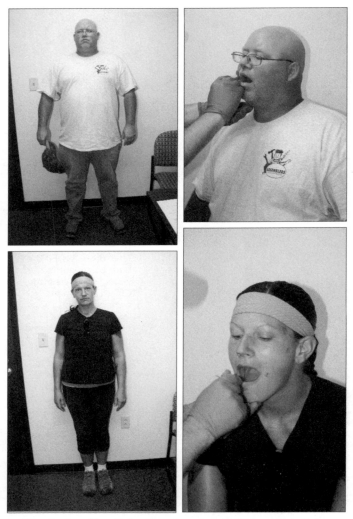

After the Iron River Police Department and Michigan State Police searched the Cochrans' home, the couple fled to Indiana, where they were located, photographed, and swabbed for future DNA comparison. *(Photos Courtesy of the Iron County Prosecuting Attorney's Office)*

Kelly Cochran walked Chief Laura Frizzo around a wooded area along the Pentoga Trail, 12 miles east of Iron River, where she claimed she and Jason buried Chris Regan's body. *(Photos Courtesy of the Iron County Prosecuting Attorney's Office)*

As investigators uncovered parts of Chris Regan's remains, they realized that his body had been dismembered, buried, and spread over an area of the forest.
(Photos Courtesy of the Iron County Prosecuting Attorney's Office)

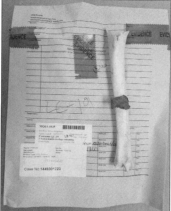

Investigators thought the reciprocating SAWZALL, found in the Cochrans' truck toolbox, might have been used by Jason Cochran to dismember Chris Regan's body.
(Photos Courtesy of the Iron County Prosecuting Attorney's Office)

Questioned further by investigators, Kelly Cochran stated that
her husband "enjoyed" decapitating Chris Regan post-mortem.
(Photos Courtesy of the Iron County Prosecuting Attorney's Office)

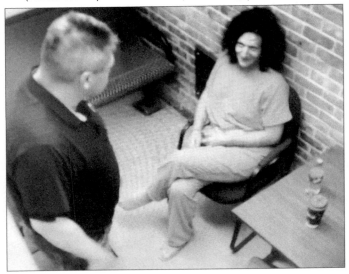

Kelly Cochran smiles for her mug shot after going on a
"meth-fueled" run following her husband's death.
(Photo Courtesy of the Iron County Prosecuting Attorney's Office)

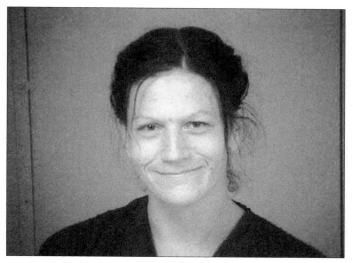

The many faces of Kelly Cochran: Here, she smiles for her mug shot
not long after her husband's death was ruled a homicide.
(Photo Courtesy of the Iron County Prosecuting Attorney's Office)

Laura Frizzo took a moment after Chris Regan's skull was recovered to kneel, reflect, and pray. *(Photo Courtesy of Roy D'Antonio)*

The reason why Kelly Cochran will spend the rest of her life in prison: the tenacious and unparalleled law enforcement work of Jeremy Ogden, Melissa Powell, and Laura Frizzo. *(Photo Courtesy of Mollie Holebecke)* burned items in the past: garbage, household debris, building materials. But this smoke smelled different. It was potent. Burning rubber? Like a synthetic, dangerous smell of melting plastic, coupled with an odor defying description of any kind Wernholm could conjure.

Approaching the Cochrans' front yard, Wernholm was certain the burning was coming from near the garage.

Kelly walked up and stopped her neighbor from going any closer. "Can I help you?" she asked.

"What's going on there, out back—what are you burning?"

Kelly didn't respond with anything Wernholm could later recall.

Wernholm told Kelly how foul the smell was and decided to go back to his house. Close the windows. Hopefully, they would finish whatever they were doing.

Just then, as Wernholm turned to leave and walk across the street, Jason came out from around the back.

Jason watched his neighbor walk away, but did not say anything.

Frizzo caught up to Wernholm in the days after the Cochran home search. He had a second story.

"When you left that night after the search of the house, it was late. I was looking across the street. I saw something."

"And?"

"A flashlight out in the yard, you know, the rays of light." Projecting downward, like a kid out on his lawn searching for night crawlers. "It was Kelly. She was out in the yard searching for something."

"That's it?"

"That's all, really. I do not know what she was looking for, but it seemed important."

"Thank you."

38

JUST RUNNING SCARED

On the morning of March 9, 2015, Chief Frizzo checked her e-mail. Jackson Roper had been staying in touch throughout the past few weeks. Careful with what she shared, Frizzo was grateful for the blending of investigatory minds. As for who had hired Roper and his partner, it wasn't important. One source gave an indication that a concerned citizen was behind hiring Roper's firm. After all, there were certain investigatory tactics a private investigator could engage in that law enforcement could not. Whoever was footing the bill for Roper and his partner, to a certain legal extent, it did not concern Frizzo. She welcomed the help in an atmosphere where she felt (beyond her own department) she had little support.

During the course of my investigation, Roper wrote that morning, *I placed a GPS tracker on the Cochrans' vehicle.*

Smart.

It was Friday, March 6, 2015, the day after the search, when the Cochrans fled. They'd packed what they could, told no one, and took off without alerting the IRPD they were leaving.

Roper encouraged Frizzo to file a warrant so he "could share this information" with her.

According to Roper, he had spoken to Jason on March 5 and had warned him: "Someone is going to come forward and show me where Chris Regan's body is located." Roper stood at the Cochrans' front door.

Jason shut the door in his face.

"That was a great move," Frizzo later said.

A bluff, obviously. The smart PI was stirring up the waters to see what type of reaction he'd get out of them. He was also hoping they would panic and head out to where the body was dumped, leading him to it.

Instead, the Cochrans did something else.

They booked.

When they left the area, they stopped their vehicle, Roper explained to Frizzo in that same e-mail, *at the intersection of US2/Honeybee Lane in Florence County, [Wisconsin], for a duration of eight minutes.*

This was important to Frizzo.

FRIZZO WAS CONCERNED ABOUT what she believed had been a "limited search" conducted by the MSP at the Cochran house on March 5.

"It had taken almost eight hours to process the west side of the house," she explained. "But *only* the west side."

As she considered it: *What about the upstairs? The basement?*

No one had gone into those areas of the property and searched with any type of detail.

So Frizzo called the lab director. "I'd like you to go back into the house."

Immediately she could tell, "He was annoyed with me."

"Laura," he said (according to Frizzo), "what do you want us to do? What will make you happy?"

"He said this arrogantly," Frizzo remembered, "and it was obvious he had been talking to the MSP detective who told him that I was wasting time and money."[3]

"What I want"—Frizzo responded—"is for you to process the rest of the house!"

---

3. I made multiple inquiries to several of the MSP detectives involved in this case, told coworkers to have them contact me for their version of what transpired, but never heard back. Not even to decline.

PART 3

THE CHASE

39
A LONG ROAD

THE DRIVE TOOK UNDER an hour. The road was desolate and repetitious in places. Trees and shrubs and brush, a dotted or solid yellow line in the middle of the pavement, the open sky and the radio.

Laura Frizzo came upon Ridgetop, Commonwealth, and Florence, traveling on Route 2, southwest of Iron River. Reaching the outskirts of Spread Eagle, Wisconsin, a town straddling the border between Michigan and Wisconsin, she pulled over. It had recently snowed, so a thick coating of the white stuff covered the ground. If the Cochrans had stopped here, which Jackson Roper's GPS device had indicated, as they fled town, maybe there was something to find. The fresh snow would help. Footprints? Tire tracks?

Getting out of her car, Frizzo felt confused. It was a busy road, especially the intersection of Honeybee and Route 2, where the GPS tracker indicated they'd stopped.

Did they toss something out here? Maybe put a piece of evidence here long ago and came back to check on it?

Frizzo found no footprints leading anywhere. No tire tracks. Not a sign anyone had stopped.

Walking around, Frizzo noticed a "two track," or a double railway track, running east to west from the highway, but it was clear no one had driven or walked near it.

The chief spent quite a bit of time searching the area, yet came up empty. Back in her cruiser, she took out her iPhone as a thought occurred to her: *They could have stopped because they were on the phone.*

"This area has very sketchy reception, so sometimes people will pull over to finish their phone call before they lose reception," Frizzo explained. "Or they could have stopped there because they were arguing and didn't know what they should do. They could have been discussing what to tell their family when they arrived in Indiana."

Frizzo drove down the road to get a better visual.

"I looked for anything that stood out. It's a heavily wooded area. A couple of campsites. A house off to the south about a quarter mile away. There was nothing I could do at that time. All I knew was they had stopped there for almost eight minutes."

40

SUSPICION

THE PHONE CALL WAS not at all surprising. Over the past several weeks, Maria Lumbar (pseudonym) had spoken to Kelly Cochran about several household items Kelly had promised Maria. Weeks ago, Kelly had told Maria she and Jason were planning on leaving the area. The two knew each other from the Citgo station in Caspian where Kelly would stop to gas up the truck, grab cigarettes and coffee. Over a few months, Maria and Kelly had become acquainted.

"Can I get those things from you, Kelly?" Maria asked. Kelly had called the Citgo a few days after the search warrant. By then, she and Jason were long gone. On their way to Indiana.

"I'll eventually get those things to you," Kelly said.

"How are you?" Maria asked.

"We're okay. I found this GPS tracker underneath our truck!" Kelly said out of the blue.

"You found what?"

"We felt someone in a tan-colored van was following us as we got into Indiana. I became suspicious. I looked underneath the truck. I found this GPS tracking device. Pulled it off. Took the batteries out. I'm saving it for evidence!"

"Oh, my, Kelly."

KELLY COCHRAN WAS SOMEONE who viewed the world differently than most. She kept a lot to herself, she later claimed to me in conversations and letters. She would go off on tangents about how all her life, those around her did not truly understand her "truth."

"Everyone thinks they know the truth, when, in actuality, only I do," she said. "Throughout a lot of this, I have shared *pieces* of the truth. But when you lived in 'my world' so long, you know that 'normal people' can't handle the truth."

Kelly explained her "world" as a place the general public had "never [been] exposed to." Most people, she added, have never had to "watch life leave someone, in ways that I had to." As for what happens to the soul after: "Life doesn't go on after that, regardless of what you do."

She made a point to say that the "entire truth will hurt too many people. After all, as humans, one of our defense mechanisms is to hide or bury the truth or reality."

Kelly talked about her "past" as a part of her life she was still trying to make "sense" of. She claimed to have a "great upbringing, great education." She called herself "too smart for my own good." She described her parents as "normal, loving" people. She admitted she'd never "been happy as a child." She recalled "only being content." She once told her mother that for as long as she could remember, she was "homicidal." She had never been "scared" as a child. She concluded, "I was just not one to be emotional or one to express emotions like most."

With all the men she was juggling at the same time—Chris, Tim, Jason—Kelly said, "They were busy days. Go to work. Go to Chris's—and then I'd go hang out with Tim."

I brought up the subject of Kelly being someone who "needed lots of stimulation to feel alive."

"I don't know if I am any particular type," she said. "I've had so many people try to profile me. I don't believe there is anybody like me. I don't think you'll ever meet anybody like me."

41

TWO TRACK

FRIZZO FELT THE COCHRANS might have dumped evidence tying them to killing Chris Regan near their Lawrence Street home. Jason walked a lot. He fished at the Caspian Pit. The burn barrel was still missing. Thus, if the chief was working under the assumption that Chris Regan had been murdered, the most important question still loomed: Where was his body?

During the week of March 16, 2015, as she worked on a second search warrant to go back into the Cochran house, specifically the basement, garage, and upstairs, Frizzo walked the area, woods, and trails around the Cochran house.

The idea that they'd taken off after that search warrant stuck in the back of Frizzo's mind. It said something. She wondered if she could have done more to keep tabs on their whereabouts at all times.

"Honestly, my first thought when I heard they'd taken off was fear for my fourteen-year-old son's safety. Then, when I saw their location and direction of travel"—toward Indiana, where they had family and once lived—"I again just thought that these silly people considered the miles between us will make me stop. But they obviously didn't know anything about me."

Another interesting moment Frizzo had heard about took place the day after the first warrant had been executed.

Kelly and Jason stopped at the magistrate's office to demand a copy of the search warrant's probable-cause affidavit. They were curious to see what evidence the IRPD had leading them into the house.

"I don't have any of the copies back yet," said the magistrate. "Plus, you'd have to go through a judge, anyway, to get your hands on the affidavit."

When Frizzo heard about this, she called Melissa Powell, the prosecutor.

"I don't want them seeing my probable-cause documents and know everything we're doing."

"Understood."

A motion was filed with the judge by the prosecutor to prevent the Cochrans, or anyone else, from seeing the probable-cause affidavit connected to the warrant.

"Kelly just wanted to know exactly what I knew," Frizzo said. "And the main reason they fled was the fear that I would be back to arrest them. They were afraid they may have missed something. That I would come back after finding, and proving, it was Chris's blood inside their house. When they fled, I knew I had them. I didn't care where they went. Honestly, my thought was 'Do they *really* think any amount of distance will stop me?' "

THEY CALLED IT THE "Two Track," an area on the outskirts of Lawrence Street. A dirt road, or pathway, running northwest from Lawrence Street, about three hundred yards directly northwest of the Cochran house, along the edge of the Caspian Pit. Frizzo thought Chris's body had been dumped, along with additional evidence, somewhere within this stretch of secluded road and woods.

As she walked, looking for anything that stood out, marking specific areas where she believed an item was connected to the case, the old Caspian dump site, located in this same general area, was of particular interest to the chief. Frizzo found a set of "unusual footprints" along a cliff line, in a "very steep area," where footprints should not have been. From there, the footprints circled a fresh mound of sand and dirt. Not a large pile, but big enough for a grave.

"It's very unusual that a mound of sand or dirt would have been placed there," a guy from the Department of Public Works (DPW) explained to Frizzo, who had phoned him.

There was still too much frost on the ground, a solid layer of about four inches, for the K9s to come out, have a sniff around, and be useful. So Frizzo was told to make note of the locations she wanted searched. When the ground thawed, the K9s could do their thing.

Not to be deterred, Frizzo continued looking. She came upon an old blanket partially sticking out of the ground, frozen into the soil. She got down on one knee. There were human hairs attached to the blanket. It seemed an odd place for a blanket.

Frizzo called in a backhoe.

She stood by DPW employee Jeff Andreski as he worked the controls and dug near the mound and a few areas surrounding it. By then, Frizzo had excavated the blanket from the ground, bagged it, and sent it to the lab.

As Andreski dug, Frizzo wanted to believe Chris

Regan was speaking to her once again, but she wasn't feeling it this time.

Frizzo sifted through the dirt as Andreski dug.

In the end, nothing came of it.

Within a day, Frizzo had located the owner of the blanket—it had nothing to do with her case.

42

FEELING THE PRESSURE

On Monday, March 16, 2015, Frizzo sent a lab request to process a specimen of Chris Regan's DNA she had obtained from the military. Obtaining his DNA directly from the military was important to avoid possible contamination by using other sources of DNA, such as a toothbrush, touch DNA from a glass inside his apartment, or a hair from a hat. She needed to find out if Chris's blood could be connected to any of the blood found inside the Cochran home—and be certain about it.

"We'll jump right on it."

Later that day, Kelly called. Frizzo was still thinking about the fruitless search at the old dump. There had to be something somewhere. There was no way the Cochrans had not utilized that wooded area, the dirt roads surrounding the Caspian Pit.

"Will you be fixing our house back up after wrecking it?" Kelly said. The resentment in her voice was obvious.

"Are you referring to the search warrant we executed back on March fifth?"

"Yes!"

"I've been trying to contact you since then to see if you have any questions or concerns, but you know what, Kelly, I haven't been able to find you."

"You took our phones—remember?"

"Kelly . . ."

"I went to the Iron County Courthouse to get a copy of the warrant affidavit, but we were unable to get one. Look, are you going to be fixing our house back up so it's once again livable?"

"The ceiling tiles can be replaced. . . ."

"You cannot get those kind anymore," Kelly lashed back before Frizzo could finish.

"We can give you back the tiles, once the lab has cleared them."

"What about our door? You ruined it."

"We didn't ruin your door. We can replace whatever hardware we took from it. And listen, Kelly, that door has a hole in it, so it's not in the best shape, to begin with."

"The hole was there when we bought the house."

They went back and forth about the house being in a condition Kelly considered unlivable, which Frizzo knew to be nonsense. Kelly was trying to give the IRPD an excuse for her and Jason leaving the area.

Frizzo wasn't buying it.

"Why are you contacting me *now* about your concerns regarding the house? Why have you waited almost two weeks?"

"We don't have phones!"

"You found the time to stop at the courthouse for the affidavit, but you were unable to find time to stop at the IRPD and discuss your concerns about your house?"

"You don't treat us very well. So why would we want to come there?"

"We all treated you with respect during the search warrant, Kelly. Please. We allowed you to sit in our patrol car. We also brought you twice to the restroom at the local gas station while we searched."

Kelly ignored the chief and asked again if they were going to put the house back into its original condition.

Frizzo repeated herself.

Kelly wondered, without being asked, if Frizzo had found blood inside the house, adding that it was from her dog, who had been "in heat."

"Kelly, look," the chief said, ignoring this, "I'm going to be straight with you. You might want to contact an attorney at this point." As Frizzo talked, it was clear by Kelly's response that she was not "able to comprehend what I was saying." Frizzo later detailed this observation in her report about the call.

As Frizzo continued to speak, Kelly hung up on her.

Frizzo raised her eyebrows, cradling the phone.

The chief then took a call from a cellular phone company connected to the military. They had recently extracted a bit of information from Chris Regan's cell phone, which was not yet reported.

"Go ahead," Frizzo said.

"It appears," the phone tech explained, "that his cell phone was turned on at nine thirty-nine on the night of October 14, 2014. . . ."

"Thank you."

43

(RE)SEARCH

IN THE DAYS THAT FOLLOWED, the investigation into Chris Regan's disappearance would become darker than anyone involved could have ever predicted. On March 27, 2015, that second search warrant was granted. Frizzo, along with officers from the MSP and Iron County Sheriff's Office (ICSO) pulled up to 66 Lawrence Street.

As a formality, Frizzo knocked.

No answer.

She banged.

Nothing.

"I'm going in through the back."

After letting everyone else in through the front, Frizzo stood and looked around.

"Immediately," she recalled, "I could tell the Cochrans had been packing household items to permanently" leave the area.

Pictures had been taken off walls. Clothes and other items left on the floor. The bathroom had been "completely" cleaned out. The upstairs was barren, save for a few major pieces of furniture. It was as if whatever the Cochrans could take and carry out, they did.

Frizzo opened the basement door and walked carefully down the stairs. She could smell a heavy aroma of marijuana. There was a room with a lock on it. Frizzo popped the lock and stepped in. There were eight dead pot plants.

"This tells me they departed hastily, for sure," Frizzo said.

Jason Cochran would not have left behind that much weed if he wasn't looking to leave in a hurry.

As Frizzo studied the basement, her concern for Chris Regan grew. The basement stairs appeared to have been removed at one point. She leaned down, looked underneath.

Fresh dirt was below the stairs.

"Look at this," said one forensic specialist.

Frizzo looked up the top of the stairs.

After spraying luminol on the wall leading down into the basement, it glowed. Frizzo stepped up to take a look. It was an "oddly shaped" section of wall—and the only section, Frizzo noted, freshly painted.

As she rummaged through a pile of debris and odd household items in the basement, Frizzo came up with a spiral-bound notebook. She opened it.

Jason had written this particular notebook while he was in the hospital after suffering his psychological meltdown in September.

"He talked about how he was 'going crazy' even while on the meds he was taking, how he wished his wife would at least just call him."

Another notebook the chief picked up was a bit more interesting. In this one, Jason described how he was working on a book about his life, describing a person who "beats his wife and has a 'hit list.'"

Frizzo placed it in an evidence bag.

Out in back of the house, Frizzo and members of the team focused on the garage. As they entered and looked carefully around this "very unusual structure," they noticed boards on the north side "that looked as though they had been recently placed." Fresh wood planks nailed in between old ones.

Frizzo lifted up one of the boards.

The "dirt foundation was found to be very loose."

Forensic techs removed a larger area's boards to take a closer look.

They brought in tools and equipment. They dug in an area underneath the floorboards that seemed to have been previously excavated.

"The roots were freshly cut."

They dug deeper.

"Hold up," someone said.

"What is it?"

A set of bones.

44
RUMOR HAS IT

A RUMOR BEGAN TO CIRCULATE around town that Chris Regan's body had been found "in or near the Caspian Pit." This prompted Kelly to become further agitated.

Kelly called the prosecutor's office (PO) a few days after that second search. She was livid: "Who authorized a second search of our house?"

During that search, firearms ammunition was seized for a .22 pistol, .30-06, .380, twelve-gauge shotgun, and Winchester .25 automatic. No additional guns had been located, however, other than the .22 revolver and the twelve-gauge shotgun Frizzo and her team had found during the March 5 search warrant.

Since finding and studying the *Where Monsters Hide* notebook Frizzo found during the second warrant, she realized Chris Regan had been likely murdered by both Kelly and Jason.

As it turned out, however, those bones found in the garage, underneath the recently nailed boards and fresh dirt, were probably from a dog, skunk, or possum. And the bloody ceiling tiles, walls, and carpet had been so contaminated by chemicals—bleach and paint—that no DNA comparison could link the samples to Chris's DNA.

Still, Kelly was under the impression that the IRPD had found Chris.

The PO explained to Kelly that the recent warrant sworn in front of the magistrate, along with the accompanying probable-cause affidavit, were sealed. It would be to the Cochrans' best interest, the office explained, to obtain legal counsel.

Since the time of that second search, K9s had been brought out to the house to sniff around. They hit on the garage and an area in the back by the garage where it was clear a fire pit had once been located. Beyond that, the dogs led team members down to the Two Track area and the Caspian Pit, where they picked up a path leading down into the water.

Something was there. Frizzo stood by the water, staring, thinking. She could feel it. She wanted divers and underwater camera equipment to have a look, see what the Cochrans had tossed into the water.

For weeks, Frizzo had been calling the Cochrans in Indiana. She'd left several voice mail messages for Jason's parents. Since then, she'd also come up with a cell phone number connected to Kelly. When she called it, the voice mail message "sounded like Kelly's voice," so Frizzo left multiple messages.

No one ever called back.

Finally, on April 15, 2015, Kelly called. It was seven twenty-five a.m., and Kelly was angry again. The pressure Frizzo had applied was beginning to work.

"Would you and Jason be willing to submit to a DNA sample?" Frizzo asked. "We need it for investigative—"

Kelly did not allow the chief to finish. "No!"

"It's important for us and comparative purposes regarding the case—"

"No! Jason and I have been cooperative enough."

"In what ways have you been cooperative, Kelly?"

"We've given you our phones. We've allowed you to search our house."

"Kelly, we had a search warrant for both," the chief said. Did she need to explain that with or without Kelly and Jason's consent, the searches would have been done.

"You destroyed our house. That's why we left."

"Kelly, you should know that we've switched our case file class on Chris Regan from a 'missing person' to a 'homicide.' The lab needs your DNA for comparison tests."

The phone call ended.

Frizzo wrote a warrant for the DNA. A few days after speaking with Kelly, she contacted the local police in Hobart, Indiana, the town where Kelly and Jason were now living. The chief indicated she was going to need assistance in collecting Jason and Kelly's DNA.

Meanwhile, the Cochrans got wind of what might be happening. Never had the vise been so tight. They could feel it. Jason had called the prosecutor's office on April 21 to ask if any charges had been filed against him or his wife.

"Fishing" was how Frizzo later explained it. "They began to call and fish for any information they could find out."

Frizzo had been trying to phone Jason all morning long on the same number he'd used to call the PO. Finally, that afternoon, he picked up.

"Funny you called the prosecutor's office *after* I was calling you all morning," Frizzo said.

"Well . . ."

"When I spoke to Kelly last week, she said you two would submit to DNA, and I was calling to see when you two would be available for this."

"I have been thinking about this and we spoke to a lawyer and we will not be doing this."

"Why wouldn't you be willing, Jason?"

"I'm tired of you harassing us. Our attorney says you need a warrant for our DNA."

Frizzo rolled her eyes. "I will have a warrant, Jason. Don't worry. So now you're refusing to give up your DNA and you also refused a polygraph. I would say you both appear to be very uncooperative. I really would like to talk to you. I will say that you may not like the way things seem to be heading. It's important for you to talk to me, Jason, and, you know, give me an explanation of certain things."

"What number can I reach you at?" Jason asked.

Frizzo gave it to him.

"If I don't hear from you by, let's say, Friday, April twenty-fourth, I am going to assume you are not interested in talking to me."

As the warrants were prepared, the K9s, along with Mike Neiger, conducted searches of the park-and-ride and woods nearby, as well as a wooded region around the Cochran house, the Caspian Pit, and several Googled locations investigators had extracted from the Cochrans' home computer.

Frizzo read through the old MSP reports. Of interest to her were the neighbors, David and his uncle, Todd Saylor. They had spoken briefly to the MSP. Frizzo wanted to reinterview David and Todd and find out what more they knew. These were the closest people to Jason Cochran in Michigan. The night Todd Saylor reported hearing power tools, but nothing seemed to be refinished at the Cochran house, had always gnawed at Frizzo. She felt it was significant.

Frizzo called the Saylors and they agreed to meet her at the IRPD on May 14, 2015.

"Sit, get comfortable," Frizzo said as they walked in and introduced themselves.

Todd and David sat. Both seemed nervous, but also cooperative and willing to share whatever information they could provide.

"Have you ever seen this vehicle at the Cochrans' house?" Frizzo asked, describing Chris Regan's car, showing them a photo.

Both said no.

"You remember that time in early October when Jason Cochran borrowed some of your power tools? Did he ever give them back to you?" Todd asked David.

The mere mention of power tools sparked a memory. Both talked about that week after Chris went missing, when Jason borrowed the tools.

"We even joked a few times," David said, turning his attention to Frizzo, "about how, right after Chris Regan disappeared, the Cochrans invited us over to their house three times within one week and they had an *enormous* amount of meat, like kebabs one night, pizza with a ton of meat on it another, and then tacos. We couldn't understand how they had all this meat, seeing that they were always so poor. Even their dogs' bellies were hanging on the ground! We discussed the idea that maybe they cut up the missing guy and that we had eaten him."

Frizzo looked down. Took a long, hard swallow. Horrific. The idea of this possibility made her lose herself in thought.

"You need to understand," Frizzo later recalled, "this is after David tells me about the sawing he heard all night long. I thought, 'Oh. My. God. Could this be true? Could they have cut him up?'"

Could they have fed Chris Regan to the Saylors?

Frizzo looked back up. The Saylors seemed to be joking about this in some respects, but it was, she now understood, a strong possibility.

"What kinds of tools did you have that you lent to Jason?"

David Saylor mentioned a SKIL saw (one of those round, circular saws carpenters use to cut plywood) and a SAWZALL.

Todd recalled an incident: "I could hear fighting one night going on outside and then I heard tires squeal. . . . This would have been right around the time Chris Regan went missing."

Frizzo asked again about the night of March 5, when the search had been going on. Could they add to what they had already shared with the MSP?

Todd Saylor reiterated: Jason was acting quiet and seemed nervous.

"What did he say?" Frizzo asked.

"It was what *I* said," Todd explained. "I told him that if the forensic lab is over at the house that they would find everything. They'll go through your house with a fine-tooth comb, and if there is something there, they'll find it. He got really nervous at that point. He said, 'I didn't know that.' I couldn't believe how red his face became. . . ."

They talked about how the neighbor/friendship developed over the time they knew each other. Todd said Jason warned him and David about Kelly, calling her a "big flirt." He confessed to them that he knew she was cheating. He said she loved pills. Would take any opiate she could get her hands on. It didn't seem to bother Jason much, Todd explained, that his wife was stepping out.

They both claimed Kelly went "out of town" a lot, according to Jason.

"Jason was really interested in the pit, how deep it is. Like he asked *specific* questions. He wanted to know if there were any other pits around."

This seemed weird to them.

Todd addressed David: "You remember when you helped Jason haul out that big freezer from their basement?"

"Yeah, it was sometime over the winter. They said they were selling it. It was empty, though."

"How do you know that?"

"I looked inside."

Those large meat meals they had eaten at the Cochran house came up again. Todd and David talked about how fat the dogs had gotten post-October. Both said they found it odd that Jason would come over all the time, pre-October 13. He'd show up alone for bonfires they had out in back of the house. Never with Kelly. But after Chris went missing, Kelly and Jason were inseparable. They never went anywhere alone.

In the days after Chris's disappearance, both men said, they witnessed Jason leaving the house with a backpack, something he'd never done before. They thought it was strange.

Both Kelly and Jason "were paranoid about the search and definitely left town because of it," the Saylors said.

Frizzo ended it there and said she'd be in touch during the coming weeks and months.

After the Saylors left, Frizzo called a dive team to set a plan for going out to the Caspian Pit and conducting an underwater search.

"I knew there was something there—I just needed to find it."

45

DIVER DOWN

Frizzo and Mike Neiger, along with a team of K9s, went to work at the Caspian Pit. The dogs cleared the wooded areas around the pit as well as the south end. As they started sniffing around a specific area northeast of the pit, quite a ways back from the water, the K9s picked up a "line of detection." It ran at an angle across a sandy region, heading toward the water.

"Over here," someone yelled.

The dogs stopped at the water, were barking, and walking in circles. Neiger put a K9 and its handler in a kayak.

They set out.

Fewer than five minutes into the trip, the K9 hit on an area in the water located on the south side of the pit, near a dock, approximately ten feet from the end of the dock.

"Here!"

"That's a precise and clear indication of human remains," the K9's handler said as the dog went wild. "But let me also say that this is not specific to the area and could mean there are remains within the area she's out-lined, if that makes sense."

Frizzo understood.

While the dogs searched the pit, Frizzo went over to the Cochran home to look for anything they might have missed. She was interested in finding a saw or some other indication that the Cochrans had dismembered Chris Regan and—as ghastly and horrendous the thought—had fed parts of him to their neighbors and the dogs.

Mike Neiger helped. Together, they collected all of the ash found in back of the house. As Neiger carefully picked up each shovel of ash and dumped it slowly into an evidence bag, he spotted something.

"Hold up."

"What is it?" Frizzo asked.

It was a small SAWZALL blade, blackened from a fire, sitting in ash, entirely intact.

"Why burn the blade?"

They looked at each other.

Also inside that same portion of ash Neiger and Frizzo found the metal components from a pair of Old Navy jeans, same brand Chris Regan had pairs of inside his apartment. Buttons. A zipper. Two grommets.

"Oh, my . . ."

Standing, thinking about this, Frizzo felt a chill. The testimonial from the Saylors echoed. Now a saw blade. Remnants from a pair of burned pants.

Where was Chris Regan's body?

They might never find it.

As the chief and Mike Neiger continued to sift through the ash, several other pieces of debris interested them. Wearing latex gloves, Neiger picked up something that resembled a small, chipped-off piece of rock.

"Looks like bone," he said.

* * *

BACK OUT AT THE Caspian Pit the following day, May 19, 2015, a dive team headed into the water, utilizing sonar and visuals.

The pit was cloudy and murky. The bottom, it turned out, contained about an eighteen-foot-deep layer of silt, which made it difficult to see anything beyond it. If anything had been tossed into the water, with such a deep mud base, it was probably gone for good.

"We got something," one of the divers came up and reported as Neiger and Frizzo waited along the shoreline.

"What is it?"

They found an area of the pit with no silt, about eleven feet off the shoreline, a shallow region along the eastern middle portion of the water.

"A barrel," one of the divers reported.

An old, rusted fifty-five-gallon drum.

Frizzo and Neiger looked at each other.

After the barrel was taken out of the water, it was clear it had been used as a fire pit. It also had a clothesline attached. On the opposite end of the line was a cement block to hold it underwater.

Frizzo tracked down the Cochrans' next-door neighbor, who had the exact same clothesline in her backyard: color, rope texture.

"Yeah, they had one just like it, but it's gone now," the neighbor said.

Frizzo had a quick look around the Cochran yard.

She found several cement blocks identical to the one used to hold the barrel underwater.

46

PUSHING FORWARD BACK

THE BURDEN ANY INVESTIGATOR faces during a case that feels static is to stay resilient. Practice restraint as well as persistence. For any investigator searching for a missing person or murder suspect, there is an intensity of pressure—from the public, and the weight they place on themselves—to make something happen. A lack of progress can lead to an adverse effect on the lead investigator's performance. An investigator is resigned to follow her instincts as far as she can, and then rely on the evidence to guide her beyond that. Resource allocation is something the greatest detectives understand, utilize, and employ. At some point in any investigation, this can end up being the key component to success. Which was why, as Laura Frizzo took in Upper Michigan's bright June sun halfway into 2015, she felt the answers would be in breaking the Cochrans. Frizzo admittedly did not have much experience in this sort of cat-and-mouse game Kelly was playing. The chief had investigated murders, and was in the middle of a child killer case she'd taken on before Chris went missing. Yet, dealing with such a deceptive, sketchy, angry creature as Kelly Cochran was wearing her down. She needed help. She needed someone experienced with where the right opportunities existed to punch holes in the Cochrans' stories.

As each new witness was interviewed, along with those who came forward, Frizzo persevered. A woman who lived down the block from the Cochrans reached out to the IRPD on June 12, saying she'd recalled an incident that might be of some importance.

"Bring her in," Frizzo said.

The period in question, so claimed this new witness, was mid-October, the same time frame turning up under every rock. The woman recalled being "awakened by something that sounded like a gunshot coming from [the Cochrans'] residence" one night in mid-October.

"I got up and looked out my window. I heard a door slam, like from a house. There was a car parked outside the Cochran place, running, its headlights on."

"Color of the car, ma'am?" Frizzo asked.

"I couldn't make it out."

"I heard a woman in distress shout, 'No! No!' Then I heard a voice say, 'Let's get the hell out of here.'"

The car—and she was certain it was a car, and not a truck—backed out of the driveway and took off.

Was it Chris Regan's?

The woman said she didn't get to know the Cochrans until after October. She'd invited them over for Thanksgiving dinner. They were totally in love at that time, she said.

"Kelly and I got to talking about Chris Regan," the woman explained.

"How so?"

"I asked her if she had ever been in Chris's car and she said no. She told me that it was Chris who had fired her from her job. She told me she'd cheated on Jason, but would not say with whom."

"Was there anything else?"

"I heard the boys," she said, which Frizzo knew to be the Saylors, "ask them if they did anything to Chris. They both just said, 'No!' and that was it."

47
HELP

HOBART, INDIANA, IS A solid six-hour drive south from Iron River, Michigan. Even for a cop traveling well above the speed limit. The Hobart Police Department (HPD), on East Fourth Street, downtown, has a small waterway called "Duck Creek," which ran north-to-south behind it. The police department is housed inside a redbrick, whitewashed building, along with the City and Community Center. The entire area has a small-town, Americana feel. Hobart gives a comforting sense of what Midwestern country living is truly like.

In early July, Frizzo made contact with the Lake County Sheriff's Department (LCSD) and the Hobart PD, having no idea how vital HPD was about to become in the search for Chris Regan. Frizzo needed help in serving a warrant to the Cochrans for DNA extraction. During a meeting on July 24, 2015, it was decided that HPD would grab the Cochrans, haul their asses downtown, and swab their cheeks.

"As of now, we have been unable to locate their vehicle—they may have gotten rid of it," the LCSD informed Frizzo. "That, or they've left the area."

Great. One more hurdle.

Frizzo now worried the Cochrans were gone for good.

Back in Iron River, Frizzo found another one of Kelly Cochran's conquests, a local man. Scouring through Kelly's phone records, looking for numbers she frequently called, Frizzo found him.

"I met her at Mr. T's Restaurant," the guy explained. "Realized she was a freakin' weirdo after a few weeks. I started to ignore her calls."

Frizzo wanted to know more.

"Kelly told me Jason knew about all her affairs and that she was having 'many' affairs with coworkers at Oldenburg. [Jason] would go through her pockets and find all sorts of things connecting her to other men. She always seemed strung-out, like a druggie."

"You think she used a lot of drugs?"

"She definitely had a pill issue. She preferred painkillers, but would take just about anything. She picked at her face, too, so she might have done heavier things."

A meth head?

"Have you heard from her?"

"Just once. She called and said she left Caspian and was living in Indiana because you guys were harassing her."

The man talked about how he'd once spoken to Kelly about knowing where Chris Regan was or what happened to him.

"Did you kill him?" he asked.

"No."

"What about Jason?"

"No. He's in a place for crazy people. I'm done with

him. He freaks me out and he puts me in the corner. He is abusive, controlling, and jealous."

"That was it?" Frizzo asked after he outlined the brief conversation.

"Yeah, but I wondered about this crazy husband of hers I had never seen, and how she was always out and about." If Jason was so dangerous, abusive, and controlling, how in the hell had she managed to leave the house every night of the week and sleep with so many men? "I have no idea if anything she ever told me is true."

"She ever mention to you about her shoulder?"

"Yes. She said it was rotator surgery that did it."

"Nothing about a car accident?"

"Nope," he said. "It's funny. She got a kick out of all the guys she was getting with at Oldenburg—it was a game to her. She called them her 'conquests.'"

Another Mr. T's employee walked over to Frizzo as she stood with the guy in his front yard. Frizzo introduced herself, and the woman explained that Kelly had been fired from the restaurant for stealing money.

"Throughout the time she was working there, she never talked about her husband. I never even knew she was married—she flirted with all the guys. Then, [in] the middle of October, she starts showing up at the restaurant *with* her husband." The woman was taken aback by this: Kelly sitting with her husband, having the gall to show up and eat at the same restaurant she had stolen from. It showed how shameless, brazen and unfeeling she was, not to mention how deaf to the feelings of her former employer and the people she'd worked with.

"Thanks—we'll be in touch."

Frizzo headed back to the station.

* * *

DURING THE SECOND SEARCH WARRANT, in a pile of debris on the floor of the basement, the chief found an old photo of Jason and Kelly. It was one of those pictures many families have had taken at the local department store. Jason and Kelly stood in front of a mock celestial-type background, their two heads touching, cheek to cheek. The impression was that of a "normal" suburban couple. No doubt encouraged and staged by the photographer, Jason had one arm wrapped around Kelly's waistline; Kelly had a hand on Jason's chest. Kelly was noticeably heavier. They came off happy. Content. A couple celebrating some sort of special moment with a professional photograph.

Frizzo already had a photo of Chris Regan that his family had provided. She placed Chris's photo underneath the date of October 14 on a calendar tacked to the wall in her office, directly in front of her desk. She took the Cochran photo and tacked it just underneath.

"I wanted to keep my mind on them all during the day," Frizzo later said. "I guess I wanted my subconscious to see them constantly. It's hard to explain. No matter what else I was doing or working on, just glancing at them, even if I didn't realize it was happening, kept me driven to find out what had happened to Chris. They never left my thoughts. I wasn't going to stop."

48
SAGE ADVICE

ON FRIDAY, JULY 24, 2015, Frizzo drove to Hobart to witness the DNA extraction and, with any luck, get another crack at talking to Jason and Kelly.

When she arrived, the chief was greeted by Detective Steve Houck and a lieutenant. Houck had prepared a room for the DNA extraction. HPD had a solid lead on the Cochrans, knew they were staying at Kelly's parents' house, a rock toss southwest of Hobart. It was decided two cops would head out and bring them in under the warrant. Frizzo waited at HPD with Houck. They talked about the case, Frizzo noting her frustration at not being able to get much information out of Jason or Kelly.

"I wish Jeremy was here," Houck said. "He'd know what to say. He could get them to talk."

Frizzo confided she was chasing two murderers and was not, as she put it, "a seasoned homicide detective."

"I can't get either of them to give me what I want."

Jeremy Ogden, the detective Houck referred to, was out on a work-related injury. Ogden, a rugged, experienced, tenacious detective, had been torn apart by a K9 while clearing a house. He was at home recuperating.

"I can take a ride over and see Jeremy, if you want," Houck suggested.

"Any help would be greatly appreciated."

TWO HPD COPS KNOCKED on the door of Kelly's parents' house.

Jason answered.

They explained why they were there and asked if he was prepared to go downtown.

Jason didn't have a choice.

"I had a feeling this was related to the Iron River case," Jason said. He seemed terrified. "Sure, I can go with you." As he said it, Jason began to "shake uncontrollably," both cops noted.

"Kelly here?"

"No. She's working."

They walked Jason to the car. "You have anything in your pockets?" one cop asked.

Jason looked at them. Reached into his pocket and took out a knife.

He sat down in the backseat of the cruiser.

The knife was "suspicious" to the cop because of what the officer later described as "discoloration," a reddish tint, on the blade.

Frizzo walked into the room where Jason was waiting. She had a notebook. Not the *Where Monsters Hide* outline, but a second notebook she'd recovered from the Caspian house. Work-related stuff from Jason's time as a pool installer. By then, the LCSD had taken DNA from inside Jason's cheek, and HPD had a warrant to have the knife forensically tested for blood.

"That your handwriting?" Frizzo asked Jason, pointing at the notebook on the table in front of them.

"Yes, it is."

Frizzo asked about Chris Regan.

Jason became agitated and nervous. His face "reddened and he continued to take large gulps, but would not offer information other than [saying] he had never met Chris Regan."

"Come on, Jason. . . ."

"I want an attorney."

"Would you be willing to talk to me if I was able to get you an attorney?"

Jason laughed. "Uh, no way."

Frizzo left the room. By then, two HPD cops had located Kelly at work and brought her in.

After the LCSD CSI unit took a DNA extraction from Kelly's inner cheek, Frizzo greeted her.

Kelly smiled. "Detective?"

"Hi, Kelly. Listen, I was wondering if you'd still like to be on record as saying that you have no idea where that park-and-ride is located?" This was a carefully thought-out path the chief believed might help lead her into a more productive conversation. Frizzo had direct proof Kelly had lied about this.

"I do not know where it is, Detective."

"Would you like to have a look at your own text messages, where you're making plans to meet up with other individuals at the park-and-ride?"

Kelly dropped her head. Shook it back and forth. It was clear Kelly knew she had made—among many others—a mistake. She had no idea how to get out of it.

"Kelly, can you answer me?"

"I want an attorney."

* * *

DETECTIVE STEVE HOUCK SAT with Detective Jeremy Ogden at Ogden's house and talked over the case the HPD had become involved in. Both Ogden and Houck understood the chief had been trying to break Jason, the weaker link, since October 2014 and could use some guidance.

Before leaving for Iron River, while she'd waited that day, Frizzo had heard a bit about Jeremy Ogden and realized the guy was a first-rate detective who had been involved with scores of cases. He had a "gift" for questioning suspects and getting them to open up, Frizzo was told. People trusted the guy for some reason. He was revered for his investigatory tactics and overall knowledge of murder investigations. As Frizzo walked around HPD and ran into photos of Jeremy Ogden, she thought he was cute, too.

As Houck and Ogden talked, Ogden offered some advice.

"Steve, someone needs to follow Jason Cochran for a day and, when he's alone, approach him and tell him it's our duty as police officers investigating a murder to let him know that through our investigation we believe his wife is planning to kill him. We offer him an out to come forward and tell the truth."

"Right," Houck said.

"Or take his chances."

49

SINK OR SWIM

FRIZZO LATCHED ONTO A lead pointing her in the direction of a local landfill in Iron River. Several town workers and a Dumpster company employee had reported a smell—the like of which they had never come across—radiating from one particular Dumpster in town back in October. To these guys, rotten meat and putrid food smells were the norm—they were used to raunchy odors out on the road every day. But this was the smell of death, they said. Not an animal. Not a discarded deer carcass tossed by a local hunter. This smelled of a rotting human being. It had taken quite a while to zero in on the site where that particular Dumpster had been unloaded, but through an intense search, Frizzo and her team located it. Frizzo made a call to the Federal Bureau of Investigation, specifically the FBI's Emergency Response Team (ERT). The landfill was in Wisconsin.

Frizzo felt a resurgence of confidence after a meeting she attended with the FBI, including special agents from several different field offices. She had e-mailed a narrative of the case thus far. After reading it, they agreed and "felt this case had powerful and condemning circumstantial evidence" against the Cochrans.

Finally, Frizzo thought, *someone on my side. Someone is listening to me.*

THE CHIEF DEVELOPED an informant who had been routinely communicating with the Cochrans since they'd taken off from town. Randy (pseudonym) called Frizzo and recounted a conversation with Kelly back in late July, just after the Hobart DNA extraction. Randy had been hanging around Jason and Kelly. Kelly, especially, was feeling the pressure after the DNA extraction.

"What did she tell you?" Frizzo asked.

"Well, she said, 'They haven't found a body yet or we would have been arrested.'"

Randy described how defiant Kelly sounded on this particular day. How determined and willing she was to continue playing cat and mouse with Frizzo and the IRPD. By the end of the call, Randy said, Kelly had gotten straight to her main point.

"What was that?" Frizzo asked.

"She said, 'They're never going to find a body.'"

"You stay in touch with her, okay?"

"I will."

THE FBI WANTED TO conduct its own search at the Cochran house. Everyone felt there was more to be learned from that scene. They could not be certain the Cochrans had not buried Chris Regan somewhere on the property, or that the police had exhausted the inside of the residence for evidence. On August 31, 2015, the Detroit Division of the FBI's ERT went to work processing 66 Lawrence Street for a third time.

Frizzo observed. There was serious money behind the case now, not to mention the backing of the nation's top investigative division. She felt a bit of momentum. Prior to this, she had called the MSP to ask for assistance in extracting the DNA in Hobart. According to Frizzo, she was told, "Look, we don't have the time or money to be helping you with this case anymore." She was on her own.

The FBI took dozens of items from the Cochran house: wooden planks and sections of drywall, doors and carpeting, shower and drain traps, garden hoses, a second baseball bat, the bathroom sink, and a good-luck charm.

Frizzo found the rabbit's foot interesting. The FBI had located the "trinket" or "good luck charm," as they called it, in an odd place: under the west entryway porch, beneath a board with a corner of it chipped away, like perhaps it was marked.

Had it fallen and landed there without anyone knowing?

After placing the good-luck rabbit's foot in a ziplock evidence bag, Frizzo made a call to Terri O'Donnell, Chris Regan's ex-girlfriend.

"Terri, listen, I have something I want to ask you. Did Chris ever have, like, a rabbit's foot charm you might keep for good luck's sake? Do you recall anything like that?"

It was white, with a cotton-candy-like blue tint to the fur.

"Yes, as a matter of fact, he did. I remember distinctly seeing it when he lived in Suttons Bay and then again in Iron River, on his kitchen table."

"No kidding?" Frizzo wondered how Terri recalled such a detail.

"Well, we had a discussion about it one night. Chris was a very superstitious person. He would carry that rabbit's foot in his pocket whenever he was feeling worried or was hoping for good news or good luck." Terri went on to describe how "unique" it was, since it was a "real rabbit's foot . . . with a brass or silver top to attach to the keys. . . ."

Further, Frizzo learned, the area of boards where the rabbit's foot had been found "tested positive" for the presence of blood.

FRIZZO TOOK A CALL from her informant, Randy, near the end of August. Randy had more information.

"What's going on?"

Randy explained he'd gone up to Hobart to spend some time with Kelly and Jason at Kelly's parents' house. The conversations they'd had were chilling.

There was one night when they got talking about the IRPD and the search warrants.

"They're going to find Chris Regan's blood in our truck," Kelly said. "Yup. It's gonna be there. He cut his foot one day while we were hiking. He bled in the truck."

Frizzo was curious.

"Jason often talks about the different ways in which to kill someone," Randy added. "He's homicidal. And Kelly, before they even moved up here from Michigan, she started an affair with someone in Indiana she was getting drugs from. Jason found the guy. He went to his house and told him, 'If I ever see you with my wife again, I will kill you.'"

"Anything else?"

"After you guys left, you know, when you took their DNA, Kelly told me that if they are arrested, to grab money from their safe and put their dog to sleep. Kelly is also heavily involved with a guy she works with—and very much deeply into meth. I think Jason might be having an affair, too, and he seems 'doped up' most days. He asked me one night, 'Doesn't everyone hear voices in their heads?'"

DURING THE SPRING OF 2018, Kelly sent me a letter. We'd been talking periodically for nearly a year by then. She hadn't said much of anything significant. Small talk, mainly. The same sort of runaround and rhetoric she'd displayed with Frizzo and the MSP. By then, I knew more about her life than she thought—especially her and Jason's secrets.

"I hate germs," Kelly explained.

After what she would reveal in this letter, I thought that was ironic.

She wrote of *so much pain and loss I have never had a chance to grieve.* She talked about "many people" not understanding her—*or my heart or my decisions and that's okay.*

She claimed that out of all the losses in her life, Chris was the "biggest."

Then an incredible statement tossed into a letter that seemed to jump all over the place.

I still hear [Chris's] screams while Jason was cutting him up with me tied to a chair. I can still taste his blood. . . . I begged for Jason to kill me.

She claimed Jason said he was going to "keep" her alive: *to let me remember all of the horrors [I'd] just witnessed.*

Kelly tried suicide three times before the year 2016, she claimed.

Jason had at least three girlfriends that Kelly knew of,

she said: *I actually hoped he'd leave me for one of them someday, but they bored him.*

Jason was only with these women, according to Kelly, because of a mutual interest in S and M, which she referred to as "torture," noting that Jason was into inflicting pain during sex: *He loved to choke me. He loved to tell me that I loved it, too.*

Kelly said she's not afraid to die: *Living is the hard part.*

Regarding the Saylor neighbors and Jason feeding them Chris's body parts, Kelly said no, it never happened. That wasn't Jason's MO.

His history spoke of something equally horrific, however.

The thought of Jason cooking Chris's body parts and feeding them to neighbors was "ironic," Kelly concluded. Because in the past, she maintained, Jason had murdered scores of people and fed those body parts to the pigs the Cochrans then raised—that is, before selling the human-flesh-fed pork as local, organic, fresh local meat.

50

CLOSING IN

THE NEXT FEW MONTHS involved lots of tedious paperwork, studying and sifting through reports and cellular phone records, on top of those seemingly mundane tasks consuming an investigation of this scope. All of it, however, was an essential part of the case for Frizzo. She needed to detail and map every move the Cochrans had made during the times in question. The investigation was inching toward the one-year mark. The IRPD had made progress, of course, but in many ways, the chief was right back where she'd started.

No body.

No arrests.

The FBI wanted to dredge the Caspian Pit more carefully to see if divers could turn up anything. (They didn't.) Frizzo and the FBI also went back to that Honeybee Lane/U.S. 2 section of highway in Wisconsin, where the Cochrans had sat for eight minutes. Law enforcement wanted to see if they could find anything there. (They didn't.) A case was building, no doubt about it. But without a body, it was going to be difficult to convince a magistrate that an arrest warrant for one or both was prudent. Prosecutor Melissa Powell encouraged Frizzo to keep pressing, keep digging, keep the faith. Utilize the FBI. These things take time. There were murder investigations that were ten, fifteen, and twenty years old. Meanwhile, Frizzo had a solid informant in touch with the Cochrans on a regular basis. Maybe it was a matter of patience—allowing the Cochrans, both of whom seemed now to be actively involved in heavy drugs, to make a mistake. Sooner or later, Frizzo was confident, they were going to reveal themselves.

As Frizzo focused on the case involving a baby homicide she'd been working on since June 2014, months before Chris Regan went missing, she could have never known how prophetic HPD detective Jeremy Ogden's piece of advice to Steve Houck had been: "Let [Jason] know that through our investigation we believe his wife is planning to kill him. . . ." Or how far a turn the disappearance of Chris Regan was about to take.

"I had a strange, spiritual-like feeling," Frizzo later explained, "that something was going to happen to Jason, Kelly, or both. I can't explain it."

Arguably, and hotly debated, human beings have six basic emotions: fear, anger, disgust, surprise, happiness and sadness. A cop's instinct, no doubt about it, should be seven.

PART 4

MURDER PACT

51

THE SOUNDS OF SILENCE

HE WAS BARELY BREATHING. With their ears up to his mouth, paramedics could hear a faint "breathy" sound coming from his lungs. Yet no "epigastric" noises were present—the upper central region of his abdomen, in other words, was not moving.

If he wasn't dead yet, it was a matter of minutes, maybe seconds. His body was shutting down.

The call came in as an "unresponsive male" on February 20, 2016, near seven p.m.

"He's barely breathing," the woman told the 911 operator. She sounded shaky, rather angry, at times mumbling, at others clear as cellophane, with several inaudible moments throughout. Still, within it all, she displayed no panic—as if, perhaps, calling was more of a nuisance. "I don't know . . . he's throwing up. He's sweating. I need an ambulance. Right away."

"Okay, are you in a hotel—is that a hotel?" dispatch asked.

"No," she said. "I'm in a home." At this point, she sounded out of breath.

"And how old is the person?"

"Thirty-seven—just get an ambulance here. Right now!"

"Okay . . . You said 'difficulty breathing'?"

"Barely . . ." She called out his name. Her desperation counterfeit, like she was putting on a performance. She then took a few quick breaths in, as if gasping for air herself. "He *is* still breathing. . . ."

The caller said a number of things next. Most of it hard to make out. Then became focused, clear, and direct: "I need an ambulance here, right away. . . . I gotta tend to him."

She hung up.

When paramedics arrived, family members hovered around a 284-pound man described in first-responder reports as "mildly obese." He was propped up in a seated position on the floor, his head dangling off to one side, eyes closed. His skin was warm to the touch—but purple. There was vomit on the floor around him, as well as inside his mouth and on his clothes.

The emergency medical technicians (EMTs) administered cardiopulmonary resuscitation (CPR) and placed him on his back, on the floor. The way in which he was situated, in addition to his weight, was going to make it impossible to get him onto a stretcher and into the ambulance in a usual manner. For one, they were on the second floor; second, the narrow walkway down the stairs was going to make it impossible to place him on a stretcher and slide him down the stairs as though on a sled.

"Tarp," one of the EMTs said. "Get the tarp."

They placed him inside a tarp—same way biologists might harness a beached dolphin, hammock-like—and carried him down the stairs, a pair of first responders on each side.

He was so big, a report of the incident claimed, that while they were working on him, trying to keep him breathing, the balloon (on the breathing apparatus—which a medic repeatedly squeezes to keep air flowing into the lungs) ripped.

"Damn."

They got him into the ambulance with a struggle. By now, he was secured to a cot and meds were being pumped into his veins. As the ambulance raced toward the hospital, "Good wave form was present"—meaning he had a heartbeat—"and bilateral lung sounds [were] confirmed."

Despite whatever trauma he had been through, barely hanging on to life, the man was still somehow alive.

52

UNSURPRISING SHOCKER

Frizzo sat in the courtroom for the first day of trial and stared at twenty-six-year-old Brittany Russell. Russell had been charged with homicide in the death of a three-month-old girl under her care. Frizzo had been investigating this case longer than Chris Regan's disappearance.

The trial was going to be emotionally taxing. But also all-consuming. Frizzo would have to focus. Take her mind off Chris Regan, Kelly and Jason Cochran, for the time being and dedicate herself to this trial until it was over.

As the process of picking a jury began, Frizzo felt her hip buzz.

She looked down.

Damn it.

"I have to take this," Frizzo told prosecutor Melissa Powell. "I'll be right back."

Frizzo stepped out into the courthouse hallway. The call was from HPD's Steve Houck.

"Yeah, Steve, what's up?"

"Jason Cochran is dead."

"Jason Cochran is . . . what?"

"Dead. . . . Detective Jeremy Ogden is back to work and is looking into it. He'll be in touch with you soon."

Frizzo had heard right. Jason Cochran had not made it. As it turned out, Kelly called 911 after "finding Jason unconscious." A further, more detailed report of the incident clarified that although Jason's body was "warm" to the touch and "clammy" from sweat, he had no pulse and was not breathing on his own when medics arrived. Furthermore, once they got him on a machine inside the ambulance, his weak pulse flatlined. No lung sounds could be confirmed. He had stopped breathing on his own.

"I remember saying for months that I just had a feeling that something significant was going to happen in the Regan case while I was in the Brittany Russell trial," Frizzo commented. "I just knew it. Not a few minutes into picking a jury, there you go."

The next call Frizzo took was from Special Agent Mark Hoff of the FBI.

"We received a call on the tip line," Hoff told Frizzo, "from a guy named Walt Ammerman, a friend of Jason's, telling us Jason was dead and that Walt felt 'something wasn't right.'"

Early indication was that Jason had died from a heroin overdose. He would soon test positive for THC, opiates, morphine, and codeine. A test for fentanyl, which was killing scores of heroin addicts lately, was negative. Still, massive (killer) amounts of heroin had been found in his system.

Maybe too much?

"I knew two things," Frizzo said, referring to the last time she saw and spoke with the Cochrans during that DNA extraction. "That one of them would end up dead, if not both, and something was going to happen while I was in trial that would prevent me from much movement."

Frizzo went back and sat down next to Melissa Powell, completely stunned by the turn of events. She had a strange feeling. People were talking in the courtroom. A trial was going on before her, but she wasn't hearing any of it.

"There's this odd but obvious spiritual happening taking place. Indescribable."

It was all around her. Frizzo could feel a presence.

Walking out of the courtroom that day, Frizzo got a text from HPD detective Jeremy Ogden. He wanted Frizzo to e-mail him the case reports so he could begin right away.

This one gesture gave Frizzo "a huge sense of relief that this detective everyone spoke so highly of was back to work, and on the case. I knew right away this would be the end for Kelly. Honestly. I just knew this guy, Jeremy Ogden, wasn't going to let up until it was solved."

Frizzo collected herself. Took a moment.

For the first time in months, she believed finding Chris Regan was a reality.

Frizzo called Jeremy Ogden that night. Thanked him. Told him she would get him the entire case.

"If there's anything you need to know, call me, text me, whatever. I am here to help."

"I won't stop until that butterfly is put in a cage," Jeremy said.

53

PINPOINT

JEREMY OGDEN HAD A particular look to him. Salt-and-pepper goatee, his hair buzz-cut on the sides, cropped about an inch straight, like a brush, on top. Built solidly, Jeremy had been with the HPD for almost twenty years. Before that, two years with the New Chicago Police Department (NCPD). For HPD, he had started, like most every cop, in patrol, but he was quickly assigned to the K9 Division, where he'd stay for the next eight years. After that, he cut his detective teeth in the Drug Enforcement Administration (DEA) and a specialized undercover narcotics group for an additional five years, before heading into Homicide. When the Jason Cochran death dropped into his lap, Jeremy was HPD's general-assignment detective, having previously been the commander of the Investigations Division. It was clear, as Frizzo began to learn about Jeremy's career, that she could not have ordered a finer, more gifted investigator to jump aboard and help. Jeremy Ogden was just what this case needed at a time Frizzo needed it.

A godsend.

In more ways than one.

Ogden knew right away something wasn't right about Jason Cochran's death. He could tell from the way medics explained to him how at the scene Kelly had tried everything she could to get in the way—most likely out of fear they'd save Jason's life—to what he was now hearing from the coroner Dr. Chow Wang.

Ogden stood by as Wang sliced and diced, cutting Jason open, weighing his organs, studying his inner-chest cavity, checking his arteries, and weighing it all against the toxicology reports.

"What do you think?"

"Look here," Wang said. He focused Ogden's attention on dozens of pinpoint hemorrhages on Jason's forehead, nose, and sides of his face. The left cheek, in fact, had a "visible mark." A bruise.

"But look at this," Wang added, beckoning Ogden in for a closer look. The doctor took Jason's eyelids and folded them back, inside out. "Look at those eyes."

Petechial hemorrhage.

"That's due to pressure, suffocation to the face and neck."

It was the only answer.

Wang pointed to Jason's back. The blood (lividity) had settled there, so it was clear he was on his back when death occurred. There could be no disputing it.

"That rules out positional asphyxiation." (Jason suffocating on his own after overdosing.) "Also, although his coronary arteries were ninety percent occluded, he did not have a heart attack, as there is no sign of myocardial infarction."

That statement was ironic because Jason would have likely had a major heart attack in the near future and probably would have died from it.

"Look at his neck," Wang said.

Additional petechial hemorrhage.

"That is *inconsistent* with an injury during CPR."

Wang said he was going to rule the death homicide.

As Jeremy Ogden was leaving the autopsy suite, someone from the coroner's office stopped him.

"The wife, Kelly Cochran, Detective. She has been calling here asking if we know of a cause of death yet. This is extremely unusual."

Ogden thought about it: Jason Cochran had enough dope in his system to drop a hippopotamus, and yet someone had suffocated him. He had been murdered.

Or, actually, Jeremy Ogden now knew, silenced.

JEREMY OGDEN WAS ONE of those investigators who dug his heels in, buried himself in the available material, and followed the evidence to a place he believed was going to be productive. Frizzo had done so much in the disappearance of Chris Regan. She'd followed her instincts. But questioning Jason and Kelly had become Frizzo's Achilles' heel. With Ogden now involved, providing a fresh set of eyes and experienced investigative mind, the case would change course.

Ogden went home and watched all of the videotaped interviews. He listened to the audio interviews. He stayed up through the night, jotting down notes, posing questions, making observations. Within a few hours of absorbing the case, he understood Kelly Cochran had the answers. She knew what happened to Chris Regan.

"I need to get her into an interview room," Ogden told Frizzo. "That's what I'm focused on right now."

Speaking to the EMTs who were on the scene, Ogden found out that as they worked on Jason, Kelly had reported to them, "Jason had died in his sleep." She said he went in for a nap and never woke up.

"He's in poor health and has been battling cancer," Kelly said as EMTs asked about Jason's overall health.

None of that, Jeremy Ogden knew, was true.

He set out to visit Kelly at her parents' home. Ogden wanted to see the layout of the house and maybe get a firsthand account from Kelly. The more times she told the story, the more opportunity existed for her to trip over herself.

Kelly came out of the house as Ogden parked in the driveway, got out of his car, and approached the door.

They stood in front of the house.

"Why are you here?" Kelly asked. She was agitated and angry. Wired.

She's on something. . . .

"I'm Detective Jeremy Ogden from the Hobart PD. I'm here to investigate the death of your husband, ma'am."

"Are you . . . are you . . . going to be asking me about anything else?"

That's odd, Jeremy thought.

"What other reason would I have for being here?"

"Look, are you going to be asking me about *anything* else?"

"I don't understand your question."

"Forget it."

They discussed Ogden's need to get inside and have a look around, to see where Jason had died. Jason's parents, Mary and Chester Cochran, were there visiting. Ogden indicated he wanted to talk to them, too.

Kelly balked at first, saying her house was a mess, but eventually she allowed him in.

Ogden asked who was present during the incident.

Mary said the four of them: Jason, Kelly, Mary, and Chester.

"The medical attention given to my husband was horrible," Kelly said. "The 911 dispatcher hung up on me."

"I took the phone from Kelly," Mary explained, "so as to direct the ambulance here. The house isn't marked well."

"The medics did not know what they were doing," Kelly added, butting in.

"Can I see the room you shared with your husband?" Ogden asked. "I'd like to have it photographed."

"The room is a mess."

Ogden asked what happened.

"We were both in bed. He was lying there," Kelly explained as they approached the room. She pointed to the foot of the bed. "I woke up and he was blue in color. I got on top of him. I began smacking his face. I yelled, 'Wake up! Wake up!' I was straddling him. I then put my arms under his and pulled him into a sitting position and then pulled him off the bed and we both fell on the floor, with him on top of me. He was throwing up."

Jeremy Ogden listened, noting that as Kelly talked through the incident a few times, she had said in one instance Jason vomited while on the floor and in another while on the bed.

Discrepancy.

Another detective arrived and began photographing the room. Kelly would not "leave the threshold and kept a constant watch on" the photographer as he worked his way around the scene.

As Ogden tried talking to Kelly, she drifted, her focus on what the other detective was doing.

But the biggest tell of all: Kelly showed no emotion. She did not seem one bit broken up about her husband's untimely, unexpected death.

54

SEX, LIES, AND VIDEOTAPE

CHIEF FRIZZO CALLED Detective Ogden. They discussed the progress he had made since coming aboard, along with several recent developments. Ogden said he believed Kelly and Jason had murdered Chris Regan—and Kelly had, subsequently, murdered Jason to quiet him, because she was afraid he would talk. Not much new there. Yet, Ogden added, he was certain Kelly would, at some point, tell them where Chris's body had been dumped. But that was only the beginning.

"E-mail me a photo of Chris Regan," Ogden said.

"On its way."

Hanging up, Ogden sat back in his chair. He noticed something between him and Frizzo besides this case. A connection.

"I knew there was something there, before even meeting Laura," he recalled. "She's an incredible person, with such a beautiful heart. I was so taken aback by her struggles and determination to get answers. I'd never met a woman like her before. And she's beautiful, on top of that. What a bonus."

As he stared at the phone, a thought occurred to him: *Somehow, we're going to spend the rest of our lives together.*

Beyond that personal connection, there was something profound and compassionate in Frizzo's voice.

"It was so clear to me how much Laura cared for Chris Regan's two boys. We'd talk about the Regan family for hours. Laura wanted nothing more than to give them the answers they deserved. As for me, I was strongly attached to the case from the beginning because Chris Regan had served his country for twenty years. He deserved someone going the extra mile to find him—and tell his story of death. And those responsible, clichéd as it sounds, they needed to pay the price for what they had taken from Chris Regan and his family."

Back on February 29, 2016, Ogden explained to Frizzo, Jason's parents came into HPD to sit and talk with detectives. Before even sitting down, Mary Cochran said, "I sure hope Kelly didn't have anything to do with Jason's death."

Why would she even mention this?

"I made contact with Kelly's girlfriend," Ogden told Frizzo.

"With whom?"

Jeremy proceeded to tell quite the tale—all of which had come directly from Kelly and, after he caught up to her, Kelly's girlfriend.

AFTER SPEAKING TO KELLY at the house, Ogden was able to convince her to stop at HPD and sit for a proper interview. A few days later, she showed up.

Ogden asked, "Have you had any relationships with females?"

"I have," Kelly said.

Kelly explained how she was picking up chicken one afternoon at a popular local fast-food chain near Hobart. She flirted with one of the girls behind the counter as she picked up the order. When the girl went on break, she and Kelly continued talking in the parking lot. Her goal at that time, Kelly claimed, was to find a female sexual companion for Jason. Someone with whom the two of them could have a ménage à trois, an idea Kelly had hatched about two weeks prior to Jason's death.

"Because of the things I have done in my life," Kelly told Ogden, "I felt I owed it to him. This woman was kind of like [me] paying him back for all the things I had done."

After exchanging numbers with the girl, Jason, Kelly, and the girl met on three occasions, Kelly explained. In a hotel, another time at Kelly's sister's house while Kelly and Jason were babysitting, and a final time inside Kelly's mother and father's house, in their bedroom. Jason and Kelly's sexual life had become unusual, violent, and complicated.

IN A LATER STATEMENT, Kelly talked about the day before Jason's death. Between eight and eleven that night, Kelly claimed, she and Jason "spent time in foreplay." They "attempted sex, and did some role-playing." Jason tied Kelly up and took photos of her. "I spent a lot of time and effort getting him to go through the entire sex process and come, but he had some problems performing." She said his "daily meds" prevented Jason from being stimulated and sustaining an erection. "He enjoyed tying me up and choking me to where I'd lose temporary consciousness. . . . He was never one to want to choke me during sex until we went to

the motel/hotel with [the fast-food girl]"—a total contradiction to what Kelly would later tell me in an interview.

"The [fast-food girl] asked him to choke her, and he
looked thrilled by it." He did it "maybe seven or eight
times" that first night. Kelly said she "also allowed the
two of them to do the same to" her. The entire sex game
scared Kelly, she said. She agreed to it to please Jason.
There were times, she added, when she'd black out and
come to, with Jason having sex with her lifeless body.
This was after they'd invited a belt into the situation,
using it to choke one another out.

"He also liked to whip me."

AFTER INTERVIEWING KELLY THAT day, Jeremy Ogden
found the fast-food girl, Elisha Horton (pseudonym),
hoping to verify what Kelly had told him.

For the most part, Elisha backed up Kelly's version.

"The first time, though," Elisha explained, "she picked
me up at work and brought me back to their house and we
did drugs—various pills. I wasn't even sure what Kelly
was giving me. That night, I went out to a bar and I ultimately wound up getting very sick and was throwing up
outside the bar. Jason and Kelly were there, too. We were
actually supposed to go to a hotel that night, but I was too
ill."

A few days later, however, Kelly texted Elisha and
asked her to be exclusive with her, a lesbian affair, and
cut Jason out. Kelly wanted Elisha to herself.

Something Kelly had not shared with Ogden.

Kelly had turned her phone over to Ogden during that
first interview. He'd read through texts between Kelly
and Elisha and it was clear they were carrying on, just the
two of them. He then looked through the photos. Among

them, Elisha had snapped pics of Kelly lying nude on a hotel bed, a belt around her neck.

"Kelly liked using a belt on Jason and herself during sex," Elisha told Ogden.

The next time they talked, Ogden asked Kelly if she was having sex in this manner the night Jason died.

"Yes," she said.

As they talked, Ogden changed tactics. He needed to bring Chris Regan into the conversation and gauge Kelly's reaction.

"Look, Kelly, Chris Regan deserves to be found, you know. He served his country for twenty years in the U.S. military and his family should be able to have a proper burial [for him]. It's important to his family to have closure."

Kelly became nervous. Agitated. A subject that clearly bothered her.

Ogden knew Kelly was responding to him and liked to talk to him. There was a rapport building.

Still, she wanted nothing to do with talking about Chris Regan.

"Things have occurred in your life, Kelly. I know this. Your situation has changed and you have a unique opportunity at this time to come forward and be a witness rather than a suspect."

Ogden had used this same line (witness/suspect) different ways, a number of times.

"I don't know anything," Kelly said.

"Kelly, come on . . . help me out here. This guy's family is looking for closure."

"No, I do not know anything."

"Kelly . . ."

"Let me ask *you,* do you think Jason killed Chris?" Kelly asked, hoping to deflect focus.

"I think something happened, like maybe spur-of-the-moment type of thing."

Ogden said it—but it was far from what he believed.

"We commonly talk to people and tell them what they want to hear in order to get them to continue to talk to us," Ogden later explained. "It's how we solve investigations."

They got back to the subject of Elisha. He wanted to know where Kelly and Elisha had hooked up. Kelly had mentioned a "hotel." He pulled out a map. Asked Kelly to point it out.

She told him.

Kelly said Jason mainly watched. He participated on one occasion.

"Kelly, at some point, you are going to need somebody. I will be there for you. I will be ready to talk to you when you're ready to talk."

"I don't need anybody. I'm pretty self-sufficient."

"Tell me about Chris Regan's death?"

"You shouldn't be asking me questions about something I don't know nothing about."

There was a line here Ogden had made a decision not to cross early into the relationship he was building with Kelly. He did not want to push too hard. He needed to find out how far Kelly was willing to take it, hoping it would set the stage for future talks.

"If you push people too hard . . . early on, they generally won't come back."

As they talked, Ogden started to "dance around Chris Regan's murder" and Kelly's or Jason's involvement. He was vague, stealthily referring to the theory that Kelly and Jason could have killed Chris together, but only Kelly was alive to talk about it now. So she held the cards. Controlled the narrative.

At one point, Kelly looked at him and smiled. Dropped her head. Looked back up, smirking: "If I am going to have any respect for you, Detective, you might want to just say how it is."

Silence.

Inside, Jeremy Ogden was pumping his fists.

"It's the hook. That moment where she changed the table and she is the one now engaging to talk to me. She is now going to try and seek information from me. This was very important."

The detective mentioned Kelly's family. What if someone had hurt one of her family members? What would her response be?

"I'd hunt them down and kill them," Kelly said.

Ogden was reeling her in.

"Kelly, did you go out looking for Chris when he first disappeared? I'm just curious."

"Well, I called him for about two weeks, and I have all those texts. . . ."

"That's a common tactic people implement," Ogden explained later. Kelly knew exactly what he meant: During a missing person's investigation, the responsible party will often text the person who was "already gone or deceased." They will generate phone calls to try to create an alibi. They will act like they are involved in caring about the person's whereabouts.

"That's what you were doing, right?"

Kelly did not respond.

They discussed how common it was for people to go over to the missing person's residence during those early days after the person went missing and act like they were concerned, looking for the person.

"When you already know what happened to him. I'm going to say it again, Kelly. You can be a witness or a suspect. You decide. . . . You hold Chris Regan in your hands right at this moment."

Ogden was curious about Jason being out of the picture for good now. In the scope of what Kelly had told the MSP and Frizzo, Jason was no longer a threat to her.

"You do not have to worry about him anymore, Kelly."

"He was a loving, great guy," Kelly said. "Best thing that ever happened to me in my life."

As Ogden sat and listened to Kelly talk, thinking about all he had learned from videotapes and audio interviews, reading through reports, a theme developed.

Bring him home.

The victim. Ogden's only goal.

The interview concluded. Ogden did not expect to get anything substantial out of Kelly early in their talks. However, within that one smile Kelly had given him, Jeremy Ogden knew it was far from over. Kelly would be crawling back soon enough, eager to talk.

"They all do."

55

PERSISTENCE

DETECTIVE OGDEN KNEW Kelly Cochran had a deep desire to divulge her secrets. There was no question that, for whatever reason (ego, uncontained narcissism, or that she believed she was smarter than law enforcement), at some point Kelly was going to talk about what had happened to Chris Regan. Still, it would have to be on her terms, when and where she decided.

In early March, after those first few initial interviews, Jeremy Ogden met with Kelly. Continuing to build that rapport, which needed to be done casually, he decided on a neutral environment.

"Culver's in Merrillville?" he suggested. A chain restaurant. Lots of people. Clanking glasses and dishes. Background conversations going on. Sports on television.

Kelly agreed.

Ogden put a three-man plainclothes team in the parking lot. One detective in the restaurant.

"I wasn't going to meet her anyplace alone."

Not out of fear, but from common (police) sense.

They sat in a booth and Ogden brought up the idea of

Kelly being a suspect or witness. He needed to drill this point into her. Make her believe she had a choice. Force Kelly to play a card.

From there, the detective went back to Chris's family. Closure. The waiting. Wondering. He asked Kelly to think about what Chris's family was going through.

"Look, Kelly . . . bottom line here. I am willing, I cannot do it today"—Ogden looked at his watch as if he had somewhere else to be—"I cannot leave today, but I can leave tomorrow if you're willing to go up to Michigan. Whenever you want."

Kelly thought about this. She stopped talking.

Another point he made was how bad Kelly had been treated by Michigan authorities and how she would not have to deal with them any longer because he was now involved.

"Don't worry about them."

Kelly stared at the detective. "I know one hundred and fifty percent that *that* is just not true!" she seethed. Frustration rose on her face. "If we are going to have *any* type of relationship, Detective, you are . . . you are *not* going to lie to me—do you understand?"

"I do."

This, too, had been a preplanned investigatory tactic. Ogden needed Kelly to feel as if she was in control. That aggressive statement about the IRPD gave Kelly that impression.

"I had flipped it right back around to what she did to me during the first interview."

Ogden talked about the witness/suspect dilemma, making sure this stayed at the forefront of Kelly's mind. Then he pulled out another tool: "Kelly, look, you can pick and choose your story in this of how it all happened." The implication was that Jason was gone. Ogden wanted

Kelly to latch onto the notion that she was now the only one who knew what had happened to Chris Regan. "Something had to have gone on between Jason and Chris, Kelly. I know this. You guys did whatever it was you had to do in order to go on living. Am I right?"

With that, Ogden made Kelly believe he'd lessened her culpability, making her believe there was a way out of this.

With no response, he went back to the witness/suspect theory, explaining it in more detail, telling Kelly that, if she chose, she could play the passive victim in it all. But she had to come to the table with information.

"A suspect will play this game with us back and forth, trying to convince us that they're not really involved," Ogden said later. "That's all this was. I knew if I waited long enough and stayed patient, she would crack."

Kelly left the restaurant with the door wide open, as the detective put it. Just as he'd planned. He had her. She was slowly crawling to him on her hands and knees, considering giving it up. He needed to get her there and be ready once she was willing.

Like any long investigation, however, the tables continued turning. In Jeremy Ogden's case, a huge break fell from the sky and landed in the detective's lap.

56
THE LETTER

Frizzo called Ogden on March 12, 2016. She had something. A friend of Jason's from Michigan had called the FBI and stated he had a suspicious feeling about Jason's death and wanted to talk to someone.

Forty-nine-year-old Walt Ammerman, a technician for a machine service, spent his days traveling, making repairs. Walt liked the work. It got him out of the office and meeting new people all the time.

"He's a really personable guy," Ogden said. "He had spent time with the Cochrans and invited them up to his lake property. He'd communicated with Jason quite often. Kelly knew him well. He has a really successful business. I thought, 'This is the guy to do what I have planned—as long as he's willing.'"

In early 2013, Walt met Jason while playing the game Battle Pirates on Facebook. They'd meet up online, talk, and play for hours and hours. It wasn't long after, while passing through the area one day, Walt stopped by the Cochrans' Caspian home to introduce himself in person. Walt said later he'd visited about five times, with Kelly and Jason dropping by his house a few times, too. He'd been down to Indiana also to visit them, after they took off from Michigan. But the main relationship had been online: Walt and Jason speaking nearly every night while playing the game.

Walt had called the FBI a few days after hearing Jason had died. He thought Jason's untimely death "was somewhat odd." Walt had known there "was someone missing since 2014 . . . and they, the Cochrans, were being blamed for it. . . ." He had talked about it with Jason and Kelly numerous times. What he found particularly odd was that the same person accused of being responsible for a missing person was dead now. It didn't add up. Acting on instinct, a concerned friend had made a Good Samaritan call to the FBI. If there was nothing to it, so be it.

"I got your number from the FBI," Ogden said when he got hold of Walt on March 14, 2016. "I'd like you to come down to Indiana. I need your help. I have a plan in the works."

Walt was willing, he said, but curious about the detective's plan.

"I want you to call Kelly and tell her that Jason had mailed you a letter back in December and told you that if anything ever happened to him, he wanted you to send this letter to the . . . Iron River Police Department. We'll record this call. You'll do it from here. We'll be with you. You'll have protection afterward."

Quite a task. Walt was nervous. He wanted to help.

"Okay," Walt said.

"Listen," Ogden added, "if you feel like you shouldn't do this for any reason, I can get a lawyer or somebody else from Indiana to do it. It's just that it would mean so much more coming from you."

The call would have more validity in Kelly's eyes

coming from Walt. She was both street- and book-smart. Kelly was not easily fooled. She was running on adrenaline and paranoia; any mistake could send her into hiding, on the run, or lawyered up.

"I'll do it," Walt said.

They met a few days later in the parking lot of a movie theater in Merrillville, Indiana, not too far from where Kelly lived. Several detectives, including Ogden, stood around Walt as he dialed Kelly.

Walt came up with the idea that the fictitious note accompanying the letter would have to be signed Quack-Quack, Jason's nickname. This would seal the deal with Kelly.

Walt paced as the phone rang.

"Hey, hey . . . ?" Kelly said.

Walt said hello, what's going on, how are things. Then: "Kelly, um . . . listen. . . . This has really been bugging me. You know how we (Walt and Jason) met up a few times in December?"

"Yeah? Yeah?" Kelly sounded flustered. Restless. Concerned about where the conversation was heading.

"Jason asked me for my address. Okay?"

"Yeah? Okay . . ."

"I got a letter, like January fourth or fifth, something like that." Walt came across as sincere, convincing. "And inside is a note from him. I don't know how to . . . The note says, 'Drock,'"—"Drock" was Walt's nickname—" 'if something were to happen to me, please send this in a week. Do not open it. Thanks, Quack-Quack.' There's an envelope in there, with no return address, addressed to the Iron River Police Department. I mean, it's been three weeks. It's been bugging me and I haven't been talking about it."

Kelly took a breath. Then: "Oh . . . shit."

"I'm supposed to mail this and I just wanted to tell you."

"Oh . . ."

"Well . . . ," Walt said.

"Please don't," Kelly pleaded.

"I don't know how *not* to," Walt responded. "I mean, all I can picture is his mom saying, 'You were his best friend . . . how could he do this to him.'"

"Oh?" Kelly sighed.

"So, look, I just wanted to tell you . . ."

"Um, you gotta do what you gotta do," Kelly said. She laughed. Then started weeping. "You're serious? You're not fucking with me?"

"I am *not* [screwing] with you."

Kelly wailed.

"I really gotta go. I don't know what to do," Walt said.

"Do whatever you have to do."

THIS LETTER, ACCORDING TO KELLY, was a ruse she saw through clearly. Explaining herself, she added: "First off, Jason would never write a letter. Because why would he own up, for one?" She paused. Threw up a hand in a gesture toward me as we Skyped: "We'll leave it at that. . . . I also knew that he would never write just Walt a letter. He would write me a letter."

"Okay," I said. "I get it."

"In his actions against Chris, he was hurting *me*. That was against *me;* it had nothing to do with Chris."

A DAY AFTER THE CALL, Kelly texted Jeremy Ogden.

He did not respond.

So she called.

"Things might be coming out really soon . . . ," Kelly explained, her voice beset by nerves. "There is some letter being sent . . . it's a letter from Jason written to the Iron River PD."

"A letter?"

"Yeah. It's on its way to Iron River now."

Ogden listened to Kelly stumble through words, trying to articulate what was happening, while revealing as little as possible.

"She's struggling. . . . She's worried," Ogden observed later.

He had her.

After Ogden asked Kelly what was in the letter, she said the letter was going to answer all of the questions he had asked about Chris Regan.

A major discloser: This was the first time Kelly had admitted she had actual knowledge of Chris Regan and perhaps even where his body had been buried. Walt had said nothing about Chris Regan. This information had come directly from Kelly.

"You see, she knows that Jason can disclose information about Chris Regan through this letter—that is what she is thinking," Ogden explained. "This tells me that *she* knows what happened."

"Do you think this letter will disclose Chris Regan's location?" the detective asked.

Kelly spoke in a deep, raspy voice. "I don't think Jason knows," she said.

How interesting.

Ogden asked Kelly if she was willing to go up to Michigan and show him where Chris Regan's body was located. "You know where he's at, Kelly. Let's get into the car. Let's go. Right now. I'll come and get you."

"I think *you* think I know more than I do."

57
STALKED

JEREMY OGDEN SAT IN his black Dodge pickup, parked in his driveway. It was early morning, March 21, 2016. Throughout the night, he had developed a feeling. Something was happening. The letter had worked. Kelly was on the move. She was going to react to this letter in some way. Ogden put surveillance on Walt, in case Kelly decided to hurt him for sending the letter. Since that call Walt had made, Kelly started calling and texting Walt every day, each time more desperate to get any additional information she could out of him.

Whenever Kelly called Walt, Walt repeated, under Ogden's direction, in one form or another, "I know nothing else," which kept Kelly continually on edge.

Looking in his rearview mirror, preparing to back out of his driveway and head into the station house, Ogden saw Kelly Cochran's white pickup truck driving by directly. There she was driving up the road, turning her head as she drove by, projecting a laser-like stare at Ogden's house.

Damn, he thought. *I got her.*

Kelly did not see him sitting in his truck.

Ogden waited a minute and pulled out of his driveway. He made sure to stay back far enough so Kelly didn't see him.

Kelly drove toward the center of Hobart. Just outside the downtown city limit, she turned onto Third Street. Then she drove past Lakeview Park, before taking a right into the parking lot of Jerry Pavese Park, which hugged the northeastern shoreline of Lake George Dam and its lake.

He stayed back. He watched as she parked her vehicle. He then drove past the parking lot and sped to the other side of the lake.

"I raced around the lake and parked in front of a friend's house. I called my friend as I was walking into her backyard. I told her not to be alarmed if someone calls the cops. It was just me . . . in her backyard."

Kelly got out of her white pickup truck.

Ogden found a spot on the opposite side of the lake, a clear view of the Jerry Pavese Park parking lot. He had a set of high-powered binoculars, took a minute to find his target, dialed it in.

"I had a dream a couple nights before this," he explained. "Look, I'm not big on this stuff—don't get me wrong—but I will take direction from wherever it comes if it seems good. This dream was surreal. In it, I stood at the base of a big tree that had been burned. I had a shovel in my hand. When I awoke, I was at peace. I felt as though I had found Chris."

Kelly walked around a swampy area of the lake for a few minutes. Then she found her way up into a heavily wooded area, disappearing from the detective's view, before stepping out into an open space by the water.

Ogden had her back in focus.

She sat down on a fallen tree.

"It was the perfect view for me to watch her," he recalled. "So when I saw her go into this section of woods, then walk down by the water, I stared closely. I could tell with my optics that something was not normal. . . ."

The tree Kelly sat on had fallen on its side after being struck by lightning. The base (trunk) was burned out.

Ogden made note of where she sat. He knew the basic location fairly well. It meant something to Kelly, for sure.

He watched for about thirty minutes and Kelly did nothing more than sit and think.

After he was certain Kelly was gone, he found the location.

"The tree had been struck by lightning and was charred. I ultimately sat right where she did and thought about things."

Staring at the trunk of the tree and the charred portion of it, Ogden came up with an idea.

"I left that day without implementing it, but I couldn't stop thinking about it. I thought about it all that night. I knew this was going to change the case. I knew when I did this, it was going to get Kelly talking."

58

PRESENCE OF EVIL

JEREMY OGDEN PLANNED A trip to Iron River a few days later. He wanted Frizzo to show him around, take a first-hand look at everything. As he was backing out of his driveway: "Damn it all, if it wasn't Kelly driving up my street again."

Ogden pulled back into his driveway and scooted down so she wouldn't see him.

Kelly passed his house and drove to the same spot in the woods by the lake.

There she sat on that fallen tree once again.

What is she up to?

If Kelly was stalking *him*—and there could be no other way to perceive her behavior because Kelly had no reason to be on the same side of town where Ogden lived; it was nowhere near her house or place of employment—then Jeremy Ogden would do the same.

Hours passed, the cat with his mouse in sight. Ogden observed as long as he could. He had a dinner planned with his youngest daughter that evening.

"And I wasn't going to miss it."

He left with Kelly still sitting on the tree.

"It was time for me to implement my idea."

After his father-daughter dinner, Ogden packed a bag and drove through the night to Iron River.

"Arriving early in the morning," he remembered, "the sun was coming up. As I was driving into town, I was amazed by how big and vast the woods were in the area. And I realized immediately that Kelly was going to have to tell me where Chris was buried—or we were never going to find him."

Ogden checked into a local hotel. He rested. Then he hopped into his truck and set the GPS for Kelly and Jason's Caspian home, 66 Lawrence Street. Five minutes away, when he pulled up, a complete, "remarkable, uneasy feeling" washed over the detective. Ogden could feel "a presence of evil" lurking, hovering over the house.

After parking his truck, he walked around the garage, house, and woods in back, heading toward the Caspian Pit.

He could feel it: complete maleficence. Whatever happened in that house was beyond description. There was no doubt Chris Regan had been murdered inside the Cochran house.

Jeremy Ogden spent the next two days in Iron River. Chief Frizzo drove him to all the locations and shared all the detail she could recall about the case. Her feelings. Thoughts. Theories. They drove the routes Kelly and Jason would have driven and discussed how hard it had been for Frizzo to get any relevant information out of Kelly.

Frizzo knew right away the case was in great hands and Ogden was going to finish what she had started long ago. But also, Frizzo later said, "I knew I had found my soul mate."

They'd spoken on the phone countless times. There was always something there. But now, in person, it was more than a spark. More than a connection he had felt when they spoke long-distance. There was an energy between them.

Chemistry.

DETECTIVE JEREMY OGDEN RETURNED to Indiana a few days later. He woke up one morning at five, dressed in his gym clothes, and drove out to the park. He needed to put that idea into play.

Ogden found the spot where Kelly had sat. He knew she'd be back. So he took out a pocketknife and carved *CHRIS IS HERE* in the trunk of the tree, where she was sure to see it. Then, to the right of where he knew she usually sat, he carved *REGAN*.

A big, bold statement by the detective—a psychological rook moved into place.

Checkmate.

A day later, Ogden had morning court. Before session began, he wandered around the hallway, stopped and stared out a window. It was gorgeous outside. A sunny and warm day. Quite a rarity for Indiana in early March.

She's going to the park today.

He had a feeling.

"Jeremy?" someone called out behind him, startling the detective.

"Yeah?"

"Court is canceled today."

Ogden said nothing. He dashed out the door to his truck and took off for the park.

As he was driving south across the bridge heading for

Jerry Pavese Park, he spied Kelly's white pickup truck pulling into the parking lot.

Son of a bitch!

He drove to his spot across the lake as Kelly parked and walked out to sit on the fallen tree.

Ogden grabbed his binoculars. Jumped out of his truck. Made his way to his observation point. Just as he got into position, pointed the two circles on her, Kelly became flustered and ran from the fallen tree, disappearing into the woods.

Moments later, she was in her truck driving away.

Had she been spooked by what she saw?

Ogden ran to his vehicle.

He was too late. Kelly was gone by the time he made it to the parking lot.

"I really never saw what was carved into the fallen tree," Kelly told me later. "When I had heard that he did that, I mean, that's . . . sick. Touché if he really did that—because I never saw it. I used to go there to get high. But I never saw that carving in the tree."

"This day was very important," Ogden said. "I decided to drive over and talk to the Cochran family."

He caught Jason's brother at the house.

"You have a few minutes?"

"Sure," he said.

"Can you tell me about Kelly and what's been going on lately?"

Jason's brother described how he'd stood, watching her, on the back porch of the house on the day Kelly spoke to Walt.

"I thought she was going to hyperventilate and throw up."

As he spoke to Jason's brother, Ogden's phone blew up. Kelly.

Texting.

I need to talk.

I need to talk.

Please.

I need to talk to you.

This cannot wait.

Kelly finally said she was going to head over to Veteran's Memorial Park in town and would appreciate if Ogden met her there.

"She's desperate right now," Ogden recalled. "I actually began to worry that she might hurt herself."

If Kelly died, Chris Regan's whereabouts were going to be buried with her.

Ogden told Jason's brother he had to run.

Pulling into the parking lot of Veteran's Memorial Park, he looked left toward the memorial of six flags, five monuments. There were two benches in front.

Kelly wasn't there.

He looked straight ahead into the parking lot.

Her white truck was parked in the south corner.

Ogden pulled up. Parked. Jumped out. Approached Kelly's vehicle. Looked inside.

Oh, shit . . . , the detective thought. *Son of a bitch.*

Kelly was slumped over in the driver's seat.

59
CHILDHOOD

Jeremy Ogden's childhood was not your typical American dream, culled from the wistful Midwestern image of a white picket fence, golf-course-green lawn, or some old dude sitting on his porch in a rocker, with a piece of straw hanging out of his mouth. Then again, in the scope of today's world, what does the American dream represent?

At eighteen, Jeremy Ogden met his biological father, Larry. Jeremy's mother, Deborah, was young, innocent, and had fallen in love with Larry, but they never married. Jeremy's sister Kimberly passed away when she was eighteen after a yearlong battle with brain cancer.

"Kimberly's death forever changed me," Jeremy recalled. "The year she fought in and out of intensive care, I had to grow up quickly. Life-and-death decisions kind of do that to the human spirit."

These types of moments in life define us. For Jeremy, memories of Kimberly drive him.

"Kimberly has been an angel watching over me my entire career. I also have a brother, Jeffrey, and a sister Jennifer."

The man Jeremy's mother did marry, Charlie, Jeremy's stepfather, became a role model, beginning with coaching Jeremy's Pop Warner football team and mentoring Jeremy throughout his youth and into adulthood. They became so close that Jeremy stood in for Charlie as his best man when Charlie married Jeremy's mother.

"My uncle, John Ogden, raised me from my freshman year to graduation. I lived with him. He's an incredible man and person. I grew up in the Calumet Township of Gary, Indiana. I went to Lake Ridge Middle School. It was like a mini gladiator academy—survival of the fittest." Jeremy explained how he was forced to "fight [his] way out of more than one situation." His mother ultimately sent him to live with his uncle John to get him out of that environment. "My freshman year I transferred to the River Forest school system in Hobart Township, Indiana. That's where I lived with Uncle John. I graduated from River Forest. During my time at River Forest, I had a girlfriend whose father and stepfather were murdered. It made me think a lot. I always wanted to know how to solve homicides. Their murders are still unsolved. This is when I really began to think about a law enforcement career. After graduation, I worked as a bagger and midnight stocker at a local grocery store. I later took a job as a carpenter."

Jeremy moved to Florida and lived with his uncle for about a year. Then he went back to Indiana and continued working as a carpenter. He married young, at twenty-one. Divorced twenty-one years later.

"I still had that itch for law enforcement and was running my own construction company at the time I returned from Florida. I applied to three different police departments at once and received offers from two. I chose Hobart."

* * *

KELLY COCHRAN WAS UNCONSCIOUS.

"I'm trying to wake her up and she's not responding. She's not waking up."

Ogden lightly slapped Kelly across the face. "Hey? Hey, Kelly? Come on."

He shook her by the shoulders.

"Kelly?"

Nothing.

"Come on, Kelly, wake up!"

She was breathing, but very shallow wisps.

"I even gave her a sternum rub"—a practice EMTs and first responders use (knuckles from a closed fist pushed into the center of the chest) to revive people who are not alert and are not responding to verbal commands.

Ogden called an ambulance.

"Kelly? Wake up!"

Before the ambulance arrived, Kelly came to.

"I called an ambulance. They're on the way," he said after she opened her eyes and realized what was happening and where she was.

"What did you do that for?" Kelly asked, upset.

EMTs arrived and checked her out.

"I haven't slept in a few days. . . . I am very tired," she told them. "I'm okay. I'm not going anywhere."

The ambulance left. Ogden sat with Kelly inside her truck.

"What's going on here, Kelly?"

They talked for two hours. Ogden had a rough time getting his recorder to work. The sun had gone down and it was getting dark. Being alone with Kelly, unable to record the conversation, was not a good idea.

"Okay," she said.

"Can you meet me at Lake Park Restaurant? Let's talk there."

Ogden felt she was ready to give up something.

"Yeah, um, I guess . . . okay."

Ogden left. Kelly said she'd be right behind him.

After a brief anxious period of not hearing from Kelly, her not showing up at the restaurant, he drove into town to look around. Then back to the restaurant.

Kelly finally pulled in.

Just before she got out of her truck, Kelly downed one milligram—on the street a full "bar"—of Xanax.

They sat down at quarter to eight in a booth inside the restaurant. Kelly wore glasses and a blue blouse. Her shirt looked as if she'd slept in it for a few days. Ogden noticed scabs and small sores all over her face.

"I know you have things to do," Ogden said. "I know you have family . . . but at the same time, all you have to do is tell me. . . . You need to close this chapter in your life."

Kelly listened.

"You can bring the family closure. You can bring yourself closure, Kelly. I mean, do you really want to live the rest of your life wondering when they're going to come and get you? Because that is what's going to happen. I promise you."

Kelly sat. Didn't respond.

"It's the truth," the detective said. "And the truth is very powerful."

As Kelly spoke, her voice cracked. She talked about life and death. "All we really have is this moment—today, if you think about it. . . ."

"I know," he said. "I almost died this past year."

"Really?"

"Yeah."

"Doing your job?"

"Yeah. Almost a goner."

Kelly was eager to say something. "What is it?" he asked.

"If you tell me how my husband died, I will tell you what happened to Chris Regan."

Kelly smiled.

She's challenging me? Ogden thought.

Kelly said it three times.

Ogden shrugged.

"Listen, Kelly, your husband was overdosed on heroin with three times the lethal dose and he was suffocated." He paused. Took a sip of his water. "And you, Kelly, you were the only other person in the room with him."

Kelly stared at the detective.

"So you think I murdered my husband?"

"I don't think. I know."

FROM THE MOMENT SHE first met Jeremy Ogden, Kelly "did not trust him." She did not think she was being treated fairly. Kelly considered herself a "very good judge of character." She "studied people."

Kelly told me: "I think he is a small-town cop who thought he could jump on something big. He toyed with me from the start and thought he was going to get something more."

AT NINE P.M., THE RESTAURANT closed. Kelly hadn't said much. She'd been standoffish and reserved, talking in circles. Yet Ogden understood he was breaking her down, day by day. Every time they spoke, she said a little more. It was coming. He could sense Kelly preparing herself to let go.

He walked Kelly to her truck. She sat down in the driver's seat, rolled the window down.

Tomorrow was another day, Ogden knew. Tenacity. Fortitude. Patience. Ogden was playing chess; Kelly was playing checkers. He was in control.

He turned to walk away. "Call me when you want to talk, Kelly. Text. Whatever."

"Hey," Kelly said.

He turned. "Yeah?"

"Jason killed Chris."

"How?"

"He shot him in the head. And it was fast. He died fast."

"We have to go to HPD right now, Kelly. We need to sit down and talk. Let's go."

By now, Kelly was nodding in and out, having great difficulty staying awake. The Xanax had kicked her ass.

"You cannot drive. You keep falling out. . . . You can jump in my truck and we'll secure your vehicle. I'll take you to HPD and we'll talk further about this in a room."

60
DOWNSIZED

GETTING KELLY COCHRAN INTO HPD to talk about Chris Regan's murder had been an uphill battle, demanding, not to mention incommodious. However, at the end of the day, Jeremy Ogden had gotten the job done. A cop's greatest skills as an interrogator and an investigator who had to deal with a narcissist—and probable psychopath—had been put to the test.

So far, Jeremy Ogden kept the upper hand.

"Jeremy is the real deal," Laura Frizzo said later. "His investigative skills are like nothing I have ever seen. He knows how to get people to talk. The first time I talked to him, I thought, 'Thank you, God. Someone who knows what the fuck they're doing.' Not many like him. During those early days of playing cat and mouse with Kelly, and trying to find Chris Regan, as we fell in love, there were many times I actually tried to push him away because I didn't feel I deserved him. I've never been so loved. It's amazing now that I've accepted and embraced it. I had no idea how beautiful life really could be."

As Ogden and a second detective sat with Kelly inside

HPD, she began talking. At first, she was "vague about everything," Ogden explained. She stuck to the "Jason shot Chris" narrative. She shirked responsibility onto Jason, which was what Ogden had pushed her into doing. Yet, if Ogden thought this was some sort of typical homicide, one that he'd seen many times as a Homicide detective, Kelly cleared that up with one sentence: "Jason dismembered Chris and we took him out into the woods."

Lot of detail missing from that, Ogden knew. Still, it was a solid start. An opening. Kelly had admitted being party to a murder. She wasn't going to be able to walk away from this now. Ogden understood that half of what she was saying at this point were lies. *Just keep her talking. Keep her feeling as though she was in control. Keep her believing it was all on Jason.*

This, mind you, while HPD built a case against Kelly for Jason's murder.

The first story Kelly told placed the onus entirely on Jason.

His idea.

His plan.

His savage acts of cruelty.

"I was told what to do," Kelly said. Then she talked about Chris coming to 66 Lawrence Street that night for dinner, October 14. Jason wasn't supposed to be home.

A patent lie. Kelly had told the opposite story to the MSP in October, claiming she went over to Chris's apartment to heat up lasagna. The evidence proved she had been lying about this, including phone records Chief Frizzo had obtained, placing Kelly at home.

Ogden knew Chris Regan had been lured to the Cochran house. There was no other explanation.

"Chris and I were having sex near the back door and Jason suddenly appeared," Kelly claimed in this first interview about the murder. "Jason shot him and Chris fell on me, and we, the two of us, tumbled down the stairs into the basement."

The way she described the scene, Jason stood at the bottom of the basement stairs, hiding in the shadows, his shotgun butted against his shoulder. He had his gun pointed up the stairs. He waited for Chris Regan to finish having sex with his wife. Then shot him in the head.

Kelly claimed Chris was doing her from behind, doggy-style, while standing on the landing area down into the basement by the open door. She faced the wall, her hands above her head bracing herself. Just after Chris ejaculated—"He waited for him to finish," Kelly would later say—Jason fired one round.

Chris and Kelly then tumbled down the stairs together. Chris was dead.

Although this story would change later, Kelly said she immediately began giving Chris CPR to help revive him after getting up off the floor of the basement.

But it was too late.

Then Kelly told Ogden, "Jason downsized him."

"He what?" Ogden looked at his colleague.

Downsized?

"Machete, knife, and chisel."

Jason also took a SAWZALL—an electric reciprocating saw used for demolition, its jagged-edged steel blade pulsating in and out, able to cut through nails and metal and thick hardwood—and cut Chris Regan into pieces, which she was "made" to bag and carry upstairs.

"How long?" Ogden wanted to know.

"About an hour, hour and a half," she guessed, referring to the amount of time it took Jason to dismember Chris Regan.

Ogden took a break from the interview, stepped out,

and called Frizzo. He needed to make arrangements for Kelly to be brought up to Iron River to show Frizzo and the team where she and Jason dumped Chris Regan's remains.

Inconceivably, while she was dating Chris Regan, Kelly had gushed, "I tried to pamper, treat him like he was the amazing man I was falling in love with . . . That anyone who was able to be in a relationship with Chris was very lucky because of how awesome of a guy he was, all the way around."

Frizzo was quite taken aback. How awful. Where was the truth in all of it?

Ogden explained he felt Kelly was not sharing the complete story. It would come. But she wasn't there. Still, within every lie a perp tells, there is a basis of truth. So there was no reason not to disbelieve the ghastly notion that Chris Regan had been dismembered.

Frizzo thought about the Cochran neighbors the Saylors. How Jason had borrowed the SAWZALL from them. Then, incredibly, all that fresh meat the Cochrans had on hand after October 14 and the three meals the Saylors had been invited over for.

"I will never forget that interview with the Saylors. Sitting in my chair, listening to them talk to each other. I think it's highly probable they did this. On that day of the Saylor interview, I sat there thinking, 'Oh, my God. They cut him into pieces. Possibly ate him. Could this be real? In Iron River?'"

That interview with the Saylors was the first time dismemberment had entered Frizzo's mind, but now with the call from Jeremy, her worst fears were confirmed.

They might never find Chris Regan.

"Okay, we're ready up here when you are, to begin searching," Frizzo said.

They hung up.

After talking a bit more, Kelly displayed reluctance to drive with Ogden to Iron River and show them where Chris's body parts had been dumped. So Ogden took out a piece of paper and slid it across the table. Plopped a pencil on top.

Kelly looked up at him.

"Draw me a map."

Kelly bowed her head.

"I would have driven there by myself," he said later. "Met Chief Frizzo and done what we could to try to find him. With or without her. I was going to find this man's remains and return him to his family. He deserved nothing less."

"The map's not gonna work," Kelly said.

"Okay. So what do we do?"

"I have to show you."

Ogden ran home. Packed a bag. Took a shower. Another detective stayed with Kelly at HPD. It was after midnight by this time.

Before heading back into HPD to grab Kelly, Ogden wired the inside of his truck. A long trip. Kelly liked to talk.

For much of the six-hour trip, Kelly slept. To Ogden, the fact that she passed out and slept soundly was significant.

"This commonly occurs when somebody finally lets go of something so deep, so secret."

About an hour outside Iron River, the sun showing signs that its existence was coming around for another day, Kelly opened her eyes.

"Where are we?"

"Almost there. About an hour."

Kelly had something on her mind. She rubbed her face. Cleared her throat. Fired up a cigarette.

"Jeremy, look . . . listen. I . . . I need a letter of immunity or I'm not about to show you where he is."

Ogden looked out his window. Shook his head. There was a gas station up ahead.

He pulled in. Parked. Shut off the engine.

Angrily, "Look, I'll turn this truck around and I'll take you *right* back to Hobart. I won't even drive all the way in. We can be *done* with this—because, you know what, Kelly, I am *not* about to be going down this road with you."

Kelly stared out the window. Took a pull from her cigarette.

"I'm serious here. I'll turn the truck around and bring you back right now."

"Continue," Kelly said.

He drove to the Iron River PD.

As they pulled up in front of the building, Kelly demanded, "I want to talk to Chief Frizzo by myself. Just the two of us."

Ogden was "concerned it would blow up between them."

"All right. Let me see what I can do."

He walked into the IRPD and pulled Frizzo aside. Told her what Kelly wanted.

"But I'm going to be in the room. You're not going to be alone with her."

Frizzo walked up to the front of the station house.

"Alone," Kelly said to Frizzo.

Frizzo and Kelly went into the interview suite first and talked. She was mad-dog angry. Lashing out. Accusing the chief of tricking her and lying. Seething with that same old vitriolic spew Frizzo had been accustomed to by this point.

Ogden walked into the room. They were too close to finding Chris Regan to have it all implode.

"Are you going to leave me alone after this?" Kelly said to Frizzo.

Now I know for sure we've got you, Ogden thought.

"Kelly . . . ," Frizzo started to say.

"You've been on my ass for a year and a half and I *didn't* do anything. I *didn't* kill anybody. . . . I want immunity. I do not want to be charged or connected to Chris's death in any way."

Kelly started in on that letter Walt had supposedly sent. She was worried about it incriminating her. It was as if Jason Cochran could testify against her from the grave.

"Can I see the letter?"

"Kelly, no. . . ."

There wasn't much else to say.

"We need to leave now and go to where Chris's remains are, Kelly," Ogden suggested.

Kelly was backed into a corner. She'd admitted she knew where the remains of a missing man were located because she'd helped put his body parts into bags and dumped him there. That alone was enough to charge her with a serious crime. Why not lawyer up at this point and claim she wanted to consult with an attorney?

No one had read Kelly her Miranda rights. She wasn't under arrest. She was, in fact, free to walk out of the IRPD and go where she chose.

"Okay," Kelly said. "Pentoga Trail. Let's go."

61

DOWN A RABBIT HOLE

U.S. ROUTE 2 EAST out of Iron River takes you to First
Roadside Park, the town of Chicagon, past Chicagon
Lake, before running into Route 169 in Crystal Falls,
Michigan, near Indian Lake. From there, driving south,
you come to the Pentoga Trail. This was a popular place
of interest for Jason and Kelly: the rivers and streams,
waterfalls and parks, memorial gardens and beaten paths,
Native American burial grounds and trails, spread throughout acres of open and thickly settled countryside. The perfect place, sixteen miles east of Iron River, to dispose of
body parts.

As Ogden drove, Kelly riding shotgun, Frizzo and several IRPD officers followed. Kelly sat slumped in the seat
next to the detective, staring out the window, watching
tall, arrowhead-shaped pine and white birch trees, bare
shrubs, weeds and meadows, pass by.

Coming up "on a particular tree" along 169, Kelly sat up.

"That's it . . . right there."

"There?"

"Maybe . . ."

Suddenly she wasn't sure.

They continued driving.

A few miles later. "That's it. Right there. Yup. That's it."

Ogden pulled over. They were about a mile south, into the Pentoga Trail. The woods off the road were dense and impenetrable without the right tools and outerwear. A plus was it was early spring, so the trees were just budding. No leaves to block the view.

Ogden got out, approached Frizzo and her team. "She's saying this is it here. The remains aren't far, maybe eight to ten feet from the road in." He pointed.

"Come on," Ogden said to Kelly. "Stay right by me. Do not touch anything."

Kelly stepped out of the truck and began walking.

The team followed.

After a time, Kelly headed back to the truck, opened the door, sat down.

According to Kelly, she and Jason emptied out the bags of Chris's remains and took the bags back home to burn. The implication being they had spread Chris Regan's body parts all over, in various locations in the general area where they now stood.

Yet Kelly was, most certainly, playing a game. She knew. Ogden was well aware that a person does not forget where she dumped a dismembered human being.

For several hours, dogs and cops and detectives and deputies searched the entire area, square foot by square foot. No sign of Chris Regan.

"Kelly," Ogden said, trying to maintain his composure and patience. He needed to find Chris Regan. Now was not the time to lose it with Kelly. "Look, let's go back to your house in Caspian. Give me consent to go inside with you and let's do a videotape reenactment of what happened. Would you do that?"

Bringing her back to the crime scene might rattle Kelly into giving it all up. Perhaps they'd buried Chris in the backyard? Tossed him in the woods behind the house? Maybe dumped him in the Caspian Pit and the divers had missed it.

Kelly was feeling sick, she claimed. She'd not had any drugs with her, so mild withdrawal was settling in. Being awake and sleeping in the truck, the talking and searching, had strung her out.

"Kelly?"

"Yeah?"

"Can we do that? Go back to the house?"

62

LIFE AND DEATH

W**HEN** J**EREMY** O**GDEN** **TOLD** Kelly Cochran he'd almost lost his life the year before, he was not lying. A K9 tore a fist-size chunk out of Ogden's leg, thinking he was a suspect while the detective was actually serving a search warrant.

"I was conscious and walked away from the bite. They conducted surgery on me two days later. And I was back home recovering from the surgery."

He seemed to be on the mend.

Twenty-six days later, a massive amount of blood filled both of his lungs. The top portion of each clotted.

"I went into the ER for the clots at ten-thirty p.m., and by eight-thirty the next morning, I was in surgery. [The doctor] saved my life with a [specialized] procedure. I was in ICU for three days after that."

Ogden holds no resentment toward the K9. The dog was doing its job.

"I knew what to do during the attack, so it prevented me from being hurt worse. And the dog lived to keep working, it made a mistake."

The incident changed his perspective. He looked at life differently.

"I started realizing what was important. I decided while I was in ICU that I would begin living life to the fullest. It really gave me new direction. I wasn't focused on work so much anymore. When Kelly Cochran came along, a case I knew would be a challenge, it kind of revived my work energy."

Ogden's career began with the New Chicago Police Department, a small town in Indiana about three miles north of Hobart.

"I served on patrol for two years, working straight midnight shifts. I became a K9 handler later on . . . ran the unit until 2007. I was then promoted to corporal at HPD. I ran the 'power turn,' my crew worked eight p.m. to four a.m. That's the shift with most of the action."

In 2007, Ogden was placed with a DEA task force, where he worked high-level narcotics cases until 2012.

"During my time in patrol, we had a young man who was shot and paralyzed from his wounds initially, and then ultimately died from an infection. The case went cold for about a year. I began investigating it on the street and obtained information regarding a witness hiding out of state. I took the info to my chief and he sent detectives to interview the witness. It broke the case and the murder was solved. I continually pursued this suspect during our investigation. After he was incarcerated, my children's lives were threatened and I had to move them for two weeks while we found the guys," Ogden explained.

The life of a detective. The constant knot from the danger—not only to yourself, but to loved ones: "My first day assigned to the DEA, the leader of a large-scale gang tried to run me over while we were attempting to arrest him. I fired one round and killed him. This time, the gang threatened my family and we had security on my home for twenty days, around the clock. I went back to work seven days after the shooting, while officers watched my home."

63

HORROR SHOW

A COLD, SLANTED RAIN FELL, with ice, snow, and sleet mixing in, more late winter than early spring. The air was raw. Ogden pulled up to 66 Lawrence, Kelly Cochran sitting by his side. The front door was boarded up, the wood water-stained and rotting. The place looked abandoned.

"We're here, Kelly." She was half asleep.

Frizzo and her team continued to search that area of the Pentoga Trail where Kelly had sworn they'd dumped Chris's remains.

Ogden and Kelly walked in through the back door, which was already open. A copy of an old search warrant sat on the floor. A second detective trailed behind and videotaped the walk-through (and their conversation). As he panned the camera down and away from his subjects, focused on the search warrant, a bug crawled across the page.

In previous talks, Kelly had told Ogden that when Chris came over on October 14, they went upstairs into her bedroom and had sex on her and Jason's bed.

That was a lie.

Ogden and Kelly stood in the bedroom, the camera focused on them. He mentioned Kelly's prior contention. They both looked toward the bed, which was pushed up on its side against the wall.

"Not that night," Kelly said.

"On the fourteenth you didn't?"

"No."

"Okay, what happened?"

"He came in downstairs. We never made it upstairs."

Ogden looked down in frustration at the lies spewing from this woman, but kept his composure.

They talked while standing in Jason and Kelly's bedroom. Then Ogden said, in a more direct way, "On the fourteenth, when he came here, did you have sex at all?"

"No." She shook her head back and forth.

"Are you *sure*?"

"Yeah."

They discussed dates surrounding that October 14 night Kelly had claimed Jason killed Chris.

"So on the fourteenth, [Chris] comes over here—and was that to get his 'present'?"

Kelly smiled. Nodded affirmatively. "Yeah." The present comment was based on a remark she'd made earlier that day.

"Are you going to tell me what his 'present' was?"

She laughed. "No."

Ogden suggested they go downstairs and talk about what happened, where, how.

"Okay," Kelly said.

From the kitchen, four steps led down onto a small landing, where they'd walked into the house; the copy of the search warrant was still on the floor. If one headed down the stairs, to the left was the door heading outside (the same door they used to enter the house). Directly in front—to the left of the entryway door—was an open doorway leading down additional flights of concrete stairs into the basement.

Ogden stood in for Chris, to the left of the basement doorway, inside the door frame. Kelly stood in front of him, to the right side of the doorway leading down into the basement. They faced each other.

Kelly grinned. She wore a heavy black coat with a furry collar, the sleeves too long, covering her hands. Gray sweatpants. Her black hair was pulled back in a bun, disheveled, dirty, oily; twisted bangs brushed her cheeks. In back of Kelly, painted on the wall, a familiar, inspirational quote: *Sing like no one is listening.*

As Ogden asked questions, Kelly blurted out: "We were messing around right here." Meaning, they'd started to get frisky on the landing between the two doorways. "We didn't make it upstairs."

"You were having sex *right* here?" Ogden asked, pointing at the ground.

Kelly nodded her head. "Yes," she whispered, smiling.

"And we . . . we . . . we're getting ready to go up the stairs and . . . and that was it."

Ogden took a step toward Kelly, close to being in her face: "What happened?"

Kelly looked down. Her hands folded crossways in front of herself. She described what happened next, how she utilized the stairs and wall to help brace and position them in the doggy-style position. "He, like, stopped," she said. "His weight, like, completely fell on me."

"Which direction?"

"Back," Kelly said, pointing toward the stairs heading down into the basement.

"Where was Jason?"

"In the basement."

"Where were you?"

"I went down the stairs with him."

Ogden asked particular questions as he had Kelly act out what happened. Her story fell apart as she told it. First she said they were having sex; then they were walking up the stairs to go into another section of the house to have sex; next she walked in back of Chris as he went up the stairs; before that, she went up the stairs first.

Ogden stood in for Chris on the second stair leading up into the kitchen.

Kelly stood behind him.

"You're telling me that Jason shot him from behind?"

Ogden knew it was a lie. If Jason was in the basement, there was no way he could have made the shot, no matter how accurate his eye and hand. Logistically speaking, impossible.

"Yeah," Kelly said. She hugged herself and twisted her upper body back and forth, hands folded in front, staring down at the ground. She came across like a six-year-old girl caught in a lie, trying desperately to act cutesy to get out of it. "At the time," she added, "I didn't know he was shot."

"Okay. Then what happens?"

"He fell back. . . ."

"Okay, so he fell back and both of you tumble down the stairs?"

They discussed the layout of the stairs and where Kelly and Chris landed.

"So Chris is lying down there," Ogden said, pointing again, "and he's on top of you?"

Kelly nodded her head. "Yes."

"Where's Jason?"

"He was . . . there. . . ." She pointed down the stairs.

"Is he standing down there, to the right?"

Kelly nodded yes.

"What's he doing?"

"Holding a gun."

"What kind of gun is he holding?"

"It wasn't a shotgun? . . . Um, maybe it *was* a shotgun. It wasn't a handgun."

"It wasn't a handgun. It was a long gun?"

"Yeah! I had the handguns. He had the shotguns and rifles."

"Okay, so what kind of rifle would it have been?"

They spoke in detail about Kelly's story, which continued to fall apart. She mixed up small details and lied about others. Yet, within the story, the truth existed somewhere. Once more, it was about patience. Allow her to think she was smarter. Controlling this. And she would eventually give up everything.

Kelly said she split her forehead open when she and Chris tumbled down the basement stairs. Ogden wondered how bad it was and if the wound had required stitches.

"It did," Kelly said. "I stitched it up."

"You what?"

"I stitched it up."

"You stitched up your *own* head?"

"Yup."

Kelly said she blacked out for maybe five minutes while Chris was on top of her at the bottom of the stairs.

"What happened when you came to?"

"Everything I said . . . that . . . the way it happened."

This response was not going to fly. "Huh?" Ogden said, gesturing toward her.

She shrugged.

"Did you do anything to Chris then—check him for a pulse, anything?"

She shook her head. "No. He was gone."

"Did you have blood on you?"

She perked up. "You know, I don't think so. None at all."

Kelly said she wore a pink tank top and jeans.

Ogden tried to understand this. He pointed to the stairs leading up into the kitchen: "So, okay, right here, he's inside you? You're having sex? What did you do, just drop your pants around your ankles?"

"Yes."

"Okay, what does Jason say to you?"

"Nothing. He just looked at me."

"Look, eventually he says *something*!"

"Not that day."

"The *whole* day he stayed silent?" Ogden had his hands in his front pockets. He shook his head. Stared Kelly in the eyes.

She nodded. "Yeah." Nodded again, not looking him in the eyes. "Uh-huh."

"Okay, then, so what did you guys do at that time?"

Kelly coughed. Then looked down the stairwell toward the basement. "Only thing Jason said was 'We gotta take care of it.'"

She interpreted that to mean get rid of Chris's body.

"Did you throw up . . . down there?"

"Yes," she said. She vomited on the basement floor, on the stairs, and upstairs in the bathroom.

64

ROLE REVERSAL

I HAVE BEEN HAUNTED by this for so long, Kelly wrote in her final statement, which she gave after that walk-and-talk, pretend simulation she put on with Jeremy Ogden inside her house. *This horrible thing happened on October 14, 2014, at approximately four forty-five . . . at six p.m. Chris was killed at our house. . . .*

From that launching point, Kelly broke into a history of her relationship with Chris. For the next six, single-spaced pages—and perhaps so blinded by her extreme narcissism, she didn't realize it—she trashed the guy. Kelly justified every one of her actions, while minimizing her role in what was a premeditated, planned, brutal murder and horrific body disposal.

I tried to pamper him like he was the amazing man I was falling in love with and tried to convince him he was worth it . . . , she wrote, as if Chris had suffered from self-esteem issues (which he certainly did not).

Kelly could wax intelligent and articulate, but also come across as crass and foolish. She more often than not spoke with a drifter's, drug-using, streetlike temperament: *I believe every time we had gotten together we had sex, or at the very least I gave him a blow job.*

After that line, she then spent several sentences describing oral sex between them, using raw, tactless detail.

For the next few pages, Kelly talked about what she believed were Chris's faults in and out of the relationship. It was a strange way to show any type of sympathy. And the truth is, Kelly, a tried-and-true psychopath, harbored no empathetic emotions.

Kelly is full of self-validation and blame of others. She does not know how to love.

After a long explanation of the relationship, Kelly wrote, *On the night of . . . ,* before breaking into her first version of what happened.

KELLY TEXTED CHRIS early afternoon, October 14, 2014.[4]
   You coming over my house?
   Generally, they "kept" the relationship and time they spent together "towards [Chris's] house because of my respect for Jason. . . ."
   Chris arrived at 66 Lawrence Street near four-thirty. He parked his car in the back of the Lawrence Street house, in an "alleyway," so no one would see it. He'd driven his car "this time," Kelly said. But would usually meet her in his truck.
   Kelly was cooking lasagna. She heard Chris come to that back door by the basement, right off the kitchen, where she and Ogden had talked. She walked from the kitchen to greet him at the door.

---

4. I have chosen to italicize Kelly's version of events, and to include quotation marks at pertinent sections, because she is the only source for it.

"Dinner's ready," she said.

"Great!"

Then, without another word, Kelly *"dropped down to [give] him"* oral sex *"since I had been blowing him off lately."*

She talked about not being mad at Chris, though the relationship was becoming too much for her to handle because of her marriage and seeing several other men at the same time. She didn't have the time or energy for Chris anymore, and he was sensing an end to the relationship.

"It was hard to keep up with all of them [the men] and their sexual needs," Kelly wrote. *"I tried to see all of them every single day."*

She went to work on Chris there in the entryway, dropping to her knees. Not using the most refined language, Kelly wrote: *"After I had sucked his cock for a little while and he moaned with pleasure for the entire time,"* she stood, dropped her pants, turned around, and *"had him put it in, from behind, which I really enjoyed with him especially for how large he was."*

At that moment, she claimed, while they were having intercourse, she *"might have"* heard a shot. She wasn't sure. Yet, within a second, Chris's *"lifeless"* body fell on her back. This threw her off balance and they tumbled down the basement stairs.

The way she described it, Kelly had no idea what happened. She claimed she did not know that Jason was even home.

She had no explanation for how she knew Chris *"was only shot once and he died instantly,"* adding there were *"no movements or sounds,"* with the exception of *"me cracking my head open."*

Hitting her head on a board halfway down the stairs, Kelly blacked out.

Coming to sometime later, Kelly opened her eyes to see Jason standing over her, his .22-caliber rifle was pointed directly at her head.

"This is your entire fault," Jason uttered. "If you weren't such a stupid fucking whore, I would not have had to kill him."

Jason "yelled at" her "briefly" and continued to call Kelly "mean and nasty names."

Scared and disoriented, Kelly tried to stand. She was dizzy and out of it, blood trickling down her forehead. Chris's inert body was slumped over her. She had a hard time getting up.

Jason turned, walked away, and began looking for something. Kelly didn't know what he was doing.

After having a difficult time pulling herself out from underneath "Chris's heavy, dead body," Kelly found her bearings, wiggled herself out, stood, and watched her husband.

Jason rummaged through a toolbox. Found something. Then turned around.

Kelly looked closely into the darkness of the basement.

A set of hemostats? she thought, realizing what Jason had in his right hand.

Forceps. A pair of medical pliers, a surgical tool used mainly for clamping and controlling bleeding.

Jason walked toward his wife and placed the barrel of his .22 on her head, handed her the forceps.

"Get that fucking bullet out of his head."

"What?"

"Pull that bullet from his head with those."

Kelly bent down and acted as if she was extracting the

bullet from Chris's head, saying later she was able to convince Jason she found it and flushed it down the toilet.

Jason put his gun down and dragged Chris into the middle of the basement floor. Stood and took a long look at him. Then he turned and began to "gather tools for a way to dispose of or minimize the size of Chris's tall, big body." At fifty-three years old, Chris was just over six feet tall, a slim 170 pounds. In excellent physical condition.

Chris was lying in the center of the basement floor. "Let's get rid of his car now, so no one is suspicious of it," Jason said.

It was getting late. It was dark out by this time.

"Don't fucking draw any attention while we do this, understand?" Jason said.

"Okay."[5]

"I'm going to drive it off a cliff into a lake so no one finds it," Jason said, then hopped into the driver's seat of Chris's car.

Kelly claimed she was told to follow close behind in their truck.

"How 'bout that parking lot in Bates?" Kelly suggested just before they left. She wanted Chris's car to be found, she claimed. If Jason drove it into a lake, it would "be decades before" it was discovered.

Jason agreed—though she never said why—and headed for the park-and-ride in Bates.

Jason pulled in first. Parked the car. Hopped out. Jumped into the truck.

---

5. Within all of this recounting, Kelly plays the role of subordinate wife, scared of her husband. She presents herself as a timid, cowering woman, willing to do anything he wants, fearing for her life. My professional opinion, and that of two law enforcement sources, after studying this case, is that Kelly reversed these roles.

"Hurry now, go," he said.

Kelly took off back home.

"Drive faster," Jason urged. Kelly didn't understand his sudden need for speed, because the last thing they needed was to get pulled over.

"He had me race toward Ice Lake Road," Kelly said. "I had really hoped we'd get pulled over, but the luck I was hoping for wasn't there that night."

65

BLOOD WILL TELL

*W*HEN *THEY GOT BACK to 66 Lawrence Street, Kelly jumped out of the truck and "started throwing up."*

Jason stood over her, yelling.

As she finished and was wiping her chin, Jason got in her face: "Go inside and make me a burger and fries."

The guy was hungry.

"I wanted to run and escape, but was paralyzed by what I had just seen in front of my eyes."

As Kelly flipped burgers, tended to the fries, she vomited into the frying pan. Jason went back down into the basement. Ten minutes later, as she cleaned up her own puke, she could hear Jason walking up the basement stairs and into the kitchen.

"After all I have done for you, you're so fucking weak. So . . . stupid. I cannot believe you did this to me."

Kelly stared at him.

Jason grabbed the frying pan and hurled it across the room. Grease and hamburger meat smashed against a newly painted kitchen wall.

"Clean that up," he screamed. "Now, bitch."

On her hands and knees, Kelly scrubbed the wall and floor as she cried.

"This comment stuck in my mind for such a long time," she said in her statement, *"because he took the man I loved (Chris) from me in such a horrible, senseless act, right in front of me."*

"You know why I did this?" Jason said. He laughed. *"I did this specifically to hurt you. For no other reason than to make you hurt. Feel pain."*

Kelly stood and stared at her husband.

"I'm teaching your whore ass a lesson."

Jason turned and walked back down into the basement.

Kelly finished cleaning up the kitchen and heated up the lasagna she had prepared for her and Chris.

As Kelly got the food ready, she heard loud noises coming from the basement.

Power tools? *she thought.*

Curious, she walked down the stairs, unsure of what to expect.

Jason stood over Chris's body, a SAWZALL in his hands, a knife in his back pocket.

There was blood and body parts everywhere, Kelly claimed. She didn't say anything at first. The scene was so surreal, so abnormal. She had no idea what to make of it.

"It was scary to see this" was about all she recollected in her statement about the moment she first saw her boyfriend cut into pieces.

As she turned to walk upstairs, "to make him his plate of food," Jason beckoned her.

"Hey?"

Kelly turned.

Jason held one of Chris's hands, which he'd just cut from the body, above the wrist. He had blood all over his face and clothing. He waved Chris's dismembered hand at her, saying, "Bye, bye, Kelly . . . no more being a whore to your husband." Then Jason laughed.

Kelly claimed she fell to the ground, starting wailing and blubbering "like a baby," having no control over her emotions.

Jason grabbed his rifle, walked over to Kelly. Pointed it in her face.

"You see, whore, this is what will happen if you ever *do this again and hurt me. I'd like to kill you, too, be-cause you do not* deserve *to live for what you've done to me. I've loved you. You need to learn a lesson, bitch. Understand?"*

Kelly went upstairs while Jason "cut him up completely."

Later, Kelly heard Jason yell for her from downstairs: *"Bring me the large garbage bags. We need to get the pieces together so we can transport him to the final desti-nation for dumping."*

Kelly found the bags and walked downstairs.

"Help me package him up."

Kelly looked at the room. Blood spread from one end to the other. Body parts scattered all over the floor. Chris's head cut off, sitting in a small pool of blood by Jason's feet.

"I cut him up. You will put him in bags."

"I can't, Jason. I just can't."

It wasn't the disturbing nature of what he wanted her to do, Kelly said, that bothered her. It was the possibility of her throwing up and "then my DNA would have been all over the body parts."

Jason paced.

He stopped. Waved his index finger at Kelly.

"Hydrochloric and muriatic acid. We dissolve his body

parts instead of dumping them and taking the chance of getting caught."

"There's no way we can get that much acid and do it in this house without killing ourselves from all the horrible vapor."

"Get the fucking acid! We do the hands and head so he can never be identified."

"Please, Jason. Please. No. We cannot do that. It will never work. Please."

Jason thought about it.

"He eventually decided it would have been too risky and take too much time to complete."

Kelly said Jason ended up bagging all of Chris's body parts in *"10–15 bags (black 33–39 gallon approximately),"* Kelly wrote. Jason *"had to double bag"* it all.

"Go back the truck up to the house."

Kelly ran upstairs, grabbed the keys, doing as she was told.

Jason loaded the bags into the truck.

Done, Jason hopped into the passenger seat and told Kelly to drive.

She drove to Lake Emily in Bates Township first, about a twenty-minute ride northeast of Caspian.

They pulled up to the water.

It was deserted.

"Not here. Drive, whore."

Kelly found another small lake nearby. But again, Jason did not like it.

As they continued driving south along Road 639, the Pentoga Trail came into view.

"There," Jason said. *"Right there."*

Kelly was satisfied with this location because it was hunting season. She felt Chris's remains would eventually be found if they dumped him there.

Jason looked at the area. He became quiet.

As Kelly drove along Road 639, the Pentoga Trail, they passed trailers and cabins and campers and hunting lodges. This was a heavily populated area of the trail during hunting season. Kelly was surprised Jason was considering dumping Chris's body parts here.

"Drive around and let's see what the best place for this is," Jason said.

Kelly drove slowly.

"Stop here."

Jason turned to his wife: "Watch out for me and be a distraction, should someone come by. Understand?"

"Yes."

Jason jumped out and disposed of the remains by dumping out the bags in various places "good distances" from the road, deep into the woods.

As Kelly looked out, two cars came by.

Neither paid attention or stopped.

"When I saw his body parts from the road," Kelly explained near the end of her statement, "I knew that the yellow leaves around the parts would and should highlight it and make it more noticeable."

They said little during the ride back to the house.

When they got home, Jason said, "Get your whore ass downstairs and clean up that mess."

"He made me stay down there for hours before letting me sleep."

During the time she scrubbed and cleaned all the blood, Jason would periodically go down and scream at her.

"You do not deserve to live. But this, this *right here,"* he said, pointing around, *"this is your chance, whore, to do right by me."*

66

BURIED SECRETS

As Jeremy Ogden finished his walkthrough/interview with Kelly at the house, it occurred to the detective that Kelly was spiraling. Making up parts of the story as she went along. Kelly would stop, think about the available evidence they had against her, then tailor her response to it.

"How each situation, in other words, was going to fit into her story," Ogden said later.

In total, Ogden conducted between "one hundred and 150 hours" of interviews with Kelly. She still wasn't under arrest. Kelly could refuse to talk at any time. She could stake claim to her Miranda rights and walk away.

But she kept coming back.

During many of those interviews, Kelly appeared "carefree" about what happened. She tried to show emotion, but couldn't dredge up even the most basic form of empathy or sympathy.

"She carries on with casual conversation," Ogden recalled, "about things that are horrific . . . and all we see is crocodile tears." (This lack of so-called normal, expected reactions is the same trait most psychopaths reveal.)

Interviewing Kelly, Ogden noticed she'd admit to various aspects of the murder and body disposal, jumping around, leaving important details out.

"Souvenirs," Kelly said during one conversation.

"What do you mean?" Ogden asked.

"From Jason's kills . . ."

Kills? Plural?

"Kills!"

Kelly refused to elaborate.

According to Kelly, Jason hid various "souvenirs"—trophies—in one of the Lawrence Street basement cabinets. It was Kelly's job to bury them out at the Pentoga Trail, where they'd dumped Chris. Pentoga Trail was her idea, she told Ogden.

"When?"

"Several weeks before Chris's murder."

The location that Ogden, Frizzo, and the team had first searched with Kelly was not the location where Chris's remains had been dumped. Kelly admitted this near the end of March.

Another admission surrounded the simple act of who drove which vehicle to the park-and-ride.

"I . . . ," Kelly said, before stumbling and correcting herself, "*he* told me to drive."

As for the trash bags, she maintained that Jason carried the bags and dumped them—this admission happened after first claiming they had put Chris in "rubber bins."

Her narrative was evolving.

"I argued with her about this," Ogden said. Since Jason had a bad back, why would she allow him to carry all that weight? If he was the dominant—and he made her clean up all the blood and then make him dinner and would scream at her—why would he not *make* her carry the bags?

She never wavered on this.

After concluding the reenactment video at the house, a short visit to the Caspian Pit and a few other locations close to the house, Ogden drove Kelly back to Indiana.

As the road and landscape passed them by, he began a "casual conversation." Kelly was more than willing to talk. They discussed "schooling"; Kelly said she "took forensic training and psychology."

He thought about this. Then: "You're a cheater."

"That's fucked up," Kelly said.

"I don't mean because of men."

Kelly looked at him.

"I mean, because you went to school to learn all these things and you didn't go to school to learn these things for the greater good of mankind. You went to school to use them to be able to get away with things."

Later, Ogden added: "She didn't educate herself to become a productive member of society. She went to learn how to effectively get away with killing. It was never for the greater good."

Kelly laughed.

"Joke it all away," Ogden said.

There was a quiet moment. Then he said, "So, Kelly, when you going to take credit for your work?"

Kelly stared at him, but held back.

"Come on, talk to me here."

Kelly lit a cigarette and stared out the window.

WHEN THEY ARRIVED IN HOBART, Ogden sat down with Kelly inside HPD. It was March 31, 2016.

"Deep River Park," Kelly said.

"Yeah?"

"I can show you the location of where Jason disposed of a body."

Deep River County Park, out on the Old Lincoln Highway in Hobart, is a gorgeously landscaped, historical park, with a playground for kids and an old gristmill transformed into a visitor's center. The tranquil Deep River runs through the property.

Ogden told Kelly she needed to meet him there.

Along with another detective, he drove to the park and met Kelly.

"Kelly will get you close," Ogden explained, "but still wants you to have to pick for it." That is the power and control characteristic of her psychopathic, serial killer personality. "I always had it in the back of my mind that she was setting something up. I briefed everyone to keep their eyes open. We were walking into the woods or another location with a killer who, I knew, could hide a weapon anywhere out there. . . . I mean, she really wanted us in those woods. I wondered if she was going to put me in a position to have to kill her in defense of myself or others."

Kelly brought them to a specific area along the shoreline of Deep River, a place just beyond the gristmill heading toward a wooded area. Secluded. No one around.

"He put a body in the water," she said, pointing.

"No kidding?"

"Yeah, right here."

The water level was high at the time they stood looking around.

"The level was down a bit when he did it. There was, like, a sandbar over there," Kelly said, motioning toward the middle of the waterway.

They stood for a time. Moved some brush around.

Ogden wasn't biting. He could tell this bothered Kelly.

"Because I wasn't, for example, calling a bunch of people out there to start checking the area and digging and excavating."

"You're not going to say anything?" Kelly asked.

"Well, look, I'm going to need more proof than your word, Kelly. Like who is this person. Then I can confirm a missing person."

Ogden felt like she was leading "us on a wild-goose chase in order to divert the investigation from her role in the Chris Regan murder."

They eventually left. Ogden never tried locating a body near Deep River Park.

Some days later, after a barrage of texts and calls, Kelly never letting up, she claimed to know where a second body was dumped, on the other side of the park.

They went back out. With shovels this time.

"He buried the murder weapon over there."

They dug for a while.

Found nothing.

"You can go, Kelly."

OGDEN SAT AT HIS desk inside HPD working on another case. He had no doubt Kelly was devising another plot to play cat and mouse. It was a matter of time.

Ping.

I found a body. Bones. You need to come here right now. The Park.

Eye roll.

"I'm not functioning on her time schedule, you know," Ogden said later. "She's going to do things on mine, and it's going to be safe for me and my team."

I'm not coming to the park, Kelly.

Come on.

You're telling me you found human remains. You can take a picture and you can send it to me.

My camera is broken.

Well, OK. We'll meet another time.

Not long after, Ogden met Kelly out there. When he arrived, Kelly greeted him with one of her mocking smirks.

"Hey, Kelly, can I see your phone a minute?"

"Sure." She handed it to him.

He took a picture of her and handed the phone back.

"There's no bones out here, Kelly. Quit wasting my time."

67
READY AND WILLING

Jᴇʀᴇᴍʏ Oɢᴅᴇɴ ᴍᴇᴛ ᴡɪᴛʜ Kelly at that same restaurant in Hobart where, while sitting in her truck that night, she admitted Jason had killed Chris Regan.

It was April Fools' Day, 2016. Kelly wanted to talk.

Ogden agreed, though he was growing tired of the runaround. Tired of playing games. Tired of the lies.

He sat down.

Kelly sat across from him.

Ogden recorded the entire conversation on his body cam.

Meanwhile, back in Iron River, Laura Frizzo got busy coordinating a team to search for Chris's remains along the Pentoga Trail. The location Kelly had brought everyone out to was a ruse. Another way for her to delay the inevitable. They were prepared for Ogden to get a new location out of her.

Kelly and Ogden spoke for a time at the restaurant and then drove separately back to HPD. Ogden needed to contain the conversation. Get her in a space he could control. Intimidate her a bit. Ratchet up the pressure.

"I have more information about Chris I want to tell you," Kelly said.

"Okay, good, start," Ogden said, walking in.

They sat down.

"Look, Kelly, one bone. That's all I ask for. I don't care if it's a rib bone, a piece of backbone, whatever. But there's not one bone out there where we've been— and that doesn't make sense to me."

"It doesn't make sense to *you*—but it makes sense to me. I was there."

AS THEY CONTINUED WORKING together, romantic sparks flew between Ogden and Frizzo.

"We texted daily about the case," Frizzo said later. "And, yes, I am immediately in love with this man's mind. In all of my years of working in law enforcement, I have never worked with anyone who thought the way I did—or, especially, the way Jeremy did." The respect she had for his skills was beyond her feelings for him personally. "He saw things exactly how I did, and when I couldn't figure something out, he did. It's like, as clichéd as it sounds, he was the end of all my unfinished sentences. . . . I was completely in love with him. In March, when he came up to see the area to better help him in his investigation, that first time I ever saw him, it was like I had known him forever and I fell even further in love. He didn't know how deep I fell, but I think he could certainly sense it. It was, seriously, like the chemistry was so strong between us, even just on the phone."

There was one day in April 2016 when Ogden and Frizzo conversed nonstop about the case. After one particular exchange, Frizzo said: "Can I ask you a question?"

"Yes."

"Do you want to kiss me?"

Jeremy paused.

Frizzo got nervous. Had she crossed a line?

"Yes," Jeremy said.

Frizzo smiled.

"And our relationship took a very hard turn. And our work together became even better. We had to be careful, though, because there is no way we could allow anything at all to hinder this investigation. We had to always be completely professional, so this was going to be complicated."

FRIZZO AND HER TEAM searched the Pentoga Trail, around April 3, looking for anything that could lead them to finding and identifying Chris and then charging Kelly. Frizzo was up a ways, ahead of the team, walking along a ravine. The water off to her right glistened and sparkled, reminding the chief of the immense beauty she had lived around for most of her life. Save for the fact they were searching for a dismembered body, the landscape was magnificent. It was a sobering moment, the juxtaposition of darkness and light.

As she walked, studying the water and shoreline, Frizzo stopped. There was something in the water.

An arm?

The sight startled her.

"Took my breath away."

Taking a knee, Frizzo went in for a closer look.

"Then I realized it was a branch with small branches at the end of it that looked like fingers."

Deep breath. Her heart in her throat.

The mind and how it could trick you.

"That was one of those points during the investigation," Frizzo later remembered, "when I realized God was trying to prepare me for finding Chris Regan. I knew it would happen."

So certain of what she'd experienced that day, as Frizzo started searching again, she felt something. As she focused on the ground, and scanned the leaves and brush and water, she heard a voice. "Without a doubt, I heard it. A very clear voice."

"Are you ready?"

68

"GAME ON"

JEREMY OGDEN SAT WITH Kelly Cochran at HPD. He wanted answers. She knew damn well where Chris Regan was buried, because she'd admitted the dump location was her idea.

"Kelly, come on . . . just sit down and tell me one time. Just tell me the truth from beginning to end. Just lay it all out here for me."

Kelly rubbed her face. Took a breath.

"Okay."

Kelly broke into what would later become a more thorough, formal statement. She was still telling lies, still shirking the blame, still trying to avoid responsibility and escape justice.

Ogden listened, knowing the story was full of mis-truths. Yet he understood that every time Kelly opened her mouth, the truth was that much closer. So he allowed Kelly her narcissistic rants and self-aggrandized digressions. Sooner or later, Kelly would divulge. Why? Because she could not stop herself. She needed people to know who she was and what she was capable of doing.

"All these stories are coming together," Ogden explained. "But you have to pick out the pieces of truth."

The one fact glaring at Jeremy Ogden was that the day Chris Regan was murdered—October 14, 2014—had been "chosen by them." Chris wasn't brought there for sex, as Kelly had tried to claim. He wasn't lured over to the house for lasagna. Or to spend quality time with Kelly. The obvious evidence supporting this theory was the notion that Jason waited for them to have sex before pulling the trigger, which Kelly had said took about thirty-five minutes.

"That was odd," Ogden continued. "He wouldn't do that if he was the jealous husband looking to kill the boyfriend."

He would have blindsided the guy the moment he walked through the door—before he had sex with his wife in front of him.

The other problem Ogden had, which he explained to Kelly at HPD in mid-April, was the idea that Jason was the bullish husband, telling her what to do, when to do it.

Not a chance.

Kelly balked.

"Look," Ogden said, "I've read some of your texts to your husband." He tossed a few on the table.

Fuck me.

Cook me eggs and fuck me when I get home!

Many of the others Ogden had read were similar: Kelly was in charge.

"And that was the day *after* the murder."

Ogden stared at Kelly.

"Pull your hair back for me."

Kelly did it.

"No scar. No marks whatsoever."

She'd never hit her head falling down the stairs, because she had not tumbled with Chris down those stairs.

Kelly looked down. She drew an invisible circle on the table with her index finger.

"Your entire face would have been black and blue for a week, had you slammed your head and cut it open."

Kelly had no response.

Another important factor was evidence transfer: If Jason and Kelly had driven Chris's car to the park-and-ride when Kelly claimed (and driven their truck to dump his remains), there would have been blood and trace evidence inside both vehicles.

Ogden brought up this uncertainty, noting that if the basement floor was covered with blood, forensics would have found—at the least—bloody footprints or spatter somewhere.

"I changed my shoes."

"Shirts, pants . . . come on, Kelly."

"He and I changed shirts and pants."

Kelly was the one to meet her lovers at the park-and-ride; so there was no question Jason followed her, not the other way around.

The walls were closing in.

"Now," Ogden said, "you said there was a twenty-two-caliber revolver, which the IRPD found, in the house, and you knew where it was."

"Right."

"So you're in fear of a man down in the basement cutting up a body, and you have this gun right there, and you do not go get that gun to defend yourself?"

Kelly stared into space.

"You don't use that gun as protection and get into your truck and drive away?" he added.

"He'd take it away from me!"

"You just shoot him."

No answer.

"You think you could kill Jason?"

"I could never."

As Kelly talked through choosing the actual dump site, she used the pronoun "we" repeatedly.

"There are so many details missing here, Kelly. You're leaving out so much. And in my experience, the only reason people leave out details in *any* investigation is to cover themselves."

Kelly shrugged her shoulders. Looked away.

"What did you two do when you got home from dumping the body?"

Embarrassed, Kelly said, "We had sex."

She laughed.

This is funny?

The following day, October 15, Kelly said they went to Walmart, then grocery shopping, and even stopped at the Peking Chinese Restaurant in town to eat.

Eventually Kelly went over to Chris's apartment that day alone, lying to Jason about where she was going. Again, another opportunity was there for her to run to the IRPD or tell someone what was going on. But she didn't. Instead, she went into Chris's apartment to grab incriminating items she'd left behind—one of which included a camera with "sexually explicit" photos and videos that she and Chris had made together.

Ogden wanted to know why she did not go to the police, tell a passerby what was happening, or relay how "scared" she was.

"I just couldn't do that to Jason."

Kelly talked about a trip she and Jason took in the days

after the murder. They drove to Ashland (two hours away) and Menominee (four hours away), Wisconsin.

Ogden knew the trip wasn't a joyride; they'd likely dumped parts of Chris Regan in various places along the way.

"I was . . . I was drugged up. I do not recall."

They discussed the Post-it note directions found on the front seat of Chris's car. Ogden wasn't buying that a veteran and avid hiker would have any trouble popping Lawrence Street into his GPS and finding the house himself.

Kelly said nothing.

"Did you cry while inside Chris's apartment—you loved this man, you said?"

"No," Kelly said, shaking her head.

APRIL 26, 2016, WAS Chris Regan's birth date. Knowing this, applying a chess move, Ogden got hold of Kelly and asked if they could meet.

"Okay."

Kelly walked into HPD later that morning. Ogden had her sit down in the interview room.

"Hi, Kelly."

"What's up?"

"Look, I know you've lied to me about lots and lots of stuff here."

Kelly admitted to tossing that camera with all the sex photos/videos into a lake where she and one of her boyfriends would go to have sex.

While they continued discussing the lies Kelly had told, he was able to get her to admit "she knew that [Chris Regan] was coming [to the house] to die" that night. She had been texting him, enticing him with sex (that "present" she said during the videotaped walk-and-talk). Equally important was the story about her phone being broken, which was why she claimed to have used Jason's phone to text Chris.

"She uses Jason's phone so what was about to occur would all fall upon Jason, not her," Ogden said.

Kelly planned on setting Jason up for it all—then killing him.

They came to the subject of trophies. Jason kept keepsakes from all "his kills" in a Crown Royal velvet bag, Kelly said.

The detective pressed her about this.

Kelly balked, then took credit, saying they were "her kills," not Jason's. "I have trophies. . . . "

On October 15, Kelly said, she spent the entire day "using gallons of bleach," cleaning up the basement. There was no domineering husband standing over her shoulder, holding a gun to her head while she scrubbed and mopped up blood. Kelly did it because it had to be done. Jason smoked weed all day and took naps.

"You like playing chess, Kelly?"

"Not very good at it."

"Well, look, I think you are pretty damn good at it." Kelly smiled. "We'll see."

This became a recurring theme, both routinely referring to "the moving of the pawns."

Ogden knew nothing about chess. He'd never played.

"Let's talk again tomorrow," he suggested.

"Okay."

Kelly left.

It took about twelve hours for Kelly to make the next move. On April 27, 2016, close to a prearranged time they were supposed to meet, Kelly texted. Her cell service wasn't working so well. She was running late.

Jeremy sensed an urgency; something was up.

She's running . . . shit.

The next day, April 28, after not seeing Kelly at all on April 27, Jeremy texted: **Are you showing up?**

Kelly was scheduled to be there at nine a.m.

It's going to be around ten. Sorry. Running late.

Where? Go to the station and text me.

Ever burn?

Jeremy didn't get it.

Pawn move?

Typo?

Ever been to the West Coast? I was driving last night.

Shit!

What's up? Are you meeting me today? Hello?

This is fun, Kelly texted. **Very interesting.**

Jeremy didn't respond right away.

A while later, Kelly sent a final text of the day.

Game on!

69
THE MONSTER

THE IDEA THAT KELLY would take off was always in the back of Ogden's (and Frizzo's) mind. Kelly was volatile, shaken, backed against a wall of evidence, not to mention using hard-core drugs. The iron fist of justice for not one murder, but two, was a reality—and she knew it.

Ogden texted back an answer to the "Game on" text.

LOL.

He called Frizzo. "I think she's on the run. . . ."

"Shit. I've been talking to Colton, Kelly's brother. He's been saying he's concerned she will take her own life."

An arrest warrant was imminent. Now was not the time, however, to push it through and make mistakes. Frizzo and Ogden needed to be certain they had enough to hold Kelly once they dragged her in under warrant. Still, the clock was ticking: Was Kelly about to end the entire thing with a suicide? With her gone, they'd never find Chris Regan.

Ogden called Lake County dispatch. "I need an emergency ping on a cell phone." It wouldn't be difficult to track Kelly down if she was still using her phone.

Turned out the dispatcher was one of Jason's cousins.

"Okay," Ogden explained, "you have to understand that what we are doing here today, you need to maintain confidentiality, and whatever you do, please, you cannot share the information with any of your family members."

"I don't like her, anyways."

Some time passed and the dispatcher called back.

"Anything?"

"It's likely she's heading to her cousin's house. She's had contact with him over the past few days. She might stop there."

"Where?"

The dispatcher gave Jeremy the cousin's address: Wingo, Kentucky.

Kelly texted Jeremy: **Your move, Detective, See you soon.**

That's funny. Why didn't you just say you were out? NO more conversations?

Ogden didn't immediately hear back. He spoke to dispatch and confirmed Kelly's cell had been used outside Wingo. She'd turn on her phone to text, then turn it off.

I wasn't going to make it that easy for you. I've worked hard, Kelly answered.

Are you going to call me? What's the deal? No more texting. Call.

Frizzo phoned to say she was going to the prosecutor to work on the legal end of things from their end. An arrest warrant would be issued soon.

"I'll call the Marshal's Service," Jeremy said.

They hung up.

Jeremy set up a conference call with the local U.S Marshal's Service, Frizzo, and legal.

"I'm just about to swear the warrant," Frizzo said.

The Marshals were already "rolling their team into Wingo," setting up on a house they'd traced Kelly to.

"I've just been told we have her truck in sight," a Kentucky State Police (KSP) officer on the call said.

The warrant was sworn. Faxed to Kentucky. It was time to move on Kelly Cochran. They had what they needed.

NEAR EIGHT ON THAT same night, Kelly Cochran was taken into custody without incident. She smiled. Laughed. It was clear she was amped up on something, likely meth, considering her face was full of sores from picking at it.

Ogden took the call. At home, he grabbed a beer from his fridge and walked into his garage. Took a moment. Over four beers, he talked to a lieutenant in Kentucky who said Kelly was requesting to give a statement, but wanted Ogden to take it.

Ogden phoned Detective Steve Houck.

"We got her. Can you come with me tomorrow to Kentucky and finish this case?"

"Of course, Jeremy."

"Let's leave soon as possible, actually."

They drove to Kentucky through the night, arriving at the Mayfield Police Department (MPD), where Kelly was being held, near six a.m.

Kelly seemed different. Her hair was shiny, greasy, and unkempt; her skin was pale, and her face full of scabs; plus, she seemed defeated. Not happy about the way it all shook out.

"She became very serious."

Ogden took out a piece of paper. Drew a square box on it:

Kelly looked at the page. Then up at him.

"You are in a box, Kelly. This is where you are. And this is where you will be."

She nodded. Smiled.

"It was after I had explained that she was in a box, and that box was a jail cell, that things changed."

Kelly became engaged in the task at hand. She even started to joke around.

"And I know at that point it's going to be a meaningful conversation," Ogden said later.

"Why did you allow this to happen, Kelly?" he asked.

Kelly dropped her shoulders. Twitched a bit. "Jason," she said. "He wanted his power back."

Ogden understood in that moment Kelly had been in control for a long time and Jason was requesting—within whatever deadly game they'd manufactured—control and power back.

"And on some level . . . he wanted his wife back, also," Ogden commented.

Kelly admitted she knew Jason was in the basement waiting to kill Chris.

"You know, I did not choose this life, it chose me."

It was clear that Kelly was saying she had been brought into this world "this way" and there was nothing she could do about it. So she embraced it.

"Really?"

"It wasn't my choice. Jason wanted his wife back. I had stripped him of too much."

"You're a very controlling person, Kelly, a manipulator."

"It's how I am. I was born that way."

"I know you loved him—loved him more than anyone," Ogden said about Chris Regan. It was another ploy. He did not believe that Kelly Cochran could love anyone—let alone a man she dated, slept with, killed, and dismembered.

She did not respond.

"What was the plan on October fourteenth?"

"Jason wanted to go over to Chris's apartment to kill him."

"That would have been too sloppy, though, right?"

"[Jason] needs me. Of course, it would have been sloppy. Jason does not think."

"So you go to work, right?" Ogden meant that she put her training in forensics and psychology into action.

"Yes."

"Look at me," Ogden said with authority as Kelly drifted off.

Kelly mumbled something about "planning this for a long time." Ogden was unable to catch whether she said "we" or "I." Still, the implication was clear: premeditation.

The "sloppy" part of the murder came up again. Kelly talked about how she and Jason fought the night before, arguing over Jason's desire to kill Chris inside Chris's apartment. It was stupid, Kelly explained, adding how Jason (the sociopath in the relationship) "had emotions" to contend with and could not think rationally with regard to the proper way to commit a murder and get away with it. However, she (the psychopath) did not harbor any of the emotions that would stop her from doing what needed to be done. She could think clearly about committing a murder the "right way," without involving personal feelings or emotions.

After a brief exchange regarding Kelly not wanting to admit premeditation in fear of walking into a "fatal funnel" (Ogden's words), a death sentence, Ogden indicated it was too late for that.

"I planned on killing Jason before he killed Chris," Kelly said.

What stopped her? Ogden wanted to know.

"My emotions clouded my judgment."

A complete contradiction.

They discussed her choices: Jason or Chris?

"There was no choice. I go with Jason."

Ogden focused on Jason, asking if she was worried he would go off on his own and kill Chris. How had she managed the anxiety of Jason, in a rage, heading out when she wasn't around and killing Chris?

"He needs me. If he were to go through with that plan on his own, he would lose. He's . . . not as smart as I am."

They talked about Jason needing Kelly's "blessing to kill Chris." No matter how much he hemmed and hawed about taking matters into his own hands, Kelly knew he didn't have the psychological skills or guts to take it to that extreme.

"He did not get my blessing."

Which meant what? Ogden thought.

All of Kelly's prior talk about Jason killing other people on his own, she might have just now admitted that, more likely, it was her doing.

As they spoke, Kelly became affectless, stoic, and dark. She expressed no remorse and could not hide it.

Killing and dismembering another human being did not bother this woman. Not in the least. Ogden even thought she enjoyed it.

"We had an agreement between us," Kelly said. "Normal people—when they get married, they share agreements or vows. The two of us, our agreement was that if one of us cheated on the other, that it was that person's obligation to kill the lover themselves. And if that person did not kill the lover, then the spouse was entitled to just kill the other spouse."

A murder pact.

Kelly gave an example, using her and Jason.

Ogden wanted to know how Tim Huntley was still alive—that second coworker she was having sex with at the time Chris Regan was murdered.

"We thought about that. You know, but I cared about him. We shared something in common."

"What was that?"

"That [Tim] didn't have a choice with what was given to him throughout his life, post-traumatic stress disorder."

Kelly talked about how Jason had actually pulled up in front of Tim Huntley's house one day and threatened to go in and kill him. But Kelly talked him out of it.

Ogden wondered how she did that.

"Jason worshipped the ground I walked on."

"What do you get out of this 'agreement' between the two of you?"

"Moving the pawns. The prearrangement of what's going to happen or what happens afterward is where the enjoyment for me lies."

The hunt. The stalk. The fantasy of what she is about to do. The constant thought of taking a life. Playing God.

Killing, by effect, made Kelly feel more alive than anything else: sex, drugs, booze, romance.

The interview bounced around. Kelly tried "misdirecting" Ogden any way she could. He kept refocusing her. He encouraged Kelly to stay on one specific aspect of the murder or cleanup, her and Jason's roles, but she'd veer off.

"I hope for a male judge," Kelly said at one point, a smile on her face. She obviously thought if she had manipulated the men in her world as easy as she had, why not a judge?

Ogden said it could be male or female.

"He wanted *me* to kill Chris," Kelly said after another digression.

"Did you have your gun on you?"

"He wanted me to either kick him down the stairs or do whatever I needed to do."

"What'd you think about that?"

"Couldn't do it. So I had sex with him. I gave him a blow job and then I had sex. It occurred in the middle of sex. I knew I couldn't kill him. I don't know why I couldn't. Maybe the feelings?"

As she thought about it, Kelly said the sex was also a manipulation—that is, not to manipulate Chris, but Jason. She knew if Jason saw them having sex, it would help dredge up the courage and rage to kill.

The reason Kelly pretended to extract the bullet out of Chris's head—but didn't really remove it—was not because she was scared of her husband. Rather, she was planning on framing Jason for the murder. It was his gun. He had shot Chris. That bullet in the head represented evidence of Jason killing her lover in a jealous rage.

She described Jason cutting Chris's body up as "creepy."

Ogden said, "You're a unicorn."

"Wait, what?"

"A unicorn."

Kelly asked for an explanation.

"You are about one percent of the population. Actually, about point-zero-seven of the population, to be exact." Ogden was tossing numbers out. The female serial killer—which he had a strong inclination Kelly Cochran was—is rare among serials, less than 10 percent. "You know, Kelly, I've worked my whole career for meaning and purpose. I want to do something good for people. You also have meaning and purpose."

"A godlike purpose. To give and take."

"You've taken a lot."

They talked about the Bible.

"Hundreds of times I've read it," Kelly said.

"Favorite chapter?"

"Romans."

"What do you think about the Bible?"

"It's fucked-up shit. . . . I don't understand why people have it or believe in it."

After she was arrested, investigators found a copy of the *DSM Manual* in Kelly's truck. The *Diagnostic and Statistical Manual of Mental Disorders* is an analytic tool psychologists use to diagnose people with personality disorders. As a professional, educational text, it is updated annually.

Kelly had dog-eared various pages describing different disorders. She was both self-diagnosing and searching for weaknesses in those around her to easily exploit.

Ogden found this interesting.

The subject stimulated Kelly.

He asked about the dismemberment. Jason did it, Kelly insisted. As Jason began, she stood by and watched.

"I loved him," Kelly supposedly said to Jason, looking on as he prepared to cut Chris Regan into pieces.

Jason looked down at Chris's body, the SAWZALL in his hands. "What piece?" Kelly claimed her husband asked.

Ogden contained his disgust.

From inside the cab of her truck, investigators recovered several suicide letters addressed to different people. Ogden focused on one in particular, which was addressed to Kelly's mother and father. In it, Kelly spoke of the reason she could never be honest: *to protect you.* She was facing her own "fate" now. Kelly wrote, *"[Most people] only knew a small piece of the bigger picture."* Concluding, she wrote: *[I know] how crazy this sounds . . . but I really did love Jason, too. . . . I know that sounds pathetic and slutty . . . Please forgive me for becoming a monster.*

She admitted killing Jason, claiming she saw it as a way to give *closure to Chris's family without Jason [ending up] in jail for the rest of his life.*

Kelly surprisingly gave law enforcement props, writing how she had told everyone in her life that cops were "tearing up" their lives during the investigation, but *[I know] they were just doing their jobs.*

Finally Kelly wrote she was surprised and "happy" that some of what took place hurt her feelings: *Because I didn't want to think of myself as a heartless monster. But, in actuality, I was the monster.*

70

HELA

On May 16, 2017, Laura Frizzo took a call from a police officer she had been working with since searching for Chris's remains. Frizzo had used Alyssa Palmer, with the Madison (Wisconsin) Police Department, and her K9, Hela, on several different occasions, along with several additional K9s and handlers.

"Laura, it's Alyssa."

"Hey, what's up?"

"I'm in the area until tomorrow if you need Hela and [me] for any reason."

Frizzo hadn't yet thought about calling in a K9. Palmer was the closest dog handler to Iron River—a seven-hour drive away. For Frizzo, this call was more of Chris Regan speaking to her: *"Are you ready?"*

Frizzo told Palmer she'd get back to her. Next, she called Kelly Cochran, who was being held in Iron County after being extradited from Kentucky.

Hanging up with the jail, Frizzo drove over to see Kelly in person.

"I'll never forget Kelly walking into the courtroom all arrogant in her shackles to be arraigned. She told the judge how she'd just spent the last few days in a 'box' while in transport and was really pissed off," Frizzo recalled.

The chief and Kelly shared "girl talk" that afternoon. Frizzo stood on one side of the bars, Kelly inside her new box.

"Kelly agreed to come with me the next morning and show me various locations. I called Alyssa back to set it up."

"Sure. See you soon. But I have to leave by nightfall to get back to work." Palmer was a full-time Madison police officer.

Frizzo hung up. She felt something. How it all came together.

Tomorrow is going to be the day.

Still, how many times had she told herself that over the past year and a half?

FIRST THING THE NEXT morning, May 17, after Jeremy Ogden sent Laura Frizzo additional intel he had obtained from his conversations with Kelly, they had a new area of focus.

Palmer and Hela met Frizzo, Kelly, and several law enforcement officers out along the Pentoga Trail, specifically in an area where Kelly was certain they'd dumped Chris's remains.

Hela, a female Belgian Malinois, was trained to detect the odor of actively decomposing and decomposed human remains. Hela's "indication" sign was to sit when she sniffed remains. She'd taken part in ten searches throughout Wisconsin, Illinois, and Michigan. She had recovered three sets of human remains while accumulating two hundred hours of field training.

It was fifty-four degrees when they got going, with sunlight beaming through thick, dark clouds. Kelly pointed Frizzo to an area just south of the actual trail, 1 2/3 miles southwest of U.S. Route 2, in Crystal Falls Township, Iron County. The area itself consisted of "thick woods, some open areas, and an all-terrain vehicle trail." It was several miles north of that original area where Kelly had brought them.

Helping Frizzo was Officer Roy D'Antonio, along with several Iron River County deputies.

Kelly said, "I don't want the dog handler or anyone else to follow us to the location until I find it. Then we're ready to call them in."

Frizzo could imagine Ogden whispering in her ear: *"She's always up to something. Be cautious and careful. Never trust Kelly."*

After some discussion with her colleagues, Frizzo had Palmer and Hela hang out at the intersection of U.S. 2 and the Pentoga Trail.

Kelly, Frizzo, and several deputies headed into the woods.

As they walked, Kelly talked. She seemed different. She had a defeated aura about her, riddled with that entitled sense of hubris she could not hide. Had she turned a corner? Was she now falling into the role of the serial killer who wants to show the world her work—the psychopath who believes she is invincible? Not all serials go down this road. Some clam up and refuse to talk to anyone; while others are far too narcissistic to contain their need for attention and the spotlight. They crave the recognition that comes with being branded one of the most rare creatures on earth.

"Over there," Kelly said. She pointed.

They walked. Kelly identified a location not too far into the woods from where they'd left their vehicles. About thirty yards.

"I discreetly marked the location she gave me with a black glove," Frizzo said later.

Frizzo called Palmer.

"Come out here and start," Frizzo said. She explained the glove.

Kelly and Frizzo stood about one hundred feet away and looked on.

Hela immediately sniffed upward, her nose in the air. Then, tail wagging, the dog took off directly south toward a tree Kelly had identified.

The K9 circled the tree a few times and sat back, indicating a possible "source."

Commanded to continue, Hela bolted east and headed for an area approximately twenty-five feet from the tree.

She circled.

Then focused on a leaf pile.

Frizzo and Palmer walked over.

A black garbage bag, somewhat embedded into the ground by the elements, was the first indication they were getting close.

There was nothing inside the bag.

Frizzo pointed it out to forensics.

For a few hours, they combed the entire area Hela had picked up on, doing what Frizzo called "a cursory search."

Hela was active and excited. Locking onto something.

Not finding any remains, they decided to move on to other locations.

Palmer drove Hela, with the team following behind, to 66 Lawrence Street, the Cochran house. She wanted the dog to sniff around. Pick up a scent of some sort. Hela had locked onto something back at the trail. To further build upon that, knowing that Chris was murdered inside the house, it seemed logical to bring the K9 to the original crime scene.

Hela sniffed around the garage out back and followed a scent into the house itself. As she entered, Hela stopped, pointed her nose in the air, sniffed.

From there, Hela ran out to the shed on the property, specifically focused on one wall.

At approximately 3:30 p.m., Palmer wrote in her report, *Hela provided a formal indication that she detected the odor of human remains.*

They did not find anything.

Inside the house, Kelly leaned against her old countertop in the kitchen. Frizzo stood nearby.

"Have some pizza," Frizzo said.

Kelly took a slice and began eating. Wiping her hands, she pointed to the counter.

"There you go."

"Excuse me," Frizzo said.

The forceps she had used to dig into Chris's skull in front of Jason sat on the counter.

As they kept looking around the house, Frizzo and her team found the magazine tube for the rifle Jason used to shoot Chris.

Kelly pointed that out, too.

"It was where she said it would be," Frizzo said later. "Two days later, divers would recover the gun used to kill Chris in the Caspian Pit, exactly where she said it would be."

Kelly was telling the truth.

Frizzo met with her team and decided, because time was running short with Hela and Palmer, to go back out to the trail.

By five p.m., everyone was tired and drained.

Palmer had marked all the areas they'd searched earlier with a GPS tracking device.

"I have to get going back to Madison," Palmer said to Frizzo.

Frizzo was frustrated and certain this was the place.

Kelly was taken back to the jail.

"Alyssa, can you please go with me to one more location? It's not too far. It's along the trail. Give me one more hour with Hela?"

Palmer agreed.

"When we got out of our cars, Hela ran back to the tree area the bag had been found. Then she started to work eastward."

Frizzo and Palmer followed.

They came to a clearing.

Hela bolted east. Started barking.

Frizzo and Palmer looked at each other.

"Alyssa was a few steps ahead of me as I was texting Mike Neiger, asking if he was available the following day to come and assist me in searching the area more thoroughly."

When Frizzo looked in the direction Hela was barking, Palmer turned and looked at Frizzo.

Palmer put her hand over her mouth.

Frizzo ran toward them.

Arriving at the scene, she looked beyond where Palmer stood, Hela nearby.

There was a large rock. Hela sat by it, staring at them, waiting for her next command.

Palmer and Frizzo walked around the rock.

A skull, partially embedded in the ground, stared up at them.

Frizzo immediately went over to it and knelt down in a prayer position. She took a moment.

"I was in shock and speechless. The tears didn't even come like I expected. For almost two years, I had imagined my reaction when or even if I ever found Chris Regan. It was always such a roller coaster. . . . I just knelt there and played the entire investigation over through my mind and prayed. I thanked Chris for being by my side and directing me to him. He was with me throughout the entire investigation. And even after."

Later that night, Frizzo stopped at the jail to thank Kelly for validating herself.

"I now knew that most likely other things she showed me that day were accurate—and, as it turned out, they were. It was a good day for Kelly. And I firmly believe that my hours of 'girl talk,' as Kelly called it, allowed her to be honest that day. Telling me she was born the way she is, [and] has no remorse or sympathy. It's nothing that happened to her during her life to cause her to be this way—it's just who she is. This is the same day she told me she lied when she said Jason kept a 'trinket bag,' the first I'd heard trophies from victims called that. Still, I knew then it was *her* bag, not his."

"I believe in evil," Kelly said at one point while they talked. "It took less than a minute to suffocate [Jason]."

"What made you choose a victim?" Frizzo asked.

"Opportunity."

71

SEARCHING

On May 23, 2017, Jeremy Ogden spoke with Kelly. She was cleaned up. A bit more pep in her step, and still that unbridled cockiness.

"How many?"

"Several others," Kelly said. She didn't want to say exactly. She handed Ogden a list, adding, "Multiple people."

The list contained the names of several people Kelly claimed to have killed.

Ogden concluded the conversation. He handed the list to the prosecutor. They would need to investigate each name to see if she was telling the truth, or building herself into some kind of diabolical female serial killer.

AT THE TIME, KELLY had thirteen butterfly tattoos of various sizes, shapes, and types up one arm and down the other.

Frizzo asked her about it. To mostly everyone involved, those butterflies were another trinket (trophy): representing victims she'd killed, a majority of whom she fed to her and Jason's pigs.

"She described that night what the butterfly symbolizes to her," Frizzo recalled.

"To me, Kelly, the butterfly is a symbol of new life," Frizzo told her.

Kelly chuckled. "The butterfly, Detective, is a symbol of death. You see, when there is a corpse, butterflies will be all over it."

Frizzo had no response.

When Ogden asked Kelly about the tattoos, she said, "They symbolize dead family members."

"Which family members?"

She couldn't name them.

"It was apparent from the beginning," Ogden concluded, "that she had this fascination with butterflies. I asked her where it began. She said that while she was in college she went on a trip to the Body Farm in Tennessee." This is a well-respected research facility on the grounds of the University of Tennessee, in Knoxville. Decomposition of cadavers is studied there in a variety of settings. Each body is viewed in a differing state of decomposition. Anthropologist and mystery novelist Dr. William Bass runs the Body Farm. "She said that butterflies were all over the cadavers while she was there, and she thought it was 'cool.'"

Later, Kelly would add to this, according to Ogden: "She claimed her butterfly tattoos were for fallen loved ones . . . but I think they have to do with her victims. Just like her drawings of large trees with the all-seeing eyes. They are significant also."

Kelly Cochran did nothing without reason or purpose.

"It's fascinating because you will find more butterflies on a decaying body than you'll ever find flies or maggots." Regarding this observation, Kelly laughed, adding: "That's not something normal people see, but . . . it's the idea of beauty (butterfly) and death (decaying body). I've thought about this a lot. It's life and death. It's life *from* death."

Kelly told me in 2018 that she no longer had thirteen butterfly tattoos.

"Nineteen now," she said with a smile.

"The reason why we did not find much blood any-where in the house," Ogden said, "was because I believe she and Jason set up a *Dexter* room in the basement." Meaning, they tacked plastic everywhere downstairs, cre-ating a clever, contained room, much like a cocoon, where they could cut up a body and then remove the plas-tic, thus discarding all of the blood and forensic and trace evidence.

"Downstairs, as I looked around," Ogden concluded, "I found staples in the joists and ceiling and all over the walls, left over, I think, from the plastic. And that smell the night of the burning barrel [that] neighbors reported? That wasn't flesh burning. It was the blood-soaked plas-tic."

PART 5

A JUST CAUSE

72

SEXUAL DIGRESSION

HE GOT RIGHT INTO IT. Henry (pseudonym) had the hots for Kelly Cochran—and was not shy about sharing his feelings.

After a series of articles about Kelly—one in *Rolling Stone* magazine, which posed the question of Kelly Cochran possibly being a notorious female serial killer—appeared, Henry began writing. "Beautiful" was how he generally addressed Kelly in his letters from the prison cell he occupied to the prison cell she occupied while awaiting trial. Kelly had sent Henry a butterfly picture she'd drawn. He thought it was "cute." Early into this letter, Henry said he hoped his support was comforting. Kelly was facing serious charges: *Worse than mine, sweetheart.* He told Kelly she was "full of love" and did not "deserve" what she was "going through."

Henry was either confused or Kelly had lied to him. He believed she had once lived in Kentucky and, because of that, had a "cute Southern accent."

Describing himself as Greek, with dark complexion and dark hair, Henry had lived back east before heading west, settling in a Michigan prison for a violent felony involving guns not long after relocating. He'd left his home, he said, to look after his ill aunt and a sick family member living in Michigan, but, instead, wound up in prison.

In another letter, Henry talked about his life behind bars: He slept until noon, ate, worked out from three to five p.m., played cards until eight-thirty, on most nights worked out again, then retired back to his cell for bedtime, where he read and wrote. Then got up at noon the following day to do it all over again.

Institutionalized Groundhog Day.

Henry mentioned tattoos. He spoke of how sexy he thought they were on a woman: *I love it, a huge turn on.* He told Kelly that butterflies are "cute," before asking "where" her butterfly tattoos were on her body and how many she had.

Kelly had mentioned in a previous letter she'd married a psychopath. Henry said he'd known a few, and they "suck."

By page nine, Henry began asking specific questions. How, for example, he preferred long letters, so Kelly could feel free to write as much as she wanted. He then wondered if Kelly was "currently seeing" someone? *"[I love an] intelligent, sexy woman, not to mention [one who rides] the wild side.* He talked about Kelly mentioning in a previous letter how much she liked all of the sexual positions he had previously asked her about. It became the main topic of Henry's letter as he presented Kelly with a sexual questionnaire he'd written specifically for her.

He loved naughty girls, and because of that, he was attempting to see "how naughty" Kelly "could get."

He asked Kelly, *"[Do you like] giving head?*

4 play?
What about being *licked up n down?*
Eaten?
Hair pulled?
Called dirty names?
Choked?
Spanked?
"Slow n gentle? Hard n fast?"

ENDING HIS LIST of twenty-one sexual questions, Henry asked if Kelly took pleasure in being picked up and "slammed against a wall" while having passionate, wild sex?

Henry's favorite sexual position was to pull his partner's hair while doing her doggy-style and spanking her ass.

Henry warned Kelly not to allow "jail to control" her. Instead, she needed to control it.

Saving perhaps his most humble and humane moment for last, Henry concluded that he was going to "pray" for Kelly. He didn't want Kelly to get wrapped up in jail life for fear of what it could do to her soul. He encouraged her to focus on getting out and them being together.

As a postscript, besides letting his new girl know he was going to send her money if the jail allowed, he wrote: *Keep a smile on that beautiful face.* As time moved on, he emphasized: *It* will *get better.*

73

ATONEMENT

KELLY SAT, WEARING A pink sweater, one leg crossed over the other. She stared at Circuit Court for the County of Iron judge Richard Celello. She seemed rather content within this formal legal setting. Attempting to present herself as the battered, innocent wife, Kelly had her hair pulled back and tied in a ponytail. After several days of jury selection and hearings regarding evidence, on Tuesday, February 14, 2017, Judge Celello welcomed and thanked jurors, banged his gavel, and asked the lawyers to begin with opening statements.

Ironically, it was Valentine's Day. The victim, Christopher Regan, represented by the state, had been Kelly's lover. Kelly was given her "day in court," where she was determined to paint Jason Cochran as a domineering and abusive husband. According to Kelly, by using fear, intimidation, physical violence, and emotional bullying, Jason had forced her to help him murder Chris Regan, dismember his body, and dump it in the woods.

In early October 2016, after discussing it with Chris's

family, prosecutor Melissa Powell presented two plea offers to Kelly and her team.

It has been my policy on murder cases to not extend any plea offer unless and until I have the family's blessing, Powell wrote in a formal plea letter. *This matter was more heinous than other murder cases committed in our area, when one considers how long Christopher Regan's remains were missing and the mutilation of the body following the killing. The family, however, is aware that without Miss Cochran's recent cooperation Christopher Regan's remains may not have been discovered and agrees some leniency may be appropriate. Furthermore, the family wants to honor Christopher Regan and put his remains to rest.*

The deal Powell had been "authorized" to make was generous. In exchange for an acceptable plea of guilty, *[and] an amended count one of Second Degree Murder and count five Lying to a Police Officer . . . the People agree to a sentencing . . . of twenty-five to fifty years and dismissal of the remaining charges,* Powell wrote.

The plea offer was set to expire at four p.m. on October 31, 2016.

Kelly rejected it.

The second offer was twenty to forty years. Again, very generous—considering that Kelly would later claim Chris was alive when Jason dismembered him in front of her.

This second offer was set to expire on January 20, 2017.

Kelly said no.

JUST BEFORE OPENING STATEMENTS began, Kelly came forward and decided she wanted the second offer.

"The jury had been selected," Melissa Powell later said, "and she, all of a sudden, wanted to plead to second-degree murder. We were pretty far into our trial preparation by that time and expended considerable resources to prepare for trial. However, we took a break. Chief Frizzo, Chris Regan's family, and myself discussed whether to proceed with trial or allow her to plead."

That discussion took several hours, "with tension running high." As a prosecutor, Melissa Powell was in favor of a guaranteed plea, if it was the right deal for everyone involved. A plea ends a murder case; there can be no appeals. "The family and Chief Frizzo felt strongly that Kelly Cochran was playing games, being manipulative, and once again calling the shots. They agreed to go forward with trial."

The one problem moving forward was that Melissa Powell intended to introduce Chris's skull as evidence, which meant that if Kelly was convicted, any evidence would be secured and would remain with the case file for a minimum of seventy-five years.

"They would never be able to lay his remains to rest—unless other remains were discovered."

LAURA FRIZZO WAS NO longer chief of the IRPD. In October 2016, Frizzo had been "officially relieved of her duties" by the city manager, David Thayer. According to various public reports, Thayer would not allow Frizzo to return to work after a short medical leave that September.

Frizzo's attorney, Roy Polich, explained publicly that Frizzo had been "put on furlough by the city on October 4, 2016." He subsequently requested ("several times") the matter to be placed on the city council's monthly agenda meetings so Frizzo could tell her side of the story in an open forum.

Members of the council declined each request.

In a press release issued by Polich, he explained that his client had asked for "personal days" off from work, following what was a long preparation period for preliminary examination testimony leading up to Kelly's trial. According to Polich, the city manager ordered Frizzo to be back at work unless she provided a doctor's excuse, meaning a note.

Frizzo provided the city manager with the requested paperwork indicating she needed time off to mentally prepare for the road ahead.

On September 23, 2016, Frizzo told Thayer she would be able to return to work on September 28. He responded by setting a meeting for October 4, requiring a "return to work doctor's report." According to Polich's release, at that meeting: *Thayer did not allow Frizzo to return to work, even though she provided the requested doctor's report, which allowed her to resume her full duties as police chief.*

In other words, Frizzo had to fight for permission to take time off from work—and then, in turn, fight to return to work.

It became a bureaucratic and public debacle. Frizzo should have been given the key to the city for sticking with her instincts and pursuing the Cochrans; instead, she was essentially fired.

The city manager told Frizzo he wanted "a second doctor's opinion," according to Polich's release. But this time, the city bureaucrats would select the doctor.

A month later, the city elders selected a physician, and on November 2, according to Frizzo and her attorney:

"She saw the appointed doctor and was cleared to return to work, but was still denied to resume her duties as police chief by Thayer."

Polich claimed the entire process was nothing more "than a ruse, contrived by Thayer to deceive the public and city council of his personal desire to terminate her," suggesting further that the city manager "has a history of animosity toward women."

Thayer "vehemently denied the allegations," and said they were untrue. His decision to fire Frizzo was rooted in a "conflict with her management style."

That December, at a town council meeting, droves of community members came out in support of Frizzo, demanding she be reinstated.

Didn't happen.

Frizzo vowed to sue the city.

WITH A BIT OF court business settled, first thing in the morning, February 14, 2017, Melissa Powell turned and whispered something in Frizzo's ear, who sat at the prosecution's table with Powell. Being the lead investigator throughout the case, she was allowed, as a law enforcement officer, to be present at the prosecution's table—regardless of the ongoing battle with the city.

Then the PA stood and walked to the lectern.

Powell took a moment to get herself comfortable. She looked directly at jurors, her back to Kelly and Kelly's attorney, Michael Scholke.

Clearing her throat, Powell began by introducing what was a ghastly theme: "Bonded in Blood." She used carefully selected photos and PowerPoint slides projected onto a large screen behind her on the wall, underscoring the most powerful evidence against Kelly.

Powell then went through the investigation, step-by-step, beginning with who the Cochrans were, the breakdown of their marriage, all those extramarital affairs, and how and when Kelly introduced Chris Regan into their lives. To her credit, Powell memorialized Chris not as a victim of murder, but as a father, veteran, and hardworking single man, who'd happened to cross paths with Satan. She also made it clear—without specifics—that Kelly chose Chris as her victim. Once she met him, she knew he would eventually be one more murder victim in what was alluded to being a long list of people the Cochrans had possibly murdered, dismembered and fed to the pigs they'd raised.

About six minutes into her statement, Powell said: "The officers began pulling people in for interviews. On October 28, 2014, Jason Cochran and Kelly Cochran were interviewed at the Iron River Police Department, separately. This is when 'Fifty Shades of Kelly' started."

"During this interview," Powell continued, Kelly explained how she'd visited Chris Regan's house five or six nights per week for dinner. "That he had come over to her house two or three times. . . ." Jason knew about the affair, Powell reiterated, "and that Chris wasn't the only man she was seeing. Her husband accepted these relationships."

Using those points to pivot, Powell spoke of a brutal, orchestrated, premeditated murder plan initiated by a husband and his wife. For thirty-five minutes, she gave jurors a taste of each aspect of the investigation and how law enforcement ultimately charged Kelly Cochran with Chris's murder.

Soft-spoken, Powell had a charming, sincere affect, concluding: "Kelly and Jason Cochran were bonded in blood. As you can see from [their] text messages [to each other], what was a failing marriage in August and September 2014 became a *lovefest* after Chris Regan was killed on October 14, 2014."

She paused. Gave the moment its due.

"At the end of this case, the people will be requesting you find the defendant guilty of all charges, but, in particular, we will be asking you to find the defendant guilty for aiding and abetting Jason Cochran in the murder of Christopher Karl Regan by plotting and planning his death and luring him to his funeral."

Powerful. Effective. Direct.

MIKE SCHOLKE HAD A mountain to climb, in a blinding wind, perhaps with snow falling. Heavyset, well-dressed, and young-looking, Scholke represented a client who'd admitted the most heinous acts of murder on record—scenes straight out of a horror film. Kelly's own admissions had been captured on video and audio; the jury would be able to deliberate and discern her recorded words. The claim of spousal abuse was Kelly's only hope at a mitigating conviction of second-degree murder or acquittal.

"In some way," Scholke said a few minutes in, "we don't concede the facts . . . *some* of the facts. We will concede, and we believe the evidence will show, that Mr. Regan was shot—shot in the head, that his body was dismembered, and it was left in the woods off Pentoga Trail."

Scholke made a point to say the defense believed "that Jason, Mr. Cochran, acted alone . . . and that Kelly had no knowledge . . . that that was going to happen."

A big, bold proclamation—especially when all of the evidence pointed to the opposite.

Kelly's polished lawyer further stated that they would stand behind one unimpeachable assertion: "In regard to the dismemberment and disposal of the body, that Jason, again, was the driving force in these acts and that any role Kelly had was the result of her fearing for her life and safety."

Kelly Cochran's own recorded admissions would patently contradict several of these points.

Scholke brought Jason's "mental health issues" into his opening, specifically his "hospitalization" near the time of the murder.

It all fit, Kelly's attorney suggested.

Although the prosecution would present some "fifty witnesses," Scholke said, "none of these people can tell you with any certainty what happened in that house. . . ."

True. Yet, Scholke left out that Kelly had murdered the only other witness, Jason—before providing law enforcement with that "certainty."

Scholke then broached the elephant in the room: Kelly's own words. He warned jurors: "I'll tell you right now, you're going to hear . . . numerous versions of the story. Facts were added. Facts were deleted. Things were changed."

There was no evidence to support this. Here was the man climbing the mountain, pushing back on the unchallengeable, pervasive elements.

Kelly's competent, smart, likeable defense attorney then used the "tip of the iceberg" analogy to explain the case from his client's point of view, encouraging jurors to wait on judgment until the "entire story" was presented.

Regarding fairness, Scholke concluded, jurors should think about the scales Lady Justice holds in her hands— the balance between evidence and witness testimony.

"Use your best judgment."

74

CRUISE CONTROL

BY TWO TWENTY-ONE P.M. on that first day, February 14, 2017, Terri O'Donnell had told her story of opening up the mystery back on October 27, 2014. Sergeant Cindy Barrette followed, along with several additional police officers. Then Laura Sartori, Kelly's ex-boss at Oldenburg, filled in the blanks surrounding that early narrative and how Kelly became a name law enforcement had focused on.

Their stories never changed.

The facts never wavered.

Truth spoke for itself.

It is, as they say, what it is.

DAY TWO, FEBRUARY 15, opened with Tim Huntley, the coworker Kelly was seeing at Oldenburg at the time of Chris Regan's murder. Tim laid down a good base of logistical facts. He pointed out how Kelly knew where the park-and-ride in Bates Township was located because she had met him there on several occasions. He said she would disappear from time to time without explanation. Seemed strange.

It was clear Tim Huntley felt fortunate to be alive. He could have easily wound up dead.

"I believe he was Jason and Kelly's next intended victim," Jeremy Ogden said later.

MSP detective Chris Bracket, sergeant Tom Rajala, and a third MSP detective talked jurors through the early aspects of the MSP's role in the investigation: The MSP questioned Jason and Kelly and found inconsistencies—and yet no major piece of evidence made investigators believe, at least not then, that Jason and Kelly murdered Chris Regan.

The evidence Powell was able to get in through these witnesses built another layer on top of a mounting case: transcripts of the early Cochran interviews, cell phone records (including texts), and various screenshots of texts. Each spoke to the Cochrans' subtle lies.

Truth is universal. It never evolves.

Shifting gears, setting her case into cruise control, Powell did a great job with her witnesses walking jurors through the A to Z narrative of the investigation, including how frustrating it had become for Laura Frizzo, who felt like she was being run in circles by Kelly and Jason.

One of the Cochrans' neighbors, David Saylor, made an appearance on day three, along with several additional law enforcements officers. All of this, including the evidence Powell introduced, set the stage for Laura Frizzo's testimony. (State evidence included phone records, the Cochran computer hard drive, and the telematics from Chris's car, proving where he went and when. There were fingerprints, photos, and additional transcripts from interviews with Kelly and Jason.)

Frizzo detailed her entire investigation, from beginning to end. She came across as honest, detail-oriented, believable, but also a little naive with regard to what she had become entangled in. Frizzo kept up pressure on Kelly and Jason even when, she told jurors, she felt push back from certain investigators. They had questioned her instincts and balked about spending money, but never demeaned her abilities. Was she chasing the wrong kite in the wind? Was she overlooking some sort of glaring truth everyone else but her could see?

Through Frizzo's testimony, Powell introduced one piece of crushing evidence after the next, burying Kelly bit by bit. Videos. Kelly's revolver. The forceps (which Kelly had pointed out on the counter inside the house). Basement floor swabs. The Cochran back door. Ceiling tiles. Calls Frizzo had with Kelly. Hats with hairs. Lab reports. A video of a "field trip" Frizzo had taken Kelly on into the woods to search for Chris's remains. The charred SAWZALL blade used to cut a human being into pieces. The pit. Interviews with neighbors and siblings and friends.

On, and on, and on, the evidence piled up, supported by testimony explaining how Frizzo followed this case relentlessly. Clearly, without the chief's dogged tenacity, Chris Regan's murder would have never been solved—with additional victims likely murdered.

Another absolute fact.

The majority of the forensic case the state built was going to be in the hands of the jury once deliberations began. The technical end of it would come into play with the medical examiner and forensic examiners, but Frizzo's work involved assembling and presenting that evidence. How the chain of custody was followed by the book—plus, how thorough and constant Frizzo's persistence had been to prove that Kelly and Jason Cochran had murdered Chris Regan.

Frizzo closed out the first weekend, February 17, a Friday. Then she took the stand to conclude her testimony on Monday, February 20.

Frizzo had taken this case on, with Chris Regan guiding her in spirit, and she followed the evidence, making sure not to cloud anything she did with personal feelings. Scholke tried as best he could to poke holes in Frizzo's work, but the facts were strong, sobering, and unshakable. Frizzo followed the evidence, which repeatedly led back to two people—never anyone else. And when Jason died by Kelly's hand, one suspect was left—one culprit to keep pursuing.

Throughout that day, the FBI sent in its representative to break down all of the phone records connected to the case; Hobart PD detective Steve Houck explained his small—but important—role; a forensic specialist explained the blood and trace evidence; and retired MSP detective, Mike Neiger, now a body hunter, spoke of how he helped Frizzo during a tireless search for Chris's remains. Witness after witness was able to show jurors through his or her work that the case had been driven by Kelly and Jason Cochran's admissions.

Nothing more.

By the time Jeremy Ogden took the oath and sat inside the witness-box on Wednesday, February 22, all of the groundwork for his cat-and-mouse game with Kelly was set.

After Ogden went through his impressive credentials, Powell asked about his introduction to Kelly.

"What, if anything, did she say to you regarding 'other relationships'?"

Ogden talked about Tim Huntley and Chris Regan. Kelly seemed open to discuss only those subjects she felt comfortable with and where she believed she could manipulate the situation. Early on, she was composed and collected, while being backed into a corner. Ogden had always made her think she had the upper hand.

He had asked Kelly about her lesbian relationships, adding how Kelly was open about the girl she met at the fast-food restaurant. She'd recruited the girl for Jason, he told jurors, but she had begun a sexual relationship with her separately.

Kelly was firm, especially when it pertained to talking about Chris's murder, telling Ogden: "'You shouldn't be asking me questions about something I don't know nothing about.'"

As Ogden and Powell talked about Kelly's demeanor, body language, and "tells," he said, "She smiled at me [at one point], and she told me that if I wanted her to have any respect for her—and she for me—that I would have to tell it like it is."

"And was her response important to you?"

"Yes."

"Why?"

"It's the hook. It's the moment where she changes the table and she's the one who's engaging to talk to me. She's now going to try to seek information from me—and it's *very* important."

Patience.

Persistence.

Rapport.

All of it was part of Jeremy Ogden's arsenal of investigative tools to get Kelly to talk about what actually had happened.

Ogden went through many of the interviews he'd conducted with Kelly, which allowed Powell to introduce a series of body-cam videos into the record, including several recorded inside HPD.

Ogden's testimony went into Thursday, February 23. He opened that day discussing how he used Chris's birthday as a way to rattle Kelly.

And it worked.

By then, several months into their cat and mouse, Kelly was talking details of the murder plan. Ogden had caught her in so many lies it was hard for Kelly to keep track. She'd routinely contradict herself without realizing it.

Powell ended her direct examination by asking Ogden to talk about the suicide letters Kelly had written in Kentucky, which they'd confiscated under search warrant inside her truck. Kelly had admitted to being a psychopath, which she had figured out early in life. Playing a role in Chris's murder was part of her accepting who she was.

If jurors read those letters the way he had, Ogden explained, it was not hard to see she had admitted to being the mastermind behind Chris Regan's murder.

"To your knowledge," Powell asked, "is the serial killer—or 'the list' [of additional victims Kelly mentioned]—is that a dead issue or closed investigation?"

"No, it's open as long as she wants it to be. And whenever she wants it to continue, it will."

Scholke began his cross asking Ogden about the emotion Kelly displayed in the beginning of their encounter. How she could be seen and heard crying at times during the recordings, which indicated how upset she was by the conversations and events.

"During that [first] interview, she was rather emotional?"

"Or show," Ogden said, stopping, correcting himself. "She appeared to *try* to *display* emotion."

Scholke stayed on this, pointing out that Ogden was not a psychiatrist. He couldn't read people's minds. Therefore, he was basing his comments on his own personal opinions.

"You don't have some special window into Miss Cochran's soul, do you?"

"No, I don't." Ogden smiled, thinking that one cannot look through a window that does not exist.

As they continued, it became obvious that Scholke could not undo the recorded past: Kelly herself, each day, under her own accord, met with Jeremy Ogden and discussed the case. Ogden's role and the information he obtained was clear-cut. Fixed. Kelly had thought she was smarter than law enforcement; that she could convince Jeremy she was not involved. When pressure was applied, though, Kelly, who was high on Xanax, weed, and other narcotics, blurted out how Jason had murdered Chris. This declaration, along with other admissions, subsequently opened a new line of questioning.

Not one of Scholke's questions—by no fault of his own—did much to bolster Kelly's contention that she was one more of Jason's victims. In fact, all it did was dial in the focus more clearly on Kelly's ego. It proved how far Kelly was willing to go to try and deceive a detective whom, she believed, she could outsmart. She certainly had that arrogant attitude in the first few weeks of toying with Ogden.

Melissa Powell wrapped up her case and handed the lectern to Mike Scholke.

Scholke spoke briefly to Kelly. Stood. Faced the judge.

When it came down to it, there was only one witness Scholke needed to present.

75

SIDESTEPPING

KELLY TRIED BEST SHE could to present herself as the innocent, simpleminded wife, timid, scared, unable to walk away from a violent, abusive, troubled man. To achieve that look, she wore a brown and orange-striped sweater that fell just below her hips, a black skirt. Her hair, black and shiny as oil, was pulled back and tied in a bun. Oddly enough, she had scant eyebrow hair, giving her dark eyes a mysterious, beady quality.

She sat to the judge's left, in the witness-box, one leg crossed over the other, hands folded on the bald part of her exposed knees. She wore little makeup. Kelly had bulked up and put on weight. One source close to her said she was eating a "jar of peanut butter a day" during trial to prepare for prison. Kelly Cochran was a tough chick, regardless—but with an extra ten or twenty pounds, she'd be someone to fear.

Scholke had Kelly go through her vitals: name, age, place of birth, parents, and education. She talked about meeting next-door neighbor Jason when she was a young girl growing up in Indiana.

It took about three minutes before Scholke walked Kelly into how abusive Jason had become over the years. Scholke was smart to bring in Kelly's brother, Colton, as a witness to some of it, giving her argument at least one additional source.

Then came the testimony about animals: Jason had abused their pets and once drowned a cat when they were working on a pool.

All of this fell in line with the clichéd version of the serial killer: an abusive and violent drug addict who had a penchant for harming animals. Kelly selling this to jurors, however, was another mountain. She came across as stoic, stern, cold, and unsympathetic. Zero emotion. She sat calmly, talking about behaviors that would make most abuse victims tremble, break down, or request repeated time-outs. Yet, Kelly stared directly at her lawyer, undisturbed by the horrible stories she told.

"Were there times that he held a gun to your head or pointed a gun at you?"

"Probably about twenty."

Kelly stuck to the same script she'd drafted back when the MSP had questioned her in fall 2014. Jason was the authoritative tyrant, growing increasingly jealous and violent, while losing his mind.

When Kelly crossed paths with Chris Regan, she "fell in love" with him. She kept the relationship on "the down low," for fear of Jason finding out. As the affair blossomed, "How could I do this to [Jason]?" she asked herself. "Why was I doing this to him?"

"Did he—"

"I'm his wife," she interrupted. "Why am I doing this?"

"Did he ever threaten you?"

"All the time."

"And what would he say he was going to do?"

"Said he would kill me."

Kelly relayed a few anecdotes of Jason exploding in a rage in front of family. She talked about how she once filled out divorce papers, but Jason burned them. For five minutes, she and Scholke went back and forth, Kelly calling Jason "angry," "depressed," "unstable." She claimed he was constantly screaming at her.

It was interesting that the one person who could dispute this was dead—and Kelly had killed him.

Scholke worked his way into October 13 and 14, 2014, and those days following Chris's murder.

Kelly told the story of giving Chris directions to her house so he could come over for dinner. She chose October 14, she now claimed, because she was "sick" on October 13. She said Jason left the house. He went to a friend's to use "the spa" for his back pain. She admitted lying in the past to law enforcement, adding now that Jason had "cooked up" a plan to "lure Chris over to the house" and kill him.

"You thought Jason was gone [on that day Chris showed up]?"

"I watched him leave."

Same as she told Jeremy Ogden, Kelly said she was "performing oral sex" on Chris while kneeling on the landing just beyond the doorway, before having sex with him on the stairs. As they had intercourse, Kelly testified, "there was a gunshot and we fell down the stairs."

As they talked about what happened next, Kelly added a few minor details, explaining how Jason had given her the forceps and threatened her. Then she explained how she made dinner for Jason. Over and over, she blamed Jason for it all, placing herself in the role of the subordinate wife, another one of his victims, terrified for her life, doing what her brutal husband wanted, constantly living under the barrel of a gun pointed at her head.

"What was going through your mind at the time?"

"Survive."

"So he then grabbed the SAWZALL."

"Right."

"What happens then?"

"He uses the SAWZALL to cut him."

A few questions later: "So he took Chris's hand and waved it at you?"

"Right."

"What'd you do then?"

"Sat there."

Not once did Kelly shed a tear. She never looked at jurors. She spoke of the most horrific crimes imaginable as if talking about a day spent in knitting class.

Scholke raised the butterfly issue. He asked Kelly to explain her fascination. "I think we need to talk about [this topic]," he said, encouraging Kelly to tell jurors what butterflies meant to her.

"Couple things," she began, referencing her tattoos. "To me, butterflies symbolize . . . I . . . I had said 'death.' But it's . . . I've gotten most of these for people I've lost." The "last one" was actually for a cousin. "I mean, they're beautiful. It's freedom. . . . And then, you know, the other reason is there is a lot of [talk about them] in school and in studies and things I've seen, you know, they usually say, like, maggots and flies are on dead animals and things like that, and, actually, you see more butterflies than anything."

Scholke wanted to know why Kelly never "shouted from the rooftops, calling people up, talking to Detective Ogden, trying to call Chief Frizzo," after Jason's death.

And why wouldn't she tell them she "didn't need protection anymore . . . here's what happened."

Kelly blew that off by saying she had been in a thirteen-year marriage, and even though "he'd done a lot of horrible things," there were still "some good times in there."

Strangely, during a morning break, Kelly changed. She now wore a cream-colored turtleneck shirt, with a blue jacket/sweater, apparently trying to come across as a Sunday-school teacher. It did nothing to alter the facts, all of which were now bolstered by how impassive, detached, and emotionless her testimony sounded.

"You talked about killing a truck driver in Illinois. Is that true?" Scholke asked, trying best he could to provide a way to explain some of what she'd said about branding herself a serial killer.

"No," Kelly said.

"*No*? You just made that up?"

"Yes."

She claimed the "list of names" of people she killed was nothing more than fiction to build herself up.

All this did was illustrate to jurors how many lies Kelly had told, how often, and how easy it was for her to play with the truth.

Near the end of Scholke's direct, he asked Kelly about the so-called "murder pact" she and Jason had made.

She never took it seriously.

Finally, Scholke asked Kelly why she should be believed today, if all she'd done throughout the investigation was lie.

"Well, number one, I'm under oath. Number two, I really don't have anything to hide."

"Fair enough. Thank you."

* * *

ON FEBRUARY 27, 2017, PA Melissa Powell wished Kelly a good morning. The look on Kelly's face, a complete frown, spoke to how much Kelly despised law enforcement and the idea of having to answer questions about all the lies.

For the state's cross, Kelly let her hair down; she wore a blue sweater/jacket, a dark blue V-neck button-up shirt, black skirt, and knee-high black boots. This time, she crossed her legs and folded her arms in front of herself on her thighs. Throughout her direct, Kelly did not move. She sat stiffly, only turning her head, side to side, from time to time. Her stoicism, which she maintained throughout her direct, gave the gallery and jurors the impression that she had few ways to express herself.

Powell began with Kelly's work ethic, and her parents' description of her from the witness stand as a "hard worker."

Kelly nodded, agreeing. After she and Jason first moved to Caspian, she was working several jobs.

"Seventy to eighty hours" per week.

Powell asked for her schedule.

One job was from five a.m. to three p.m., a second from "anywhere between four p.m. and ten p.m."

She'd stopped working at Mr. T's, the family-style diner/restaurant in Iron River, "end of June, beginning of July" in 2014.

When they went back to Indiana after Chris went missing, Kelly testified, she did "some contractor work and mainly sprinkler installation, service and repair."

They talked about the pool business Kelly and Jason ran together from 2001 until it was incorporated in 2014. They built and serviced pools, occasionally repairs. Kelly said she did "a little bit of everything" for the company. By 2011, she'd taken over all of the operations because Jason's sciatic nerve problem became too much. He could only work one day a week, if that.

Powell's job was to point out the inconsistencies in Kelly's stories. Show jurors how much she'd lied by quoting statements from her interviews. Then, using investigative facts, demonstrate that Kelly Cochran was a manipulator and pathological liar, who had toyed with law enforcement for years.

Kelly gave short answers: "That's correct"; "no"; "yes, I did"; "I believe that happened"; "I don't recall."

About an hour into the cross, Powell brought up "the book" Jason had written: *Where Monsters Hide*.

"Now, in Jason's book, I think one of the things that he put . . . was monsters know the smell of other monsters the same way the hunted knows the hunter, correct?"

"Correct."

A few questions later, "And in this outline, doesn't he indicate the wife saves the day?"

"That's on the last page or the last chapter, yes."

"And doesn't he also—or I think you testified . . . that, that was an autobiographical book, right?"

"Yeah."

"And you know what *autobiographical* means, right?"

"Correct."

Throughout the day, Powell caught Kelly repeatedly lying, each one destroying any bit of credibility she might have had. She admitted lying to and meddling with Ogden and Frizzo's joint investigation.

As Powell confronted Kelly, she'd laugh under her breath, one time to the point where Powell asked if her facial expressions were a "tell."

Kelly did not respond.

Near the end, Powell asked, "Where is the rest of Chris Regan?"

"I don't know."

Powell finished her cross and Scholke had a few redirect questions.

Kelly walked off the stand and sat down.

Scholke told the judge he was done.

A recess followed, with a promise of closing arguments.

76

JUDGMENT DAY

CLOSING ARGUMENTS DURING murder trials are designed to put a bow on each case. It's a crucial moment in any trial, giving context and meaning to the evidence presented. Generally speaking, nothing new is revealed. Facts are, instead, repositioned to stand out, while unexpected and unplanned bombshell moments are either explained or amplified. A powerful closing argument has the potential to sway a juror on the fence. Conversely, a weak argument can undermine the strongest case.

On February 28, 2017, Melissa Powell stood at the lectern. She wore black-framed glasses and a black sweater dress. The case Powell had presented was ironclad: all she needed to do now was put a shine on it and get jurors to understand that despite what Kelly Cochran said or did not say, the facts of the case were never in dispute. Additionally, there was no one else with a motive. The last place Chris Regan visited—the Cochran house—was where he had been murdered. He was never seen again after that day in October when he drove to Lawrence Street. Forensic blood evidence, trace evidence, and computer forensic evidence backed up what Kelly had said during over one hundred hours of interviews.

"The Cochrans are bonded in blood. The defendant's testimony, as you heard, is that they had marital problems prior to moving to Iron River, yet she moved with him, anyway, and they bought a house." Powell said, "Those problems escalated when she started seeing numerous men, and culminated with the death of Christopher Regan on October 14, 2014." To that end: "Jason Cochran and Kelly Cochran are bonded in blood—and that bond only got stronger *after* Chris's death."

Powell paused. Then emphasizing one important factor: "According to the defendant."

This led the PA into giving Chris Regan his due as the victim, describing him as a father, Gulf War vet, and good person.

Throughout the hour and a half Powell spent summarizing the most important facts of the case, she utilized Kelly's own words to show how, if one was to pay close attention, Kelly Cochran herself was the driving force behind the murder, not Jason.

MIKE SCHOLKE WALKED TOWARD that mountain he'd set out to summit back on day one. By no fault of his own, Scholke had little to work with: a client who had told so many lies, it was difficult to sift through it all and find the truth.

Scholke used Kelly's own admission that she was a liar to her advantage, but it came out flat, sort of like trying to extinguish an apartment fire with a garden hose.

"Anything she tells you should be looked at with great scrutiny," Scholke admitted. "And the only evidence they (the prosecution) have is the word of Miss Cochran."

That was beyond the stretch of imagination.

"Numerous versions of [the murder] have been told . . . none have been proven," Scholke stated. He noted that although Kelly had lied "time after time, the amount of scientific evidence was not enough to prove her guilt." He then encouraged jurors to rely on the testimony of the only eyewitness.

"We only have Kelly's word as to what happened to Chris," Scholke said before contradicting himself. "Kelly is a liar. There is no proof that Kelly's stories, any of them, are anything but fiction."

THE JURY DELIBERATED FOR two and a half hours before announcing they'd reached a unanimous verdict. On Tuesday, February 28, 2017, the courtroom buzzed with word that Kelly Cochran was going to learn her fate.

The judge asked Kelly and her attorney to stand.

Kelly was shackled at the hip, her hands strapped to metal bracelets fastened to a leather belt. Besides rocking slightly from side to side, she did not move.

Laura Frizzo and Melissa Powell sat in their chairs, arms folded in front of themselves on the oak table.

Jeremy Ogden sat two bench rows behind Frizzo and Powell.

Kelly was found guilty of First-degree Murder, Aiding and Abetting. On count number two, Larceny, guilty. Count number three, Conspiracy to commit dead bodies to disinterment and Mutilation, guilty. Count number four, Concealing and Abducting an individual, guilty. Count number five, Lying to a peace officer during a police investigation, guilty.

Kelly never flinched. She displayed no reaction or emotion. She said nothing.

77

"OH, MY GOD"

ALL JEREMY OGDEN AND Laura Frizzo wanted was for
Kelly Cochran to be honest, admit what she'd done, and
face justice. There was a certain amount of ambiguity regarding Jason Cochran and empathy for him as a murder
victim. If one was to believe Kelly, Jason had murdered
several people, among many other heinous acts—and she
was doling out punishment to him for taking away the
one person she actually loved. Besides the clinical fact
that Kelly, being a psychopath, was unable to love, justice wasn't about Jason or Kelly. At least for Jeremy and
Laura, it was about Chris Regan and his family. It did not
matter what anyone else thought.

"I think more people dislike me now because of this
case than ever before," Ogden said later. "You have no
idea how bad this has been for me. A patrolman changes a
tire on a patrol car and gets an 'attaboy'—but they won't
acknowledge this case in any way."

How bad had it gotten? Ogden was sent back to patrol
for six months after solving Chris Regan's disappear-

ance/murder. A decision that defies logic, in so many ways.

At some point later, he left the job.

Despite the politics Frizzo and Ogden faced, Lady Justice still had work to do. In May 2017, Kelly was sentenced to mandatory life in prison; she would never get out. Eleven months later, on Wednesday, April 18, 2018, after nearly a year, law enforcement was able to drag Kelly back into court, where she sat, looking tired, far older than her thirty-five years, beaten down by prison life. After a year behind bars, much of that time in quarantine and solitary, Kelly was heavier, had wrinkles where they previously did not exist, and an overall look of a twenty-year prison veteran.

After months of negotiation, Kelly stood and pleaded guilty to injecting Jason with a fatal dose of heroin before placing her hands around his neck, nose, and mouth, smothering him until he died. Her motive, Kelly said, was that "Jason had taken [away] the only good thing" (Chris Regan) she had going on in life. Kelly had given up, despite all she had said since her murder conviction regarding promises of fighting the case against her for Jason's murder and taking it to trial.

For her admission, Indiana agreed not to seek the death penalty or life in prison. The state also agreed not to file additional charges.

Murder is punishable by forty-five to sixty-five years in prison in Indiana. Kelly's sixty-five-year sentence, which the judge handed down, would be served consecutive with her life sentence in Michigan.

After Kelly's plea, Melissa Powell issued a statement, which summed up the feelings of law enforcement in general: *I'm pleased to see a conviction in the Indiana murder of Jason Cochran. Some may believe he is not worthy of empathy due to his role in the death of Chris Regan, but keep in mind he has a mother, father, brother and other family members who suffered greatly after his death and the ensuing, horrific revelations that came with the investigation and prosecution of Kelly Cochran.* Further, Powell added: *[I am] grateful for the cooperation and assistance Iron County received from Lake County, Indiana law enforcement and, in particular, the Hobart Police Department, detective Jeremy Ogden and assistant district attorney Nadia Wardrip . . .*

Beyond that, Powell verbalized the most obvious, yet unspoken, truth present throughout the investigation: *I also want to specifically state that former Iron River Police Chief Laura Frizzo and Detective Ogden did an outstanding piece of investigative work to secure the conviction of Kelly Cochran in both Michigan and Indiana. No law enforcement officer is an island in any investigation and our thanks go out to the many, many law enforcement agencies . . . involved in the investigation into Chris Regan and Jason Cochran's murders. It should be noted that Ogden and Frizzo logged countless hours on this case above and beyond what is expected in a typical investigation and, but for their dogged determination and dedication to seeing justice achieved for the families involved, Kelly Cochran might still be walking the streets.*

No doubt, still killing.

Nothing was more accurate than that final part of the statement. Frizzo and Ogden were driven by justice for the victim; both of them had made Chris Regan's disappearance the focus of their lives. They were not going to stop until they brought Chris home.

Melissa Powell also thanked a long list of agencies involved in the case.

* * *

AFTER THE PLEA HEARING, Jeremy Ogden, Laura Frizzo, and the lawyers went back to a conference room for a chat. Family members of Jason Cochran's stepped in.

"I hate you," someone close to Jason said to Jeremy Ogden, according to multiple sources attending the meeting. "I wish you would die and rot in hell."

Ogden was livid.

"Why?" he asked.

"You allowed Kelly to cremate [Jason's body] when we wanted to bury him."

Are you serious right now? Ogden thought.

"Look, I had no way to stop Kelly at that time," Ogden tried to explain. Then: "I don't get it? We bring justice to the family and they still find a reason to hate."

IN EARLY 2018, LAURA FRIZZO was with a film crew at the location where Chris's skull had been found. They were filming a two-part documentary for Investigation Discovery about the case. Frizzo brought Hela, the K9, and her handler, Alyssa Palmer, out to the same field for aesthetics, hoping to re-create the drama of that day when they recovered Chris's skull.

As filming began, Hela picked up a scent. Everyone looked on. Frizzo and Hela's handler followed.

The dog ran over to an area and sat.

"Oh, my God," someone yelled.

There was the lower half of Chris Regan's jawbone staring up at them from the ground.

"That was from Chris to me," Frizzo said. "No doubt about it."

78
FINALLY

With that fake letter Jeremy Ogden had thought up, and Walt Ammerman put into play by calling Kelly and telling her about it, Ogden had made his checkmate move. Along with that carving in the fallen tree, Kelly had been thrown off her game and admitted details about Chris Regan's murder that only someone with knowledge of the crime could have known.

Regardless whether she later downplayed the move and claimed it did not bother her, it was a brilliant investigatory ploy.

"She will . . . never admit that I got her," Ogden concluded. "She tries to show how she is superior to everyone all the time. Just like at her sentencing, Kelly made sure her attorney told the judge she had found five grammatical errors and spelling mistakes in the agreement she signed. She wants to put people in their place. . . . Kelly is counting on the Michigan conviction to be overturned on appeal. Well, I have one for her—I got her! She is in that box for the rest of her life because of a letter that only existed in my mind and a carving in a tree that made her believe she was being haunted by her victims, even if she now refuses to admit she even saw the carvings."

EPILOGUE

AND

ACKNOWLEDGMENTS

I FOLLOWED THIS CASE from the day I saw it come over the wires as it broke. It interested me on many levels, especially Kelly Cochran, an enigma among the dozens of female murderers I have researched, written about, and provided commentary about on television. Not that Kelly is all that different than your typical female psychopath—but there was something about her extreme narcissism I found utterly compelling, and unlike what I have generally come across.

During a jailhouse interview in June 2018, which I conducted with Kelly via Skype as I finished this manuscript, I asked her about Jason and potential murders he committed in Indiana.

She paused, brushed a lock of hair covering her right eye: "Here's the thing, I am being held in Indiana, because they need information from me."

Kelly had just been sentenced for Jason's murder. She wanted out of isolation of twenty-three hours a day in Indiana, which, she claimed, was punishment for not talking about those murders in Indiana. Until that was on the table and she could go back to a Michigan prison, Kelly wasn't talking.

"So all that information about the pig farm in Indiana, what about it? You don't think he killed anyone in Indiana?"

She smiled, shrugged, nodded her head up and down.

We talked about the portrait of Jason in Michigan as a guy who smoked weed, played video games, ate, took walks, fished, slept.

As I said this, Kelly shook her head.

"No, no, no. You know what bothers me is that so many people tried to paint a picture of somebody who was not capable of so many things. So many people wanted to make me the mastermind. And you know what? I am *very* intelligent. I am *very* capable of anything. But Jason was capable of anything, and it bothers me because . . ."

She trailed off and smiled, implying he had more alone time on his hands.

"I made the money. That was [the] only thing he didn't do."

I told Kelly that Jason didn't appear disabled on those videos law enforcement found on her phone.

"No, he wasn't fucking disabled!"

"If he was able to cut up a body," I said. "He wasn't disabled."

"And carry it! I mean, cutting up a body with a tool is easy," Kelly said.

"I meant mentally."

"Oh, yeah."

During this same Skype interview, I asked Kelly if Jason lured Chris over to the house that day they killed him.

"He didn't," she responded. "I invited him over."

"Why did Jason wait until you were having sex with Chris to kill him? It does not make sense to me that he would wait—why not just ambush him when he came through the door?"

"Because he didn't kill him right away."

"You mean," I said, "going back to [a letter you wrote me of your version being confined to a chair and made to watch]?"

"Yeah, yeah . . . it took two hours, fourteen minutes, and fifteen seconds."

"You saying he tortured him then?"

"Yeah."

"He made you stay there? Watch. He was taking away something from you that you loved?"

Kelly thought about this.

"He knew . . . he *believed* that he was taking something away from me that I loved. He believed that he was hurting me. Of course, it was horrible to have that done in front of me . . . and I had real strong feelings for Chris. I don't know if it was really love, though."

I asked Kelly if she was capable of loving another human being.

She sat, staring at me, a large grin emerging. Then she laughed, before going silent for an uncomfortable amount of time.

"I believe so," she finally said, before laughing again.

"It took you a long time to answer that, Kelly."

"Yeah, it did."

"Do you think you can connect with people that way?"

She sighed. Laughed. "Um . . . oh . . . I haven't had many relationships."

I didn't really know what to say.

"Every man that I have ever been with," she said, "is either dead or is a killer. Every man."

* * *

WITHOUT THE HELP of Laura Frizzo and Jeremy Ogden, this book would have lacked the detail I was able to impart. They were always professional, helpful, quick in their replies, gracious with their time, and honest, even when it did not suit their needs. I could never thank each enough. I have met two new, lifelong friends. The fact that they fell in love during this investigation proves to me that there is hope within all of the madness found in this case.

Many entities and individuals involved in this investigation deserve mention. In no particular order: Iron River Police Department, Caspian-Gaastra Public Safety, Iron County Sheriff's Office, Michigan State Police, Federal Bureau of Investigation, Iron County Medical Examiner, the Hobart, Indiana, Police Department, Lake County Coroner's Office, various laboratories that processed evidence on a state and national level, the U.S. Marshal Service, Kentucky State Police, the Graves County Kentucky Jail, Michigan Backcountry Search and Rescue, Escanaba Public Safety, Michigan Department of Natural Resources, Lake County, Indiana, law enforcement agencies, and many other agencies and individuals.

Iron County prosecuting attorney Melissa A. Powell was a pivotal source in my research and understanding of this case at the beginning. Court reporter Sue Valenti was generous with transcripts and timely with turnaround. She did a superb job during the trial and afterward, transcribing the entire case quickly, while lawyers, producers, and writers breathed down the back of her neck. Likewise, Sue Mayo, from the prosecutor's office, was a godsend; always willing to help, providing me with documents and videos and audio I either lost on my computer, could not find, or did not receive. These are the good people, who make my job easier and keep research fluid, allowing me to meet deadlines and figure cases out. I could not be more grateful. Thank you for everything.

WITH THE AMOUNT of research I amassed during the writing of this book, I could have written an eight-hundred-page manuscript that would have been just as compelling as what I wound up with. However, the mere heft of it would have scared many readers away. I chose the most important elements of the case, and what I thought needed to be brought into the public forum. It is a story unlike any I have ever come across in writing nearly forty books. Thank you to everyone involved in this case: from the person behind the scenes who goes unnamed, to law enforcement, to the lawyers, judge, the bailiffs, and courtroom personnel. I know I've forgotten someone important and for that I apologize.

Vida Engstrand, Kensington Publishing Corp.'s communications director, has become a friend and relentless advocate for my career. Vida and I go back a long way and I wanted to publicly say that without Vida, I would be a raft in the world of publishing floating aimlessly.

Lastly, Jeremy Ogden and Laura Frizzo deserved more than the crap they put up with throughout this case and afterward. Without them, Chris Regan's murderers would have gone free and his remains would be sitting in a field somewhere. But more important, others would have been killed. Jeremy and Laura saved lives. There is no doubt in my mind about this. The lack of respect they received was surely based on ego and jealousy and personal feelings. In my opinion, there is no room for any of that nonsense in policing. Jeremy and Laura kept the focus on one thing: the victim. In any murder case, the victim is, really, all that should matter.

Everything else—the political heaps of bureaucracy and personal grudges and mistakes made by investigators—dishonors and devalues the victim, giving power to the murderer. I'm appalled, truthfully, by some of what I heard, most I did not include in this book. Laura and Jeremy are honest, good people, who believe in justice for victims of crime. Anything beyond that—their personal lives or the way they do things—is nothing but a distraction, devaluing, diminishing, and hindering their capabilities and work ethic as investigators. I find it disgusting, especially within a world today where the violence and brutality has risen and the value of human life in general has declined immensely.

LAURA FRIZZO HAD an inherent intuition of being able to feel the chemistry of those she interviewed. With Kelly, Frizzo felt there was something about her, the energy she emitted, which spoke to the darkness she harbored in her soul. Frizzo could sense it. She listened to her instincts and the public benefitted from it.

"You know, from the beginning, there was just this feeling I got from her, like nothing I have ever encountered. I have interviewed a lot of horrible, disgusting people. But with Kelly, I just couldn't let it go," Frizzo said.

Frizzo told Detective Jeremy Ogden about her feelings one day.

"Pure evil," he said. "You're sensing the evil inside that woman."

Frizzo paused. "I believe that. . . . Kelly once told me

that she could walk into a room and pick out the person like her."

Frizzo understood.

Both Jeremy and Laura are psychopath whisperers, cut from different sides of the cloth—which makes them unstoppable as a team.

"This was my life," Frizzo said. "Not once did I ever think anyone else would ever be interested in this case as a story."

In 2015, Frizzo began to believe there was a good chance Chris Regan's remains—"at least some of them"—were in an area landfill. But she had no resources whatsoever in order to conduct that search.

"When you're in it, when you're deeply involved, you're not thinking this is an amazing case. You're thinking, I need to get these people arrested and find this victim and bring him home to his family."

ANY INVESTIGATION INVOLVING a missing person requires a cop to lean on his or her ability to sift through mountains of leads that go nowhere. The bottom line in most missing-person cases is only a handful of them turn out to involve nefarious activity or foul play, where the missing person is murdered or never heard from again. Out of an average 750,000 reported missing-person cases the FBI tracks each year, approximately seven hundred thousand do not involve anything evil, deadly, or dangerous. In addition, a majority of adults who go missing leave on their own, choosing to wipe out their previous life and start a new one. It is not a crime for an adult to make him- or herself disappear. Most of the time, when a "missing person" is located by law enforcement and that person asks not to disclose his or her whereabouts, it is a request met with respect.

Missing-person cases and identifying Jane and John Does has become a passion of mine. I am involved in several cases currently. I will find and identify some of these people—or die trying.

*Don't miss the next riveting true-crime book
from* M. WILLIAM PHELPS

GETTING EVEN

THE INCREDIBLE LIFE AND
MYSTERIOUS DEATH OF MARY YODER

Coming soon from Kensington Publishing Corp.

Keep reading to enjoy a tantalizing excerpt . . .

Bill Yoder didn't need an alarm clock. On most days, the seventy-year-old chiropractor got out of bed by six-thirty a.m., walked into the exercise room inside his upstate New York home, and spent the next hour getting his blood pumping. On those mornings when Bill worked out, his sixty-year-old wife, Mary, hustled around the house, getting ready for work.

Keys? Newspaper? Briefcase?

"I generally stayed out of her way," Bill said.

After Bill finished his workout routine, a white towel slung over his shoulder, he made his way into the kitchen to rehydrate. At about the same time, Mary was ready to take off for her day of work at the chiropractor practice they owned and had run for the past thirty years. The office was a fifteen-minute drive from their modest, upper middle-class home. Bill generally kissed his wife, said goodbye, and wished Mary a great day. From there he would have coffee and read the newspaper. Maybe head out to the local Panera to write down "some thoughts" or "do some of my reflective reading." Other than that, Bill would putter around the house doing "handyman work Mary needed me to finish." Or tackle those bigger projects in Mary's prized garden.

Mary was one of those people who, with so many things going on in her life at the same time, she forever ran a little bit late. She'd be on her way out the door and realize, *Oops, I have to do this.* Off she went to accomplish what she presumed was a five-minute task that actually took her twenty.

Bill would tease her about it.

"No, no . . . Bill. I used to be, but not anymore."

The Yoder's youngest child and only son, Adam, who'd started as the practice's full-time office manager, was usually already at the office, opening up and doing a few things in the quiet of no patients. Adam had taken the job in 2013. With school responsibilities and other obligations impinging lately, the job had become too much of a burden on his lifestyle by the summer of 2015. Adam, however, had asked his parents if his then girlfriend, twenty-two-year-old Katie Conley, could come in and split the time with him. Both would work part-time, Adam explained to his parents. Katie was pretty in a girl-next-door way. Responsible. Smart. She had a royal look about her: business-like, elite, intelligent, sophisticated. She came from a family with deep roots in the community. Everyone seemed to know a Conley. The house where she grew up and lived was attached to acres of land. They had horses and livestock. Most in town who knew Katie would say she was soft-spoken and shy. Harmless and rather wholesome.

Bill and Mary had gotten to know Katie fairly well as she became embedded in the daily work of the business. They liked her. Before that, they knew little about her.

Adam had always been a private person, Bill explained, where his personal life was concerned.

"And he had been from the time he started having relationships. So we didn't really know Katie until she came to work for us."

By all accounts, when they weren't fighting, Katie seemed to make Adam happy. There were "ups and downs" throughout the relationship, but Adam was unwilling to share exactly what was going on. The way Katie came across in the office, the Yoders believed Katie might make the perfect wife one day for their son. Still, Bill later observed, "We were reluctant [to have her work at the office] because we didn't want to have any relationship issues in the business." A husband and wife running the place was difficult enough.

Adam pleaded with his parents. It would be okay, he promised. He and Katie were able to focus on work while in the office. Their personal life would be left outside the door.

"We finally said okay," Bill remembered.

With Katie running the office, Adam pulled back even further where his and Katie's relationship was concerned. For good reason.

"Look," he told his parents not long after she started working, "you've got this work relationship with her. Our personal stuff should not have anything to do with how she's treated at the office."

Fair point.

Beginning in early summer 2013, Adam and Katie began splitting office manager responsibilities. They had taken the lead of Adam's parents and rarely worked the same hours. As needed, they alternated shifts. Within a few months of Katie starting, the issue of them working together was null and void, however. Katie was more than capable of taking care of the office, competent and responsible, which allowed Mary and Bill to completely focus on patients. What's more, Adam decided to go back to school full-time that fall and Katie took over as full-time office manager. Driven, Katie took her job seriously.

The office hours were eight a.m. to five-thirty p.m., Monday through Friday. The office closed between twelve-thirty p.m. and one-thirty p.m. every day for lunch. The doors were locked. The OPEN/CLOSED sign flipped around.

Bill scaled back his hours as chiropractor almost completely that summer, focusing on the books—taxes, accounting, payroll. He worked two-and-half days a week, Tuesdays and Thursdays, with a half-day where he could fit it in. He still saw patients, but less and less as retirement seemed to be beckoning. Mary covered the other days of the week: Mondays, Wednesdays, Fridays. So dedicated to her work, Mary often headed out to nearby Amish country on certain days after working hours to give treatment to those Amish in need. It was a dangerous trip into Utica with horse and buggy, and the Amish did not want to make it.

"And that was Mary," said a friend and long-time patient. "She drove out to the Amish because they *needed* care."

An accomplished potter and avid gardener, Mary viewed both "hobbies" as an extension of her life, not something she did to tinker around and pass time. She also danced and became a Shaklee rep and sold the products out of the office. According to the company, "Shaklee Corporation is an American manufacturer and distributor of natural nutrition supplements, weight-management . . . beauty . . . and household products." Mary kept a "little shop in the back office" where she sold pottery, health-centered books and herbal supplies, with lots of Shaklee inventory always on hand. She was passionate about organic products and food. Mary encouraged people to give themselves the best chance at a healthy lifestyle. In that regard, the one absolute for Mary was her daily Shaklee protein smoothie. She kept a large cannister of Shaklee protein in the office refrigerator and mixed a smoothie whenever a craving hit. Her recipe never changed: almond milk and Shaklee powder.

MOHAWK VALLEY, CUTTING THROUGH the center of New York State, has a combined populace of about six hundred fifty thousand. Situated between the Adirondack and Catskill Mountains, as the heart of summer 2015 hit the region, Bill and Mary Yoder were actively looking to sell the practice, which they had spent decades building. Every time the subject came up, however, the thought behind the process of the sale seemed so exhausting and encumbering. A sale would involve two years of bringing someone in—that is, after they found a qualified buyer they were happy with—and training the doctor, beyond making sure patients were comfortable with him or her. For Mary and Bill, patients were their number one priority, many of whom they'd spent their careers building relationships with.

Regarding selling the practice, Bill Yoder said, "We were always too busy to do it." So they'd routinely begin a conversation about retirement and selling, but then table it.

Elizabeth Kelly had been a Chiropractic Family Care patient since 1998, seeing Mary and Bill three times per week. ·

"As my condition became better, I saw them less

often," Elizabeth said. In fact, during the third week of July 2015, Elizabeth was going to see Mary about once or twice per month. On July 20, specifically, Elizabeth checked in with Katie Conley around two-thirty p.m.

"Take a seat," Katie said. "Mary will be with you shortly."

A few moments later, Elizabeth was on her way into the back of the office.

As Mary walked into the room, Elizabeth noticed immediately, something was going on with Mary.

"She didn't seem to be as exuberant as I would know her to be. She wasn't as bright."

Elizabeth wrote it off as Mary appearing "to have her mind focused someplace else."

Was it the sale of the practice nagging at Mary? Something she ate? A personal problem?

Whatever it was, as the afternoon progressed, Mary's demeanor would change drastically. To the point where those who knew her best, along with those patients who had seen Mary for decades, did not recognize the person she became that day.

Connect with

Us

Visit us online at
KensingtonBooks.com
to read more from your favorite authors, see books
by series, view reading group guides, and more.

Join us on social media

for sneak peeks, chances to win books and prize packs,
and to share your thoughts with other readers.

facebook.com/kensingtonpublishing
twitter.com/kensingtonbooks

Tell us what you think!

To share your thoughts, submit a review,
or sign up for our eNewsletters, please visit:
KensingtonBooks.com/TellUs.